Contours of Christian Philosophy
C. STEPHEN EVANS, Series Editor

EPISTEMOLOGY

Becoming Intellectually Virtuous

W. JAY WOOD

IVP Academic

An imprint of InterVarsity Press
Downers Grove, Illinois

InterVarsity Press
P.O. Box 1400, Downers Grove, IL 60515-1426
World Wide Web: www.ivpress.com
E-mail: email@ivpress.com

InterVarsity Press® is the book-publishing division of InterVarsity Christian Fellowship/USA®, a student movement active on campus at hundreds of universities, colleges and schools of nursing in the United States of America, and a member movement of the International Fellowship of Evangelical Students. For information about local and regional activities, write Public Relations Dept., InterVarsity Christian Fellowship/USA, 6400 Schroeder Rd., P.O. Box 7895, Madison, WI 53707-7895, or visit the IVCF website at <www.intervarsity.org>.

Scripture quotations, unless otherwise noted, are from the New Revised Standard Version of the Bible, *copyright 1989 by the Division of Christian Education of the National Council of the Churches of Christ in the USA. Used by permission. All rights reserved.*

ISBN 978-0-87784-522-5

Printed in the United States of America ♾

Library of Congress Cataloging-in-Publication Data

Wood, W. Jay (William Jay), 1954-
   Epistemology : becoming intellectually virtuous / W. Jay Wood.
     p.   cm.—(Contours of Christian philosophy)
   Includes bibliographical references.
   ISBN 0-87784-522-0 (pbk. : alk. paper)
    1. Knowledge, Theory of (Religion) 2. Christianity—Philosophy.
  I. Title. II. Series.
  BT50.W57 1998
  230'.01—DC21   *98-18829*
                                                                   CIP

P   24   23   22   21   20   19   18   17

Y   23   22   21   20   19   18   17   16   15   14   13

Preface

As its title suggests, this book introduces students to some of the central concerns of epistemology while also recommending that these concerns be pursued by taking seriously our growth in the intellectual virtues. By intellectual virtues I mean qualities such as wisdom, understanding, foresight and love of truth. These are deeply anchored habits of mind that contribute to the success of our many intellectual endeavors and ultimately to our ability to lead excellent lives. While I have sought to give balanced overviews of the subjects broached, I have not hesitated to indicate how considerations of intellectual virtue and vice bear upon and even help to resolve longstanding epistemological controversies.

A traditional approach to the theory of knowledge gives pride of place to skepticism and the type of questions it motivates:

"Does the table continue to exist when I am not perceiving it?"

"Are the experiences I take to be real merely a dream?"

"How do I know that evil demons or clever scientists are not systematically deceiving me with respect to all that I think I know?"

"Do my sensory experiences mislead me about how things are in the world?"

While I usually have been able to generate interest in such questions among my students, I have always suspected that such questions remained for them concerns of the classroom and not the ongoing concerns of their lives. Matters changed as I began to reflect more and more with my students about matters of intellectual virtue and vice with their attendant concerns: Have traits such as gullibility, willful naiveté, close-mindedness and intellectual dishonesty taken root within me? Do I incline too readily to accept reports that throw the persons and views I dislike into an unfavorable light? Do I resist inordinately the fair criticisms of persons who object to my views? Do I possess traits such as attentiveness, foresight, circumspection, creativity, teachableness and understanding? And what might I do to foster my growth in these traits? In what ways does the community of which I am a part and the causes to which I have devoted myself influence my intellectual character? Such questions allow one to discuss traditional epistemological topics such as the structure of knowledge, justification and even skepticism in ways that bear centrally on what kinds of persons we are and are becoming.

There is nothing new, of course, about approaching epistemological concerns with matters of intellectual virtue and vice uppermost in mind; indeed, this approach was once the staple of Judeo-Christian as well as ancient Greek ways of thinking. One way I hope to stimulate renewed interest in epistemological matters for Christians is by connecting them with their religious beliefs and along with their attendant intellectual concerns that were once so much a part of their tradition. By bringing many epistemological distinctions and arguments to bear on students' religious beliefs one reinforces the centrality of epistemology for the concerns that matter to us most.

Because this book highlights matters of intellectual virtue and vice, many topics routinely treated in introductory texts to epistemology do not receive sustained or systematic treatment. Questions arising in connection with issues such as memory, perception, a priori and Gettier problems will be more profitably pursued in any number of more traditionally oriented texts. But traditional epistemology and its customary projects have themselves been the target of much criticism of late, so it is fitting that alternative approaches and new emphases receive consideration.

I owe special thanks for comments received on earlier sections of this book to my colleagues in the department of philosophy at Wheaton College, especially Robert C. Roberts, who has been an invaluable critic and mentor in matters pertaining to the virtues. Nicholas Wolterstorff and Linda Zagzebski commented on the penultimate draft of this book, offering numerous helpful suggestions for which I am most grateful. C. Stephen Evans not only read the entire manuscript but has been an unflagging source of encouragement and sensible criticism from the beginning. Finally, for her tireless support, patience and love, I dedicate this book to my wife, Janice.

One

The Nature of Epistemology

P erhaps you enjoy, as I do, sitting down for a leisurely read with the Sunday newspaper, coffee or tea close at hand. On a recent Sunday afternoon it occurred to me that while outwardly I might have appeared the picture of relaxation, my mind was in high gear, being challenged page after page. Splashed across the front page were reports accusing the president of unbecoming conduct. Another lead article on the politics of compassion revealed the deep differences separating Republican and Democratic candidates seeking election in my state. A related editorial urged readers to support efforts to retain social services for immigrants. The health section reported new evidence supporting the cancer-preventing qualities of vitamin supplements. A movie review in the entertainment section trashed a film I was looking forward to seeing, while another review raved about an inexpensive Italian restaurant in my neighborhood.

Each of these articles could be viewed as placing a demand on my thinking. Should I accept their claims, reject them, pursue further evidence, ignore them or respond in some other way? It was also plain that whatever I believed about these issues carried practical implications for my behavior—on how I was going to vote, eat and spend what little discretionary cash I set aside for entertainment.

At one time or another most of us ponder how best to treat claims proposed for our acceptance. We wonder also about how persons concerned to think conscientiously should deal with challenges posed against their existing beliefs. These questions, among others, are the special concern of epistemology, that branch of philosophy dedicated to reflecting on our lives as intellectual beings. As I shall try to show, the issues epistemology wrestles with are far from being mere ivory-tower academic concerns. They are deeply important issues that confront us in the routine contexts of our lives.

1.1 When Do Epistemological Questions Arise?
The short answer is almost anytime we stop to ask ourselves such questions as how we acquire our beliefs, whether what we, or others, believe is true, whether we believe rationally, or whether we ought to reconsider beliefs that have been criticized. Indeed, our lives as thinking beings give rise to these and a whole host of other epistemological issues. A few examples illustrate this.

We confront epistemological questions as we reflect on beliefs that are popular in our culture. Americans, for example, might reflect on the following findings of a 1990 Gallup Poll:

☐ A quarter of all Americans polled believe in UFOs.

☐ Slightly more than that believe that their personal destiny is controlled by the positions of the stars and planets (astrology).

☐ More than 40 percent believe in psychic healing: that if a witch doctor artfully arranges rocks and crystals on your torso, you can be healed.

A *Washington Post*-ABC News poll revealed other interesting beliefs:

☐ Twelve percent of the American people think they've been reincarnated.

☐ Twenty-one percent of Americans think it is possible to communicate with the dead.

You may be saying to yourself: *If these people were as intellectually conscientious as they ought to be, then they wouldn't believe these claims.* Are people who hold such beliefs irrational? If so, on what basis do we make such judgments? As we shall see, it's more difficult than you may think to state general principles for believing that would show persons holding the above beliefs to be intellectually irresponsible.

Our passional natures and the causes to which we devote ourselves may also cause us to confront epistemological questions. Suppose you have a passion for social justice and have as an overriding goal of your life to work for a fairer society. One day you are selected for jury duty to determine the guilt or innocence of a minority person being accused of assault and battery during an urban riot. As it happens, the prosecution's main evidence consists of some video footage of the alleged assault, filmed by a bystander. When you view the film, you judge that it is ambiguous. Looked at one way, it might appear to be a case of assault; looked at another way, it might be seen as a justifiable act of self-defense within a racially charged environment. You are also aware, however, that your passion for ameliorating the injustices done to minorities in your community might be skewing your judgment; in the recesses of your mind arises the doubt that your beliefs about this matter (or any other matter about which you have strong passions) have been reached in an unbiased manner.

You confer with your fellow jurors and discover that they detect no ambiguity at all; it appears to them to be an open-and-shut case of assault. Discussing matters with them, you find them to be no less intelligent than you are, and genuinely interested in reaching a fair verdict. You begin to wonder how, if at all, their disagreement affects your beliefs. Have your passions (however admirable they might be) overridden your sound judgment in this case, and perhaps other cases as well? Or have your passions instead given you powers of moral perception that are lacking in your fellow jurors? It is also clear to you that matters of genuine significance hang on your answers.

Epistemological questions were raised for me in a personal and powerful way as I struggled to meet criticisms of my religious beliefs. I went off to college a recent Christian convert, not at all sure that my newfound faith was intellectually defensible. During my first two years of college some professors and peers assured me that my doubts about religion's rationality should give way to full-blown skepticism. Such claims came accompanied by the standard criticisms: How could a good God allow the innocent to suffer? Can one really make sense of the Christian idea of God? Isn't all religious belief just a palliative for our fears of death and the unknown? The attitude I encountered is succinctly characterized by Norman Malcolm:

> In our Western academic philosophy, religious belief is commonly regarded as unreasonable and is viewed with condescension or even contempt. It is said that religion is a refuge for those who, because of weakness of intellect and character, are unable to confront the stern realities of the world.[1]

The antireligious polemics of Bertrand Russell, Antony Flew and others that I read at this time reinforced my fears that perhaps I was, to use Malcolm's words, weak of intellect and character. I vividly recall walking around campus feeling powerless to dispel their objections as thoroughly as I would have liked. And so things went for the bulk of my undergraduate career.

As I continued in my philosophical studies, I learned ever more sophisticated ways of responding to many specific objections posed by critics of religious belief. I also learned (thanks to many fine teachers) what is perhaps already known to you: that behind many objections to religious belief is an epistemological viewpoint detailing, among other things, what requirements a person must satisfy in order to have knowledge about anything, what steps must be taken to avoid accusations of intellectual wrongdoing, and what conditions must be satisfied before I could be said to have had a genuine experience of God. Rather than scurry to meet each objection to religious belief on its own terms, I learned that it is sometimes more fruitful to ask questions about the epistemological viewpoint motivating the objections. Where did the rules of good intellectual conduct that underlie charges of irrationality come from, anyway? Is there agreement throughout the academic world in general, and the philosophical community in particular, as to the canons of right reason? Has there been continuity throughout the history of Western philosophy about such matters? What if instead of answering the religious skeptic's demand for more evidence, I were to argue that one may be perfectly rational believing in God in the absence of evidence? I learned that defending religious belief involves us quite directly with concerns that preoccupy epistemologists.

My claim thus far, then, is that the concerns of our everyday lives raise for us—sometimes in poignant ways—the very issues raised in the study of epistemology. Moreover, as we wrestle with these concerns we are sometimes forced to reflect on how we ought to think about and orient our lives as thinking persons. Such reflections in turn prompt us to investigate the extent of our cognitive powers and their proper functioning, the reliability of our sources of belief, and related matters. These are precisely the concerns to which the study of epistemology calls us.

To grasp better the impressive range of concerns occupying epistemologists, think for a moment about the tremendous array of things you believe. Perhaps you believe (or reject) claims such as the following:

☐ It is wrong to buy and sell human beings.

☐ The universe began at a point in time as described by the big bang theory.

☐ Democracy is the best form of government.

☐ John F. Kennedy was assassinated in 1963 by Lee Harvey Oswald.

☐ God exists.

☐ One's ancestors represent a powerful spiritual force in the world.

☐ The Cubs will never win a world series.

☐ 7 + 5 = 12.

☐ The id is the core of the unconscious self.

☐ There will be a general resurrection of the dead.

☐ It is unlikely that there is life on other planets.

☐ Bach was a better composer than the Bee Gees.

☐ My boyfriend/girlfriend is in love with me.

You believe claims like these and thousands besides: beliefs ranging over matters of morality, science, politics, history, current events, mathematics, psychology, philosophy, interpersonal relations, religion, aesthetics and many other subjects.

It is clear, however, that not all of our beliefs are on a par; they do not enjoy the same status or possess the same credentials. A moment's reflection reveals that we are more strongly inclined to accept some of the above beliefs than others. Some are notoriously subject to dispute, while others enjoy widespread acceptance. Some of them are supported by lots of evidence, while others lack significant evidential support. We can imagine ourselves being mistaken about some of our beliefs, while we think it is impossible that we could be in error about others. Some beliefs are tremendously important in shaping our lives and guiding our behavior, while others could be excised from the list of things we believe without causing a ripple of disturbance in our day-to-day life. We would not hesitate to call some of our beliefs instances of knowledge, while other beliefs are of an inferior grade, meriting no status superior to highly confirmed belief, mere belief, hypothesis, considered opinion, conjecture or just plain hunch.

The striking differences in the nature and status of the things we believe permit us to express more precisely some of the major questions that preoccupy epistemologists. Must all of the things I believe be supported by evidence? And what is evidence? In what circumstances is a person intellectually irresponsible in accepting a belief? Are there minimal requirements of rationality that all our beliefs must satisfy if we are to be responsible in accepting them? Do the requirements differ for different kinds of beliefs? And if there are minimal requirements of acceptability, where do these requirements come from? Should everyone accept the same standards as binding? Is my accepting and rejecting beliefs something over which I have direct control, or is it something that just happens to me? How should we assess someone's merits as an intellectual being? Should we focus on the status of a particular belief held by that person, considered in isolation, or should we attend primarily to the overall intellectual history of the person who accepts it? This cluster of questions arises amidst discussions of what is called in epistemology "the problem of justification," a concern that dominates discussions of philosophers today.

What should I do when I find out that large numbers of people disagree with me about some of my core convictions? How should I respond if someone poses an objection whose force I feel against one of my cherished beliefs? Should I give up my belief? Should I retain it? Must I personally rebut the objection threatening my belief? Perhaps I believe that some intellectual champion from my community has offered a successful rebuttal; can I be a beneficiary of this work and now ignore the objection? How much time do I have to rebut the objection to my belief? Must I do it on the spot, or do I have some time to mull things over? What if I believe myself to have successfully rebutted an objection to one of my beliefs, but my opponent thinks otherwise? Some of these questions invite us to explore the ways that support for our beliefs is undermined, as well as strategies for preserving the support of our beliefs when they fall under attack. Epistemologists sometimes refer to these issues under the heading "defeasibility."

In fact, most of the questions one can imagine arising in connection with acquiring and maintaining beliefs fall under the purview of epistemology. A full study of the subject would require delving into the various sources of knowledge such as perception, memory and testimony, in addition to whatever faculties of understanding we may have that allow us to grasp truths independently of sense experiences. Even the definition of knowledge is a serious epistemological issue. What are the essential ingredients that make a belief an instance of knowledge, and how does one differentiate knowledge from the host of lesser grades of belief such as opinion and conjecture? The ancient tradition of skepticism, on the other hand, denies that we can achieve knowledge about anything or, more modestly, that we can achieve knowledge about certain subjects. In fact, historically many of the major epistemological theories were developed precisely to combat the challenges posed by skepticism.[2] Still more fundamentally, one might wish to investigate the very conditions that make human understanding possible at all. How is it that our world emerges out of our experiences of it as a place we can make sense of? How do features of my world such as the words on a page, the gestures of a person or a succession of musical notes ever come to be objects of understanding?

While the questions raised thus far give one a sense of the wide range of epistemological concerns engaging the philosophical community at present, they leave unmentioned an old, indeed ancient, philosophical tradition that viewed epistemological excellence as an indispensable ingredient for a well-lived life. We achieve excellence in the intellectual life, according to this tradition, when we form within ourselves qualities like wisdom, prudence, understanding, intellectual humility, love of truth and similar traits—in short, as we embody *intellectual virtues.*

1.2 Epistemology and the Pursuit of Intellectual Virtues

We are all familiar with the notion of a moral virtue: traits such as generosity, compassion, courage, temperance and patience. These are well-anchored, abiding personal qualities we acquire that reliably dispose us to think, feel and behave in certain ways when circumstances demand it. Persons who regularly maintain a calm demeanor in the face of vexatious circumstances we call patient; persons who regularly control their appetites for food, sex and drink we call temperate; persons who manage their fears in the face of perceived dangers we call courageous, and so on. The presence of such personal traits (or of their corresponding vices) constitutes our character, contributing in large measure to what sort of persons we are.

Intellectual virtues have received less attention: these include character traits such as wisdom, prudence, foresight, understanding, discernment, truthfulness and studiousness, among others. Here too are to be found their opposing vices: folly, obtuseness, gullibility, dishonesty, willful naiveté and vicious curiosity, to name a few. Certain excellences and deficiencies, then, shape our intellectual as well as our moral lives. An epistemology that takes the virtues seriously claims that our ability to lay hold of the truth about important matters turns on more than our IQ or the caliber of school we attend; it also depends on whether we have fostered within ourselves virtuous habits of mind. Our careers as cognitive agents, as persons concerned to lay hold of the truth and pursue other important intellectual goals, will in large measure succeed or fail as we cultivate our intellectual virtues.

Thinking about epistemology as encompassing the pursuit of intellectual virtue, while presently unfashionable, was the dominant way of casting epistemological concerns in the writings of Aristotle, Augustine, Thomas Aquinas and other philosophers of the ancient and medieval tradition. Your intellectual life is important, according to these thinkers, for the simple reason that your very character, the kind of person you are and are becoming, is at stake. Careful oversight of our intellectual lives is imperative if we are to think well, and thinking well is an indispensable ingredient in living well. According to this tradition, only by superintending our cognitive life (the way, for example, we form, defend, maintain, revise, abandon and act on our beliefs about important matters) can we become excellent as thinkers and, ultimately, excellent as persons.

If we fail to oversee our intellectual life and cultivate virtue, the likely consequence will be a maimed and stunted mind that thwarts our prospects for living a flourishing life.

It should come as no surprise that intellectual virtues are not fostered in isolation from other human excellences. For instance, we customarily link good thinking with bodily health. My judgments about objects of perception will be suspect if my senses aren't working properly; my judgments about the past will similarly suffer if that portion of my brain affecting memory is ravaged by Alzheimer's disease; and almost any cognitive function might be undermined by a tumor or brain lesion or a similar debility. Less often do we reflect, though, on how success as a cognitive agent is linked to moral and emotional health.

A vicious moral character can undermine good thinking just as effectively as some physical debility. The two-way causal connection between right thinking and right morality, between the intellectual and moral virtues, is a prominent motif that runs through many religious traditions; it is also attested by common sense. Arrogance, dishonesty, pride, pugnacity, laziness and many other vices undermine our ability to think well and to pursue the truth.

Father Zossima, the saintly monk of Fyodor Dostoyevsky's *The Brothers Karamazov*, illustrates nicely the connection between our moral and intellectual lives. While recounting to his fellow monks the story of his conversion, he emphasizes how youthful pride blinded him to obvious truths. As a dashing, affluent young officer with all "the polish and courtesy of worldly manners," Zossima is stationed in a town where he wins acceptance in high society. He becomes romantically attached to a young girl of high social standing, whom he fancies must of course be infatuated with him.

> Then suddenly I happened to be ordered to another district for two months. I came back two months later and suddenly discovered that the girl had already married a local landowner. . . I was so struck by this unexpected event that my mind even became clouded. And the chief thing was, as I learned only then, that this young landowner had long been her fiance, and that I myself had met him many times in their house but had noticed nothing, being blinded by my own merits. And that was what offended me most of all: how was it possible that almost everyone knew, and I alone knew nothing?[3]

Father Zossima's mind didn't suddenly become clouded, of course; it had been clouded all along by his arrogance. His pride so impaired his cognitive faculties that he had remained ignorant of what was obvious to everyone else.

1.3 The Christian and Intellectual Virtue

Christians have some special reasons to take seriously the questions and concerns raised by epistemologists. Exercising care over the formation of our minds is not a purely academic pursuit; it is also a spiritual one. God enjoins us in Scripture to pursue the intellectual virtues. The Bible is unequivocally clear that Christians are to superintend the life of the mind. "Do not be conformed to this world, but be transformed by the renewing of your minds" (Rom 12:3). God cares about *how* you think, not just *what* you think. A godly mind is not merely one devoid of vile thoughts, nor are the faithful stewards of the mind necessarily the ones who die with all their doctrinal p's and q's in place (brainwashing might as effectively accomplish this).

The concern of ancient and medieval philosophers to cultivate the habits of mind that we call the intellectual virtues is also a biblical concern. Not only do classical Greek thinkers and the writers of the Hebrew wisdom literature name some virtues in common, but their understanding of some virtues and vices seems roughly to coincide.[4] Scores of injunctions to pursue intellectual virtues dot the pages of Scripture. We are urged to be attentive, wise, discerning, prudent, circumspect, understanding, teachable, lovers of truth, intellectually humble and intellectually tenacious, along with many other positive intellectual traits. We are also directed to be able to defend our faith, to instruct others in the faith, to confute those who oppose true doctrine, and so on. On the other hand, warnings abound against laziness of thought, folly, immaturity in our thinking, being easily duped or gullible ("blown about by every wind of doctrine"—Eph 4:14), engaging in idle speculation, intellectual arrogance or vicious curiosity ("for the time is coming when people will not put up with sound doctrine, but having itching ears, they will accumulate for themselves teachers to suit their own desires, and will turn away from listening to the truth"—2 Tim 4:3-4).

According to the Christian tradition, to forge virtuous habits of moral and intellectual character is part of what is required for us to grow to the full stature of all that God intends for humans to be. Becoming virtuous is part of what makes us fit residents of the kingdom of heaven, ready and able to do God's work now and in the age to come. Intertwining moral and intellectual virtues in this way underscores the unity of our lives; these are not isolated compartments of our selves. We cannot be fully intellectually virtuous without also being morally virtuous. The converse is also true; we cannot succeed in the moral life without also displaying important intellectual virtues. When we succeed in harmonizing these aspects of our lives, we achieve what ancients and moderns alike call *integrity*.

It is helpful to juxtapose our thinking about the intellectual virtues to our thinking about the moral virtues, since much of what philosophers say about the moral virtues applies by extension to the intellectual virtues. This is especially true in thinking about the intellectual virtues from a Christian point of view, for while the distinction can be made in the Bible between moral and intellectual virtues, they all serve the same end by contributing to the purposes for which God created us.

I should like to note five parallels between moral and intellectual virtues. Interestingly, these parallels have received comment in both secular and sacred literature.

First, cultivating the virtues is a developmental process extending through a lifetime. Jean Piaget, Lawrence Kolberg and other developmental psychologists have documented the regular stages we pass through en route to intellectual and moral maturity. So too we learn from the Bible that even Jesus grew in wisdom, and St. Paul had to learn not to think as a child. Numerous remarks in Scripture suggest that moral virtue is similarly a developmental process requiring training.

Second, growth in the virtues is not automatic. Bodily growth is virtually automatic; becoming wise or saintly is not. And it is quite possible for someone to be mature in years but not in wisdom or understanding. To secure wisdom, one must conscientiously seek it out. The writer of Proverbs likens wisdom to buried treasure: it must be hunted and dug for, obviously demanding that we expend sustained personal effort.

Third, we are not alone in our efforts to become morally and intellectually virtuous persons; our careers as moral and intellectual agents are developed in a community context. In fact, recent work in epistemology is giving long-overdue attention to the social dimensions of knowledge.[5] Family, friends and social institutions such as the church contribute mightily toward shaping the framework within which our development takes place. What goals are worth pursuing, what goals should be subordinated to others, what practices ought to be avoided and which pursued, and what resources are available to assist us in moral and intellectual growth are matters shaped in large measure within families, churches, schools and other social frameworks. Imagine how the complexion of your intellectual life might vary as you were alternately a part of traditions whose chief goals were world economic domination, the biblical concept of shalom, aesthetic sensitivity, the dissolution of the self and union with God.

Fourth, we must work to sustain our gains in the moral and intellectual life, since regression is a real possibility. Thomas Aquinas warns that virtues can be undermined not only by bad judgments rooted in passion and ignorance but also by neglect; if you don't use virtue, he says, it will eventually weaken and die.[6] Consider the example of Arthur Dimmesdale from Nathaniel Hawthorne's *The Scarlet Letter*. He is presented as a model Puritan minister—scholarly, pious, kind, not arrogant—who strays from the path of virtue in a moment of passion, but whose real moral disintegration comes from hiding the sin and pretending to the virtue he has lost. We do not get the sense that Dimmesdale's fall is owing to some previous "tragic flaw." Rather, his gradual moral collapse is sealed by his refusal to accept the only treatment that can help him—the acceptance of public humiliation. Dimmesdale's life, like King Solomon's, reminds us that if we forsake careful oversight of our moral lives, we can lose our hold on the virtues. ("Use 'em or lose 'em," you might say.) But what holds for the moral virtues applies as well to the intellectual virtues. The writer of Hebrews accuses those to whom the letter is directed of having *"become* dull in understanding," of needing to be taught *again* the basic teachings of God (Heb 5:11-12). Sometimes knowledge gives way to dogmatism, understanding grows clouded, and intellectual agility and acuity become calcified and unyielding.

Finally, to emphasize a point already made in connection to Father Zossima, growing in intellectual virtue requires that we grow in moral virtues, and vice versa. Aristotle's *Nichomachean Ethics* states, "It is not possible to be good in the strict sense without practical wisdom, nor practically wise without moral virtue" (6.1144.30). The solidarity between the Greek and Hebrew traditions in this matter is evident in the following quotation from the book of Wisdom: "Perverse thoughts separate men from God, and when his power is tested, it convicts the foolish; because wisdom will not enter a deceitful soul, nor dwell in a body enslaved to sin" (Wisdom 1:3-4). The Pauline theme of "suppressing the truth in unrighteousness" (see Rom 1:18) and the epistemic blindness to which such suppression gives rise echoes earlier Hebrew writers and affirms the interconnectedness of moral and intellectual virtues.

1.4 Doing Epistemology As If Virtue Mattered

Thinking about epistemological concerns from a virtue perspective is largely absent from epistemological writings of the last three hundred years. Thus it is useful to underscore (by way of a literary example) how the approach to epistemological matters might differ as one did or did not include a concern for intellectual virtues.

Mark Studdock, the servile sociologist in C. S. Lewis's novel *That Hideous Strength,* vividly illustrates one way our thinking can go awry and serves to focus our points of contrast. We learn that Mark has suffered since childhood from an inordinate craving to be accepted by others. "Mark liked to be liked. . . . There was a good deal of the spaniel in him."[7] As an adult he is lured away from his teaching post at a small college to work for the National Institute of Co-ordinated Experiments (N.I.C.E.), a pernicious organization bent on eugenic control of the human race. His consuming desire to be accepted by others, to feel a part of the inner ring, the power elite, eventually leads him to sacrifice his professional standards, his moral standards, his friends, his relationship with his wife (for a time) and—most relevant to our discussion—his ability to think straight.

When Mark falls out of favor with the power brokers at N.I.C.E., he is imprisoned on false murder charges. Now, withdrawn from all flatterers and feeling the betrayal of those whose favor he had sacrificed so much to gain, Mark begins to see the extent of his folly. The solitary confinement of his cell and the absence of food serve as a tonic for his clouded mind, allowing him to see the truth about himself for the first time.[8]

What a fool—a blasted, babyish, gullible fool—he had been! . . . Ought not his very first interview with the Deputy Director to have warned him, as clearly as if the truth were shouted through a megaphone or printed on a poster in letters six feet high, that here was plot within plot, crossing and double-crossing, of lies and graft and stabbing in the back, of murder and a contemptuous guffaw for the fool who lost the game? . . . Apparently his folly went further back. How on earth had he ever come to trust Feverstone—a man with a mouth like a shark, with his flash manners, a man who could never look you in the face? Jane or Dimble would have seen through him at once. He had "crook" written all over him. . . . With extraordinary clarity, but with renewed astonishment, he remembered, even more incredulously, how he had felt as a very junior Fellow while he was outside it—how he had looked almost with awe at the heads of Curry and Busby bent close together in Common Room, hearing occasional fragments of their whispered conversation, pretending himself to be absorbed in a periodical but longing—oh, so intensely longing—for one of them to cross the room and speak to him. And after months and months it happened. He had a picture of himself, the odious little outsider who wanted to be an insider, the infantile gull, drinking in the husky and unimportant confidences, as if he were being admitted to the government of the planet. Was there no beginning to his folly? Had he been an utter fool all through from the very day of his birth? . . .

He himself did not understand why all this, which was now so clear, had never previously crossed his mind. He was aware that such thoughts had often knocked for entrance, but had always been excluded for the very good reason that if they were once entertained it involved ripping up the whole web of his life, canceling almost every decision his will had ever made, and really beginning over again as though he were an infant. . . . There was no harm ripping up the web now for he was not going to use it anymore; there was no bill to be paid (in the shape of arduous decision and reconstruction) for truth.[9]

What shall we say about Mark Studdock's career as a cognitive agent? Pretty clearly, it is a shambles. Mark's self-assessment includes charges of gullibility, folly, blindness to obvious truth, deliberately suppressing counter evidence to his web of beliefs, and more. But what exactly is his problem? Where did he go wrong? Many standard diagnoses of thinking gone bad fail to capture completely (if they capture at all) what has gone wrong with Mark Studdock.

Sometimes we fail to secure the truth (or mistakenly take ourselves to be justified in a belief) because of some kind of physiological malfunction: a lesion on the brain, a tumor pressing on the optic nerve, or a brain malfunction caused by hallucinogenic drugs. Sometimes we miss the truth not because there is something wrong with our internal belief-forming mechanisms but because our environment is somehow deceptive: the water makes the oar appear bent, the hot pavement appears as a pool of water in the distance, a funhouse distorts what we perceive with mirrors, tilting floors and walls out of square. But none of these diagnoses strikes at the heart of what ails Studdock. His problem is not that his physiology contributing to cognitive function is deficient, nor that his environment is misleading in some way.

Another misdiagnosis comes from David Hume, who recommends that "the wise man ought to proportion his belief to the evidence." Not only should each of our beliefs enjoy the support of evidence, Hume thinks, but the depth of assent that one gives to each belief should be adjusted to the amount and quality of the evidence one possesses for the belief. One might think, at first glance, that here is the correct diagnosis of Mark Studdock's intellectual life: he believed in the political agenda of N.I.C.E. without having first collected adequate evidence. Moreover, it seems that he failed to take due account of the counterevidence that portrayed the Institute in a less favorable light.

But to the contrary, Mark's problem is not that he lacked evidence for his beliefs. Indeed, the brief narrative above suggests that his beliefs and their justifications formed for him a rational, coherent "web." Rather, the questions we want answered (which Hume's diagnosis fails to answer) are as follows: How did Mark come to construe as evidence the various beliefs that served that purpose for him—that is, why should the items that counted as evidence be taken as such? Why did these pieces of evidence assume the importance they did in his cognitive scheme? On what basis did the relative weighting of evidence take place? Why were some pieces of evidence subordinated to others, or ranked as of little or no importance? Why, for example, did the testimony of Feverstone, the N.I.C.E. lackey, carry more evidential weight than that of his wife's friend Dimble? Seeing certain information *as* evidence, and weighting it in the way one does, requires that we interpret the information in accordance with a set of background beliefs. How did Mark's background beliefs slant his particular understanding of the evidence? For answers to these questions we cannot simply rehearse the tired formula that Mark should have proportioned his belief to the evidence. This advice leaves unmentioned the roles that moral and intellectual character play in the process of belief formation, specifically by influencing what we count as evidence, along with its significance for us. We will return to this subject in later chapters.

Mark Studdock's story permits us to highlight some specific points of contrast between approaches to epistemological matters that do and do not take virtues to heart. First, note that Mark's believing the way he does has a history: his intellectual behavior is a part of a longer narrative context (in the story we learn how the moral and intellectual traits characterizing him as an adult were fostered since his childhood). Often, however, epistemologists tend to focus on isolated beliefs a person holds, as if on a snapshot of a person's life rather than on his or her career as an intellectual agent. So they might ask, for example, "Is Mark's belief that N.I.C.E. has the best interests of the citizenry in mind justified?" or, more abstractly, "Is S's belief that P justified?" or "Does S's belief that P cohere with other beliefs S holds?" The tradition of Augustine and Aquinas would have found this approach incomplete, because insofar as it attends to the lives of knowing agents at all, it focuses only on a narrow time-slice segment.

Whether or not we are living successful lives as cognitive beings must be determined by an inspection of our belief policies and behavior (our believings, denials, withholdings and other noetic acts) over the long term. A momentary cross-section carved out of our career at a particular moment doesn't provide enough information on which to base such a judgment, any more than a single episode of generosity provides sufficient grounds for judging someone morally good. This is not to say that a snapshot of our intellectual life is not without value; it may prove quite valuable in aiding our judgments about the overall trajectory of our careers as intellectual beings. But it is not the whole story. A momentary spike in your blood pressure at the doctor's office doesn't necessarily mean you have heart problems. Your blood pressure may be artificially elevated due to "cuff anxiety" or any number of factors. A consistently high reading, however, indicates unhealthiness. An intellectual career is not formed on the strength of a single belief any more than a moral life is evaluated on the basis of a single moral or immoral action. They are instead the cumulative result of many believings, many decisions made in the course of a lifetime.

One must not suppose, however, that an isolated instance of, say, credulity is without its effect in shaping our intellectual character. For as is so often observed in the moral life, a single action disposes us all the more readily to act similarly when circumstances are roughly the same. Telling a lie once makes it easier (sometimes almost inevitable) that we will tell another. And one doesn't have to continue in this vein too long before one might become a liar. Likewise, laxity in collecting evidence for one's hypotheses on one occasion may eventually lead to one's becoming intellectually lazy and losing regard for the truth. Entertaining and believing unsubstantiated gossip about a person on one occasion may contribute toward our becoming credulous or malicious or both. Allowing ourselves to subtly shade and distort our memories of certain events may eventually contribute to our becoming intellectually dishonest. So it would be incorrect to suppose that because we are concerned about the development of our long-term careers as intellectual agents, we can be indifferent about isolated occasions of belief formation.

So the focus of our thinking about epistemological excellence, I argue, should be the unfolding careers of knowers and the care they display in orienting themselves toward ends they deem valuable. Viewing epistemological questions in career terms, as the concerns of a lifetime, requires that we attend to the processes of belief formation, maintenance and revision, not just the specific outputs of these processes. While due regard must be given to the specific beliefs we hold, we must also pay careful attention to the manner by which we acquire and maintain them. Epistemology, then, is not (or ought not be) concerned merely with the piecemeal appraisal of individual beliefs but with what kinds of persons we are and are becoming:[10] whether we are intellectually humble rather than arrogant, studious rather than merely idly curious, insightful rather than dull, wise and not fools.

Analogously, wouldn't we think it odd to evaluate the effectiveness of salespersons on the strength of a single sale? We want to see how they conduct themselves over an extended period of time. We are interested in all the facets of their work: the initiative they display in winning new clients, the courtesy they show to customers, the promptness and efficiency with which they do their work, and the way they interact with their coworkers.

To require that cognitive agents attend to the processes of belief formation, maintenance and revision might make it sound as if we are wholly at liberty with respect to what we believe, that what we believe is under our direct voluntary control. But surely this is false. Which of us can by sheer effort reject the belief that the earth is round or accept the belief that our bank account contains millions more dollars than its actual balance? Beliefs aren't subject to our direct control in this way. Typically we don't decide what to believe, but rather find ourselves believing as we do as a result of various life experiences, early training, the testimony of authorities, other forms of social conditioning and so forth, long before we come to think critically about the sources of our beliefs. If most of our beliefs come to us unbidden, how then can I say that we should preside over our accepting and rejecting beliefs?[11]

While it is true that we do not exercise *direct* voluntary control over what we believe, we can influence the processes of belief formation, maintenance and revision *indirectly*. We can, for instance, voluntarily commit ourselves to a course of study that will eventuate in our coming to accept new beliefs. We can note tendencies we might have to believe with undue readiness unflattering statements about people we don't like, or to discount unfairly the criticisms of those who disagree with our preferred ways of thinking about a subject; we can then undertake disciplines that will loosen the power these tendencies have to affect the way we believe. We can, as behavioral psychologists often recommend, voluntarily commit ourselves to courses of action—volunteer work in the inner city, for instance—that will change the way we think about, say, matters of race and interpersonal relations. Generally speaking, then, the control we exercise in forming, sustaining and rejecting beliefs is indirect, brought about either by working on good habits of mind or by engaging in behaviors such as investigating a body of evidence, undergoing experiences of various sorts, or considering the opinions of others, and so forth. One of the goals of this book is to explore some of the ways our affective nature—the complex of emotions, concerns and character—influences how we believe.

Second, some epistemologists have written as if human beings were disembodied minds, ignoring, by and large, the connections between the life of the mind and the rest of our human nature. One notable example is René Descartes, who in his attempt at managing his intellectual life writes:

> I knew that I was a substance the whole essence or nature of which was to think, and that for its existence there is no need of any place, nor does it depend on any material thing; so that this "me," that is to say, the soul by which I am what I am, is entirely distinct from body.[12]

Descartes's precedent has yielded accounts of the rational life based on a very "thin" account of the person. His is not an epistemology of the whole person but an epistemology done from the neck up—a docetist epistemology that fails to acknowledge our full humanity as knowers. We have already seen how on a virtue account one's standing as a rational being is integrally bound up with one's emotions and will. Like Mark Studdock, we sometimes fail to excel intellectually because we fail to display moral virtues that coordinate with and support our intellectual endeavors.

Our physical bodies as well as our passional natures shape the contours of our intellectual lives and obviously "fatten" a thin account of the self. Our being embodied as we are affects our intellectual lives for good or ill, depending on whom you consult. Contrast Descartes's thinking with that of some evolutionary psychologists, who see our physical natures, our animality, as the supremely overriding influence in our cognitive pursuits. According to Robert Wright:

> We believe the things . . . that lead to behaviors that get our genes into the next generation. . . . Indeed, Darwinism comes close to calling into question the very meaning of the word truth. For the social discourses that supposedly lead to truth—moral discourse, political discourse, even, sometimes, academic discourse—are, by Darwinian lights, raw power struggles. . . . Already many people

believe what new Darwinism underscores: that in human affairs all (or at least much) is artifice, a self-serving manipulation of image.[13] While such an assessment may be unduly skeptical, it nevertheless underscores an important fact often overlooked by epistemologists: we are embodied beings whose intellectual purchase on the world is mediated by our physicality.[14]

"The good of the intellect is truth," writes Aquinas, "and falsehood is its evil. Wherefore those habits alone are called intellectual virtues, whereby we tell the truth and never tell a falsehood."[15] Our success in securing truth and avoiding error, however, is not measured by sheer quantity of truth. A quick rehearsal of the multiplication tables provides an instant and inexhaustible supply of certainty. Rather, we think that securing truth about important matters, truths that have a bearing on our own well-being and the happiness of others, is what ought to preoccupy us. And herein lies a third emphasis of virtue approaches to epistemology. Recent epistemology has not usually stressed that in addition to the number of truths we acquire and the way we acquit ourselves in acquiring them, success as a cognitive agent hinges on the *type of belief* one accepts.

There are historical reasons that bland, uninspiring beliefs such as "I see trees" or "There is a hand in front of my face" emerged as the foci of modern epistemological attention, and there are important philosophical lessons to be gleaned from discussions of such beliefs.[16] To make such beliefs the sole focus of epistemological study, however, makes the discipline an unnecessarily arid undertaking, for it ignores the sorts of beliefs that animate our lives and fill them with meaning. Efforts to determine under what conditions "*S* is justified in believing *P*" once again presupposes the adequacy of a "thin" account of the self and belies the richly textured contexts in which we live and move and have our very being. Søren Kierkegaard stresses the importance of those truths that nourish the soul.

Essentially viewed, the knowing that does not inwardly in the reflection of inwardness pertain to existence is accidental knowing, and its degree and scope, essentially viewed, are a matter of indifference. . . . Essential knowing is . . . related to the knower, who is essentially an existing person [Existerende], and . . . all essential knowing is therefore essentially related to existence and to existing.[17] Finally, virtue epistemology resists the theme prominent in so much modern epistemology that there is a generic, one-size-fits-all formula for the well-lived intellectual life. Epistemology that takes the virtues seriously claims instead that the parameters of a successful intellectual life are set against the backdrop of much broader historical, cultural and philosophical contexts, which pose for us certain overriding goals and purposes. A Christian's views about an excellent life (intellectual, moral, social, etc.) are embedded within a religious framework specifying God's desires for us and the world. My success as a cognitive being will therefore be determined in part by how well I am achieving the goals my tradition sets for me (whether, say, I am closer to the beatific vision). Significant differences will no doubt mark the accounts of intellectual excellence given by Christians from those accounts of excellence depicted by, say, Theravadan Buddhists, who teach the illusory nature of a unified mental life and seek the dissolution of the self.

We ought to pause, therefore, before we accept the adequacy of an "epistemological everyman" as the proper subject of our epistemological investigations. It seems appropriate to think that whether S is a virtuous knower or not depends on who S is, the cultural and historical context of which S is a part, the roles S plays in those contexts, how S's belief that P is related to other aspects of his or her interior life, and so on. Just as we cannot do epistemology from the neck up, we cannot do epistemology in a vacuum.

I have stressed the importance of intellectual virtues and vices for any thorough approach to epistemology, and I have contrasted a "virtues approach" to epistemological matters with orientations that ignore virtues and vices. But I wish to guard against the mistake of supposing that all of the questions and concerns raised by epistemologists are reducible to the business of acquiring intellectual virtues and eschewing intellectual vices. As William Alston has taught us, there are many "epistemological desiderata," many epistemic merits that we as knowers are better off having than lacking; intellectual virtues make up only a part—albeit a very important part—of these desiderata. As we shall see in later chapters, it is good that cognitive agents be warranted and justified in their beliefs. And while intellectual virtues can contribute significantly to our being warranted and justified, they do not constitute the whole of these notions.

1.5 Is Everyone Called to Pursue the Intellectual Virtues?
Devotion to the life of the mind may be a suitable goal for college professors and scientists, historians and editors, doctors and psychologists, but must plumbers, bankers, computer programmers, waitresses, artists, nurses and others outside academia be equally concerned? Though not all are called to an intellectual vocation, all are called to pursue intellectual virtues. How we pursue them, however, depends on factors such as our circumstances (the practical exigencies we face), our abilities (our native intellectual gifts and talents) and the roles we play (whether, say, we occupy special positions of leadership and responsibility). Not all persons are called to careers like teaching or to positions of leadership in church and society that demand special sophistication and depth in the understanding of the intellectual virtues. But no walk of life is without the need for insight, discretion and love of truth, among other intellectual virtues. Parents, folks at church, neighbors and laborers of every sort require prudence and understanding in sizing up the problems they face, in appraising accurately the needs of others and in determining the most appropriate response to a given problem. In all of these contexts dullness or folly or gullibility is a liability. It is not excessive to think that most persons are able to think about the content and support for their deepest convictions. Indeed, it is hard to imagine that one could lead a normal life without coming upon occasions for such reflection.

Perhaps an analogy will help. Not all persons are called to be doctors or health care professionals, though we all ought to be concerned about matters of health. Everyone should be concerned to pursue good health by exercising, eating right and avoiding behaviors that are harmful. How much we should eat and exercise will, of course, depend on our native capacities and the roles we play, as well as the particular circumstances we are in. Our health practices will vary depending on whether we play football or sit at a desk all day, whether we are teens or senior citizens, whether we are male or female. Doctors are set apart in matters of health by the responsibilities they assume, necessitating that they give wise counsel and instruction to others. In matters of virtue as well as matters of health there are special role-relative responsibilities that attach to persons in positions of leadership. But there are also generic responsibilities to pursue virtue that attach to us simply as humans.

I have argued that—like it or not—no walk of life is immune from the need for careful and reasonable thinking; epistemological concerns saturate our lives. Whether we pursue careers in business, auto mechanics, social work, the ministry, food service, teaching, commercial illustration or whatever, we need to be aware of important truths relevant to our activities, and we need to reason well about what goals we should pursue and what methods are best for achieving them. Moreover, regardless of our occupational interests, we all have a stake in thinking carefully about our moral and spiritual lives, which also benefit from our being intellectually virtuous. The intellectual virtues regulate the manner in which we think about these important matters. Regardless of the subject matter to which we turn our attention, our thinking ought to be characterized by such traits as practical wisdom, intellectual honesty and the love of truth. These are hallmarks of good thinking. So it will be useful to know what the intellectual virtues are and how our thinking about a particular subject either embodies or fails to embody them.

Having seen why epistemological questions in general and the pursuit of intellectual virtues in particular are properly Christian concerns, we must examine further several key intellectual virtues that bulk large in the academic life and that will figure in the discussion of other epistemological issues.

Two

Exploring the Intellectual Virtues

I f we recall briefly the history of some of our beliefs, we can identify some of the major types of intellectual virtue. Think, for example, about your political convictions—most of us acquire these as we approach adulthood. Perhaps you are a firm believer in democracy, and in particular the version espoused by the Democratic Party in the United States. After acquiring your initial political orientation, you probably went on to gain a more refined and deeper understanding of its elements. In all likelihood you have had to defend your party's stand on various issues (in your own thinking, if not in conversation with others) against criticisms by opposing parties or the media. At such times you found yourself refining and maybe even rejecting aspects of your beliefs. Perhaps your zeal for your party's beliefs has led you to stump on behalf of Democratic candidates and principles in your local precinct or ward, informing and educating others as to your party's merits. Someday you might even aspire to political office yourself. Then you will have to think about how best to implement the policies of your political party to make your town, state or country a better place to live.

2.1 Types of Intellectual Virtue

From this example we may extract a rough pattern that applies to many of our beliefs. I want to discuss four different kinds of things we do with our beliefs. There are occasions when we *acquire* beliefs, circumstances during which we deliberately *maintain* them in various ways, times when we seek to *communicate* our views and times when we focus on *applying* our beliefs to concrete problems and situations. Each of these activities of the intellectual life, if it is pursued well, calls for various intellectual virtues.[1]

Most often we think of intellectual virtues in connection with gaining knowledge, what I am calling *virtues pertaining to acquisition.* Suppose you are reading this book as a requirement for a four-year course of study dedicated to gaining important knowledge and maturing as an intellectual being. To pursue such studies requires that you have in sufficient degree a cluster of dispositions (interests and commitments) and qualities of will that make up a subset of the virtues pertaining to acquisition: what might be called *motivational intellectual virtues.* These are qualities of mind and character that provide impetus to our studies, that enable us to apply ourselves consistently and vigorously to intellectual tasks and help us to persevere in them. We need qualities such as inquisitiveness, teachableness and love of truth, as well as intellectual honesty and tenacity of belief. Of course these traits normally grow as we succeed in acquiring knowledge. Being motivated to learn and grow in knowledge doesn't guarantee that we will succeed, however; other traits are required to increase our chances of success. By contriving a rough narrative we can see more easily what virtues facilitate gaining knowledge.

Consider Mary, an undergraduate journalism major who hopes one day to work for a major newspaper. Mary's teachers and career counselors have urged her to apply for a summer internship on a newspaper staff. In addition to a variety of practical benefits (money, recommendations, contacts for postgraduate employment and so on), an internship will provide Mary with an invaluable opportunity to gain firsthand knowledge about her chosen career that she might not gain simply by reading textbooks on journalism. Mary also knows that she will face fierce competition to win one of these coveted internships. Whether she succeeds will depend on whether the people hiring her perceive Mary to have the qualities of mind and character that will make her an asset rather than a liability around the office.

What will Mary's interviewers be looking for? At a minimum, they will look to see how willing and able Mary is to be instructed. As a novice she has little of the specific knowledge and skills necessary to make her a proficient journalist, but several virtues precede any such specific knowledge. First (to mention only a few desirable intellectual traits), Mary must be *inquisitive* as well as *teachable*. Indifference and a know-it-all attitude are guaranteed to make an unfavorable impression and undermine her efforts. No doubt Mary's interviewers will study her application, letters of evaluation and other sources of information to discern whether, in addition to being willing and eager to learn, she is mentally alert and will walk into the workplace ready to acquire the knowledge she needs. A willing and eager spirit cannot compensate for a mind that is easily distracted or unobservant. Instead Mary must be *attentive* and *observant;* she must have an ability to notice accurately and with adequate precision features of her environment that are relevant to her tasks as an intern. She must also be *circumspect,* that is, mindful of the company she is keeping and the circumstances she is in. Mary's demeanor as she jokes with fellow interns in the lunchroom should be different from that she displays while being instructed by a supervisor. A circumspect person is cognizant of these changes and of the sort of behavior appropriate to each situation. *Inquisitiveness, teachableness, attentiveness, persistence, circumspection:* these are a few qualities of mind that Mary must give evidence of having as abiding and not merely occasional personal traits. For these motivational traits make a person especially receptive, a prime candidate to become an apt learner.

Mary's prospective employers want to know that Mary is more than merely inquisitive and willing to be instructed; they want some assurance that she can absorb, master and retain the knowledge she needs. For it is common that students who are equally inquisitive and willing to be instructed and have equal opportunity are nevertheless not equally successful in gaining knowledge. Why? Of course, many factors might account for this, but sometimes what makes the difference between students is the presence or absence in varying degrees of the intellectual virtues and certain natural powers. Students vary in their powers to perceive (some are more observant than others), to remember (some have greater powers of retentiveness), to introspect (some are more reflective and inward), to judge (some have more developed capacities to weigh conflicting evidence fairly), to analyze (some are more incisive in dissecting ideas into their component parts, in detecting the various logical and causal relations that obtain between our ideas), to synthesize (some are better able to detect patterns and regularities, to draw disparate facts into an organized whole), to be creative (some have greater independence of thought and originality of idea and expression)—to mention just a few traits. Being successful in gaining knowledge, then, depends not just on being properly motivated and inquisitive but on being excellent in sufficient degree in whatever specific cognitive powers and intellectual virtues we employ in a variety of circumstances to gain knowledge about the world.

The virtues enabling us to *obtain* truth may differ from those needed to *maintain* it. Let's return to Mary, who, you'll be delighted to discover, got the internship. Over the years her career flourished, so that she became a Pulitzer Prize-winning journalist with a major newspaper. Obviously Mary's success shows that she not only was an apt pupil in her journalistic studies but also has been adept at maintaining her beliefs and the skills that support them by refining and deepening her understanding of them. Here I do not construe *maintaining* to mean prevention only; it includes improving upon an initial deposit of beliefs. A farmer who buys and maintains a farm does more than merely prevent it from degenerating into a worse state than when he first purchased it; he maintains the farm by improving and upgrading it.

Unfortunately, Mary is now embroiled in a controversy regarding her use of paid underworld informants as sources for some of her articles. She claims this practice is common in her profession. Law enforcement officials want her to reveal the identity of her informants so that they can be questioned in connection with ongoing police investigations. Mary refuses to divulge her sources and finds that she is being criticized from various quarters. Because her case is itself becoming the subject of editorials in her own and other papers, Mary has decided to defend her record in the public arena.

The intellectual traits Mary must now rely on differ from those that first allowed her to gain knowledge of journalistic techniques and practices. *Virtues pertaining to maintenance* include a variety of intellectual traits that enable one not only to refine and deepen one's knowledge but also to defend it when it comes under attack. Mary's beliefs about acceptable journalistic practice are being assailed as unprofessional at the very least, and possibly immoral. What intellectual excellences will benefit Mary in this situation?

Mary must make use of a variety of intellectual traits, some of which (e.g., powers of analysis and creativity) are common to other aspects of the intellectual life. But Mary will especially need a species of the virtues that we might call "dialectical virtues": those we employ in articulating and defending our beliefs orally and in writing. The virtues Mary must use parallel those of the skilled debater, defense attorney or editorialist. She will have to assess skillfully her opponents' challenge in order to see what assumptions underlie it and what logical consequences stem from it. She will have to respond to the charges creatively, clearly and persuasively if she is to be successful in rebutting her opponents. I will assume that Mary has not only superior dialectical virtue but also supporting intellectual and moral traits; she is not a mere sophist, someone skilled only at making the weaker argument appear the stronger.

What will constitute success for Mary? Ideally it would be to convince her detractors to think as she does about the use of paid underworld informants.[2] At the very least Mary could consider herself successful if she could move her opponents to a position where they acknowledge her views as among the permissible options, even if not their own. Again, if Mary is to display intellectual virtue in the dialectical arena, it matters not only *whether* but also *how* Mary is able to shift her opponents' thinking. Strident tones and deliberately sophistic reasoning show disrespect for one's opponents and for the truth. One cannot be virtuous and have as one's goal to win at any cost.

Throughout this process of defending her beliefs, Mary will have to display tenacity or pertinacity of belief, another virtue relevant to maintenance. This virtue enables her to hold on to her beliefs when they are assailed in various ways, rather than abandon them at the first sign of criticism. This virtue is a counterpart in the intellectual realm to loyalty in the moral realm. One does not abandon friends at the first hint that they are being criticized for something. But neither does loyalty require that we continue to defend our friends no matter what they do. The virtue of tenacity of belief is often seen in the attitude scientists adopt toward their theories. At any given point in the career of a theory, there are things it can't explain, anomalies that seem to be exceptions to the theory and so forth. Scientists deal with these problems in various ways: by ignoring them, by posing ad hoc, temporary explanations, or by making the theories' weaknesses projects for ongoing scientific explanation. Paul Dirac, the famous English theoretical physicist, claimed that "it is more important to have beauty in one's equations than to have them fit experiment." Timothy Ferris, in his book *Coming of Age in the Milky Way,* comments on Dirac's statement:

> Dirac meant, of course, not that one should ignore the empirical results altogether, but that a beautiful theory need not be abandoned just because it fails an initial empirical test. He had in mind Erwin Schrodinger's reluctance to publish his estimable equations of wave mechanics merely because they conflicted with experimental data. "It is most important to have a beautiful theory," Dirac told science writer Horace Freeland Judson. "And if the observations don't support it, don't be too distressed, but wait a bit and see if some error in the observations doesn't show up."[3]

You can miss the mark either by relinquishing your beliefs at the slightest provocation, making yourself like a ship "tossed to and fro and blown about by every wind of doctrine," or by clinging to them come what may, making yourself dogmatic. The virtue of proper tenacity enables us, as the saying goes, "to know when to hold 'em and know when to fold 'em."

You'll be relieved to hear that Mary successfully weathered the controversy she was embroiled in—and became something of a celebrity in the process. In fact, a prestigious university asked her to become an adjunct professor, thereby allowing her to influence in a more direct way the next generation of elite journalists. Of course Mary has always been an able communicator, possessing a full measure of what I am calling *virtues pertaining to communication.* She possesses those traits that are indispensable for a successful newspaper writer: insight, articulateness, precision, eloquence, persuasiveness and so on. But her work as a teacher will require that other virtues relevant to communication come the fore. Imparting knowledge and information in a teacher-student situation requires another subset of virtues relevant to communication. We might call these *pedagogical virtues.* Not all who excel in some area are able to teach others what they know. For example, when musicians are asked how they are able to negotiate difficult passages or improvise a cadenza, they sometimes respond, "I just let the music carry me along," or express a sort of bewilderment about it themselves.

The virtues of a great performer, whether in sports, music, chess or elsewhere, don't automatically make one a great teacher. Dorothy Delay, of Juilliard, is one of the world's most famous violin teachers. Her students include such international stars as Midori and Nadja Salerno-Sonnenberg. Delay never had a concert career and describes herself as not having been a good student.[4] But her ability to train and promote rising stars is remarkable. Her students and admirers comment on her ability to communicate with students, to move them to maturity and independence of judgment, emotion and style, and to help them understand audiences and the demands of the particular performance. One former student describes Delay as having "the most penetrating analytical mind and a matchless ability to diagnose and solve any technical problem."[5] Clearly, to be a teacher of Delay's caliber requires intellectual virtues of clarity, creativity and persuasiveness, not to mention personal traits such as empathy, sincerity and humility.

Mary's charmed career as a journalist went on to include participation on a blue-ribbon presidential commission dedicated to exploring ways journalists can help create a more informed electorate. Mary was disturbed to find out that well over half of the Americans eligible to vote couldn't name their own representative in Congress. The traits enabling us to apply what we know in order to secure specific practical goods and purposes I am calling the *intellectual virtues relevant to application*. Various virtues such as administration, organization, foresight, problem solving and strategy are features of the intellectual life apropos here.

We often differentiate between theoreticians and applied practitioners in an academic discipline. A theoretical physicist studying a particular subject may not be able to see as well as an engineer how to implement this knowledge in practical applications in, say, medicine or the military. Some persons have capacities that fit them to see how knowledge about a certain subject can be brought to bear on concrete problems or to secure certain practical goods.

A life of virtue is a whole life, in which the excellences of mind and character are blended into an unbroken wholeness; in short, a virtuous intellectual life is marked by *integrity*. An obvious flaw mars persons whose brilliance blinds them to the concerns of others. Worse still are villains like the Nazi doctors who used their powers of mind to harm and exploit others. Nature may endow some persons with intellectual traits we admire—acuity, foresight, imaginativeness—but having a trait that is generally admired does not necessarily make you an admirable person.

We must therefore differentiate between the sort of admiration we have for certain intellectual traits, considered individually and in the abstract, and the admiration we have for persons who possess them. Traits such as eloquence and a strategic mind are desirable and admirable, but we must remember that these qualities are always qualities that reside in persons, and personal excellence involves more than excellence of mind. It is important therefore to see the narrative context, the life story of the person in whom these traits reside. No doubt Hitler was a brilliant and eloquent administrator. Our deep lament is that these intellectual pearls bedecked a swine!

An incident from the children's book *A Little Princess*, by Frances Hodgson Burnett, illustrates the point about integrity. Sara Crewe is a bright and wise-beyond-her-years orphan who works as a household drudge in Miss Minchen's Select Seminary for Young Ladies. She befriends Ermangarde, one of Miss Minchen's duller pupils. When Ermangarde's father sends her a stack of history books, she laments to Sara:

"He wants me to read them," said Ermangarde, a little discouraged by this unexpected turn of affairs.

"He wants you to know what is in them," said Sara. "And if I can tell it to you in an easy way and make you remember it, I should think he would like that."

"He'll like it if I learn anything in any way," said a rueful Ermangarde. "You would if you were my father."

"It's not your fault that—" began Sara. She pulled herself up and stopped rather suddenly. She had been going to say: It's not your fault that you are stupid.

"That what?" Ermangarde asked.

"That you can't learn things quickly," amended Sara. "If you can't you can't. If I can—why, I can: that's all."

She always felt very tender of Ermangarde, and tried not to let her feel too strongly the difference between being able to learn anything at once, and not being able to learn at all. As she looked at her plump face, one of her wise, old-fashioned thoughts came to her.

"Perhaps," she said, "to be able to learn things quickly isn't everything. To be kind is worth a great deal to other people. If Miss Minchen knew everything on earth and was like what she is now, she'd still be a detestable thing, and everybody would hate her. Lots

of clever people have done harm and have been wicked. Look at
Robespierre—"
According to the Christian way of looking at things, persons and not
their individual attributes will be the final subject of praise and blame.
I will not fare any better on the judgment day because I was blue-eyed,
tall or, for that matter, naturally inquisitive and attentive. What will
matter, among other things, is how well I superintended *my* life and
the "talents" entrusted to my care, which include the way my intellectual character did or did not contribute to that life. In these matters
the playing field is a lot more level.

A clarification must be made at this point. It would be misleading
to think that an intellectual virtue—say the virtue of perceptiveness—
pertains to acquisition and only to acquisition, as it would be misleading to think that clarity and cogency are virtues that apply only when
we communicate our beliefs, for they apply as well to the defense of
our beliefs. The lines separating these four areas are admittedly fuzzy.
In fact, some traits seem to be relevant to many intellectual endeavors
(love of truth and intellectual honesty, to mention only two). It would
be more accurate to say that in the intellectual life we face a variety of
different situations or circumstances: times when we need to acquire,
defend, communicate and apply knowledge. And in each of these
situations different excellences of mind become salient.

The following analogy might help. If you are a general interested
in winning a battle, you bring your whole army to the fray. Because a
battle unfolds in phases, different parts of your army may be called to
the fore at different times: reconnaissance at an early stage, artillery
and air support at another, and infantry and medics at still other times.
But it may happen that some soldiers are active in every phase in the
battle. So it is with the virtues. As we pursue the truth, we encounter
different circumstances requiring us to draw upon different intellectual traits, and some traits seem to be in play in most of the intellectual
tasks that befall us.

Not only may the same intellectual traits be relevant to a variety of
intellectual endeavors, but the precise role they play in our intellectual
lives varies with the circumstances in which we find ourselves. Aris-

totle notes, for instance, how the same moral virtue may require different behavior from different persons, depending on their circumstances. The virtue of temperance applied to eating will look quite different in the life of an Olympic marathoner than in the life of a philosophy professor. The same point applies to intellectual virtues. We prize traits such as foresight, attentiveness and circumspection; but these same traits may issue in different behavior depending on our circumstances. Foresight before taking off on a cross-country drive may require only that I check my oil level, my tire pressure and the roadworthiness of my spare tire. Foresight in my job as a space shuttle engineer will assume a different and more demanding form, as my job and the stakes at hand require that I anticipate numerous and even unlikely scenarios. The virtue of attentiveness will demand more of a soldier in a garrison under siege than of the same soldier back on the base in peacetime. We see, then, that moral and intellectual virtues direct our thinking and actions in situation-specific ways that call for behaviors relevant to our roles and responsibilities.

2.2 The Structure of Intellectual Virtues

As we saw in the last chapter, virtues are well-anchored, abiding dispositions that persons acquire through their own voluntary actions and that enable them reliably to think, feel and act in ways that contribute to their fulfillment and sometimes to the fulfillment of those with whom they interact. They allow us to negotiate gracefully and successfully the tasks of life as they arise, and to overcome obstacles in the path of accomplishments. Vices, by contrast, are settled traits of character that undermine human flourishing. Intellectual virtues such as interpretive sensitivity, prudence and studiousness are habits of persons *as thinkers,* which allow us to live excellent intellectual lives—lives whose goals include gaining knowledge and understanding. I also claimed that epistemology as a discipline can benefit from having a number of its concerns recast so as to invoke virtue concepts.

But my recommendations remain vague, like a doctor's advice that you eat right if you want to be healthy. We want to know which foods to eat, how much and in what combinations. Analogously, we need something like a dietary chart or map to orient our thinking about the intellectual virtues. A map of the intellectual virtues will direct us to the central types of intellectual virtue and help us to see their contours and interrelationships.

Let us first consider moral virtue and vice, since its language and concepts are fairly familiar. Virtues, as we have already seen, paradigmatically dispose us to think and feel and act in ways that contribute to our and others' flourishing. Let's see, as an example, how the three component parts mentioned above coincide in the lives of compassionate people.

First, they must have reliable powers of moral perception and judgment that indicate to them persons who are in need; they see the moral qualities of the situations they are in. We find virtuously compassionate people especially sensitive at detecting the suffering of others.

Second, the judgments of compassionate persons will be qualified by, or perhaps prompted by, a corresponding emotion or set of emotions. Compassionate persons have enduring concerns that motivate them to ameliorate the suffering of others. Because they are concerned that others not suffer unnecessarily, they want to relieve the suffering of others. They will typically feel pity and sadness that some person is living in deprivation and will feel joy if another's needs are met. Their abiding concern to see suffering relieved accompanies them through life's varied circumstances, through encounters with poor and rich, sick and well, grieving and rejoicing, each case prompting them to *feel* emotions commensurate with their concerns and their circumstances.[6] Thus emotions and the concerns that give rise to them can motivate, accompany and arise as a consequence of our virtuous actions.

Third, compassionate persons *act* appropriately to alleviate need. To act appropriately, however, requires not just careful deliberation but whatever skills and knowledge may be necessary to act in accordance with the virtue. For instance, we typically find that virtuously compassionate persons have social skills that enable them to offer suitably consoling words, or a well-timed hug, or the appropriate sort of assistance. An indulgent parent or a codependent-dependent spouse may give lavishly but does not give appropriately, and hence not virtuously. To go awry in any of the parts of a virtue is to fall short of the virtue. To perceive and act to alleviate need but inwardly to resent doing so is not to act virtuously; what's missing is the underlying concern for the well-being of others. An obtuse person who simply fails to notice need, even if he or she would respond appropriately upon detecting it, is likewise not virtuous. All three elements must be present, and present in the right degree.

Virtues are *dispositional* properties, along with the concerns and capacities for judgment and action that constitute them. They are properties that we can possess even at times when we are not acting virtuously or overtly displaying them in some other way. Rather, various circumstances we encounter trigger our acting out of the virtue. I might be a courageous person even though I go a considerable length of time without becoming aware of dangers that would require a courageous response from me. I might care deeply that unnecessary human suffering be alleviated, and yet go through a day or a week when no circumstances arise to activate a compassionate response. Vices too exist in us as dispositional properties. A person with a hair-trigger temper, easily moved to vicious anger by the slightest provocation, may nevertheless pass a day in which no circumstances "pull the trigger," as it were. So virtues are deeply embedded parts of character that readily dispose us to feel, to think and to act in morally appropriate ways as our changing circumstances require.

Of course it does not follow that a person who is not maximally virtuous is automatically vicious in the worst possible way. Classical Greek philosophers distinguished among moral virtue, moral strength, moral weakness and moral viciousness. Morally vicious persons are flawed in thought, word and deed; not only do they not judge correctly about moral matters, but as a result they do not act or feel appropriately either.[7] Morally weak persons suffer from what the ancients called *akrasia* (weakness of will). They may correctly identify the path of virtue, but they lack a motivational structure of sufficient strength and development to move them to act virtuously. Morally strong persons judge rightly with respect to moral matters but must nevertheless struggle with temptation and contrary inclination. Morally virtuous persons not only judge and feel appropriately but move easily to act in morally appropriate ways; for such persons doing the right thing constitutes a "default mode."

Perhaps the late Mother Teresa's nature had been so transformed that she not only readily identified and empathized with the poor and sick but even reached out to them "on motivational autopilot," as it were, without having to struggle against contrary inclinations. She never (or very rarely) thought to herself, *Oh, let the sick kid fend for himself, I'm tired of helping others.* Here too we can note a contrast between Greek and Christian concepts of the virtues. According to the Greek conception, to have the virtue of generosity I must act relatively flawlessly with respect to my giving. Christian thinkers (following Scripture and the model of the adult convert as opposed to the aristocratically bred Athenian gentleman) claimed that this side of heaven we cannot escape contrary inclination in all areas of life.[8]

The concept of a virtue on the above analysis is rooted in the notion of human flourishing, from which it follows that contrasting notions of human flourishing will give rise to differing accounts of the virtues and their various interrelations. Traditionally theories of virtue and vice and the concepts they employ are embedded in some notion of human flourishing or happiness. Whether a trait is virtuous or vicious hinges on where our lives as a whole ought to be headed. Thus what we regard as intellectually virtuous and vicious behavior will vary as we are committed to one or another account of human flourishing. Consider how notions of human flourishing and the goals of cognition corresponding to them change as we alternatively embrace the ideals of Aristotelian *Eudaemonia,* Stoic *apatheia,* the Christian beatific vision or Buddhist annihilation.

Our analyses of intellectual virtue and vice, as well as what we take to be the distinctive features that make certain traits good or bad, are situated in larger philosophical commitments that impart to them their own distinctive *grammar.* Let me illustrate: We in philosophy prize analytical rigor; we work to cultivate skills with which we can dissect concepts into their component parts and note their various logical interrelations. Sometimes, we think, the truth about the world is revealed only after logical dissection. Zen Buddhists, however, condemn such thinking as intellectually vicious, as symptomatic of an underlying spiritual defect that keeps us bound to the wheel of rebirth. "For the attainment of incomparable satori, one has to cast away his discriminating mind. Those who have not passed the barrier and have not cast away the discriminating mind are all phantoms haunting trees and plants."[9] Though Buddhists defend my general thesis about the connection between intellectual and moral vice, they reject the Christian account of persons and flourishing that constitutes the framework for the present discussion. As a consequence, while Buddhists (as well as Stoics, Nietzscheans and Aristotelians) may invoke terms such as *compassion, courage, wisdom* and other virtue concepts, these will overlap with their Christian counterparts only to varying degrees. But this result is precisely what we should expect, for the New Testament too contrasts, for example, wisdoms grounded in different root concerns: those grounded in purely human precepts and those grounded in God.

Now let us look more carefully at intellectual virtues. Following the model of a moral virtue, we can analyze intellectual virtues as abiding, reliable traits that allow us to orient our intellectual lives—our believings, perceiving, reasoning habits and so on—in ways that contribute to human flourishing.[10] Intellectual virtues, on this analysis, ought not to be equated with reliably functioning natural faculties such as sight, hearing, memory or capacity for introspection, though the absence of properly functioning natural capacities could very well interfere with my being able to perceive, feel and act reliably as virtue might require.[11] An epistemic vice, by contrast, is a trait (an attitude, affection or disposition) that bears unfavorably on some aspect of one's intellectual life. I have mentioned traits such as wisdom, understanding and foresight as examples of intellectual virtues. Intellectual vices include traits such as obtuseness, gullibility, superstitiousness, close-mindedness, willful naiveté and superficiality of thought. We must ask, though, whether intellectual virtues follow the model of moral virtues by touching upon the way we think, feel and act.

What of emotions and intellectual virtue? At first glance we might question whether intellectual virtues follow the same structure as moral virtues. Suppose I display the virtue of discernment by picking out some especially subtle, elusive pattern found among experimental samples in my laboratory. Will my having acted out of the virtue automatically come accompanied by some particular emotion? It would seem not.[12] Despite appearances, emotions and the underlying concerns that give rise to them are connected to intellectual virtues in various ways.

Sometimes emotions motivate intellectual activity. C. S. Peirce observed that unresolved doubts leave us in an "uneasy" and "irritated" state that moves us to resolve our uneasiness by "fixing" (settling on) some belief.[13] Why should the unresolved doubts that a scientist has about a theory produce an uneasy and irritated state? Presumably because the scientist is concerned about the truth or falsity of the theory and all that is implied by it. Such a concern can assume both an "interested" and a "disinterested" form. The scientist may care about the theory itself because of its centrality in her scientific outlook and research. Her love of a subject matter spurs her to want to know more about it, to explore its nature. But she can also care in a disinterested way: even if it should turn out that her cherished theory is false, she is more concerned that her mind track the truth and that she avoid believing what is false.

Some persons, on the other hand, are relatively unperturbed upon finding that their beliefs are false or inconsistent. Because they lack our scientist's concern for truth and consistency of beliefs, they are not disposed to feel the uneasiness of which Peirce speaks and, as a result, lack the intellectual virtue of truthfulness or intellectual honesty. Persons who have "a passion for the truth," an abiding concern for the truth, are thereby disposed to a whole range of emotions, including anxiety when their beliefs are assailed by doubts, delight when some discovery resolves such doubts, and discouragement when some research program undertaken to resolve the doubts fails. To see more clearly how our concerns and the emotions to which they give rise suffuse all phases of the intellectual life, let us consider a real-life example.

Barbara McClintock won the Nobel Prize in 1983 for her revolutionary work in the transposable elements in the genetic makeup of corn. Her work was so complicated and meticulously documented that it met with stony silence when first presented at a conference of geneticists decades before she received the Nobel award; only a very few scientists were then in a position to appreciate her revolutionary findings. Despite this setback, McClintock returned to her work with greater determination. A colleague at Cold Springs Harbor Laboratory, Evelyn Wilken, commented on her work during this period: "It was a great thing to see. She was really getting such intense joy out of it."[14] When notified of her award, McClintock commented on how unfair it seemed "to reward a person for having so much pleasure, over the years, asking the maize plant to solve specific problems and then watching its responses."[15] McClintock directly linked the intensity and acuity of her observations to the thrill she received from being so intensely absorbed: "Anyone who must think intensely and integrate vast amounts of information to solve a problem must feel it too."[16] McClintock's having acted out of the intellectual virtues was accompanied by her feeling great joy.

The example of Barbara McClintock suggests several observations. Clearly she embodies the intellectual virtue of perseverance. She is not much discouraged by her failure to garner her colleagues' recognition. But notice how this appears to be grounded in the joy she derives from her work, her deep delight in the subject matter itself. Someone who cared more for recognition and other extrinsic rewards probably would not have tolerated the professional isolation she endured. McClintock's love of her subject and the intrinsic rewards she derived from researching it gave her a kind of intellectual independence or autonomy that is itself virtuous.

We see, then, that emotions and their underlying concerns not only motivate intellectually virtuous activity but also accompany our acting out of the virtues—*and* come about as a consequence of our having acted out of an intellectual virtue. We feel gratified when we have solved some difficult problem. Creative people feel joy and exaltation when they create some fine work or bring some extended research project to completion. What we care about has the potential to influence our motives for pursuing intellectual tasks and the manner in which such tasks are pursued, as well as the kinds of persons we become for having pursued them. In fact, emotions contribute to intellectual flourishing in such deep and interesting ways that I will explore this subject further in the last chapter.

For now, however, we can discern in the minds of persons suitably trained a pattern linking emotions and intellectual virtues that reflects the moral quality of emotions themselves. We think emotions are appropriate or inappropriate insofar as they reflect features of the world that are themselves good or bad: in other words, emotions must "fit" what they are about. For this reason we think it brutish to laugh at parents who are grieving the loss of a child and churlish to be resentful at another's success. Laughter and other forms of merriment don't fit with the tragedy of losing a child. A similar fit marks the emotions of someone who is intellectually virtuous. As noted, joy, gratification, delight, repose and a host of other emotions accompany creativity, intellectual success, discovery, problem solving and other activities that betoken our coming to have a better understanding of the world. By the same token, situations that thwart understanding trigger negative emotions in us. We feel frustrated when our inquiries after truth fail, annoyance at superstition, outrage at beliefs rooted in prejudice, and anxiety or apprehension when our cherished convictions are challenged. Thus we see just how close are the connections linking emotions and intellectual virtue.

One might also question the similarity of structure between intellectual and moral virtues by noting that not every display of intellectual virtue is automatically action guiding. If I have the virtue of foresight, it might require that I anticipate and make suitable plans for the future—for example, that I start saving now for an anticipated shortfall of funds. If I am virtuously teachable (docile), I will pay attention and expend effort to master material. But not every intellectual virtue issues forth in some specific action or, for that matter, in any action at all. Being virtuous in understanding or wisdom might be compatible with continuing to meditate in an easy chair. That intellectual virtues don't always issue in action is not a point of contrast with moral virtues, however, but a point of similarity. For instance, I might be virtuously truthful or humble or friendly without these virtues leading automatically to some specific action. Rather we should say that the virtues, moral and intellectual, dispose us, as circumstances require, to various courses of action.

2.3 Epistemology, Virtue and Responsibility

By saying that virtues are voluntary and acquired traits I mean to underscore the fact that whether the virtues or the vices take deep root within a person depends in some measure on the person's deliberative will. No one becomes compassionate or patient or self controlled accidentally. You could not wake up one morning to the serendipitous discovery that you had overnight become habitually wise or prudent or discerning. Rather, we bear varying degrees of responsibility for our moral and intellectual traits insofar as our choices either thwart their development or contribute to it. Consequently, we are proper objects of praise and blame when our choices contribute to our being intellectually virtuous or vicious persons. To cultivate these qualities requires that we be aware (at some level) of how we are thinking and choosing and behaving. (We can, of course, make mistakes about whether we have or lack these qualities.) If we detect deficiencies within ourselves, we can undertake various strategies to overcome them. If, for example, I believe myself to be gullible, I can resolve not to accept any testimony that is not corroborated, and then assiduously practice checking on truth claims.

Though I have stressed the role of personal choice in becoming virtuous, it is not the case that we always bear full responsibility for our intellectual and moral states. Being virtuous is not simply a matter of pulling ourselves up by our own bootstraps, as it were, but comes about as a result of our conscientiously developing what nature and early training bequeath to us. And we must admit that the playing field is not level with respect to either early opportunity or natural endowment. The role of the deliberative will is thus circumscribed by early training and native ability. So while I may bear some personal responsibility for being morally and intellectually virtuous, it may also be due, in varying degrees, to accidents of history, geography and the natural lottery. Being raised and taught in a moral environment by parents who model moral virtue and who work hard to train me in it will assuredly make my becoming virtuous easier than were I to have been raised in a thieves' den. Aristotle acknowledges, if not overstates, this point when he claims that "the difference between one and another training in habits in our childhood is not a light matter, but important, or rather, all-important."[17] Some persons are born with genius-level IQs or unusual facility in mathematics or art. Moreover, they are fortunate to be born into circumstances where such natural gifts are allowed to flourish. Others with similar native potential are born into severe deprivation, with the result that their potential is stunted or extinguished or left completely undeveloped.

Most people, however, are born with more modest natural endowments and must achieve such excellence as they can through hard work and perseverance, sometimes overcoming formidable obstacles. The story of Demosthenes (383-322 B.C.), the famous Greek orator, illustrates this. As the story goes, Demosthenes was born with a severe speech impediment and was jeered and ridiculed for his poor delivery the first time he spoke before a public assembly. He resolved to do all within his power to overcome his impairment. He put pebbles in his mouth to learn to speak distinctly and gave speeches before the roaring surf to strengthen his voice. He overcame not only the self-imposed impediments but nature's as well, and went on to become the most eloquent orator of ancient Greece. So while nature and environment don't favor everyone equally, we can nevertheless strive, like Demosthenes, to exercise such powers as we do have to regulate our lives so as to become intellectually and morally virtuous.

The roles of heredity and environment in shaping our intellectual state require that we make further distinctions between the characteristics that contribute to epistemic success and failure. Let me distinguish among purely *natural intellectual abilities, intellectual skills* and *intellectual virtues*. Someone born with perfect pitch or a photographic memory will obviously excel in discovering a certain range of truth.

Though such abilities are admirable on some level, they are not virtues; indeed, they may be found in some idiot savants. Typically persons possessing such qualities did not acquire them, nor can we say they are personally praiseworthy epistemic agents for being so gifted.[18] Similarly, a person who is defective intellectually (an Alzheimer's or ADD sufferer, for example) is in a lamentable state vis-à-vis the intellectual life but is not thereby intellectually vicious. Many cognitive defects or excellences may thwart or assist our intellectual efforts without being attributable to some underlying personal failing or effort for which we bear responsibility.

Consider next someone with an acquired skill in doing proofs in deductive logic. This person too will be adept at discovering a certain range of truth and avoiding falsehood. He or she will know, for example, the correct procedures for running a *reductio ad absurdum* argument and how to avoid adopting beliefs grounded in bad logic. Though such skill requires effort to acquire, and granted that it is better to have such skill than to lack it, it still does not constitute a real intellectual virtue.[19] For such skills can be cultivated and deployed in ways relatively disconnected from human flourishing. (Think of the Unabomber, for example.) A mature intellectual virtue, by contrast, arises out of a concern for human wholeness and, in its Christian form, union with God. A part of practical wisdom consists in one's ability to survey the shape of one's life, to monitor one's strengths and weaknesses, and to undertake strategies of self-improvement where possible. Viewed this way, intellectual and moral virtues have an integrating function; they draw together the threads of a person's life and weave them together in a coherent and vital whole.

Our map of the virtues has located only a few of the major thoroughfares and points of interest. We have noted that four general activities mark the intellectual life, and we have explored the way various intellectual traits aid us in acquiring, maintaining, communicating and applying knowledge. It is now time to explore some of the surrounding terrain in greater detail. By examining carefully a few select virtues we can better appreciate their richness and subtlety and how they contribute to an integrated intellectual life.

Three

An Extended Look at Some Intellectual Virtues

In the last chapter I identified some of the major intellectual tasks we perform and situations we face as thinking beings, and I indicated some of the types of virtues that are relevant to these tasks. Some intellectual virtues are narrower in scope than others; they apply to a more limited range of circumstances. Inquisitiveness and teachableness, for example, are obviously traits pertaining chiefly (though perhaps not exclusively) to acquiring beliefs and knowledge. Other intellectual virtues (such as understanding, prudence, analysis and discernment) are relevant to almost all the major intellectual tasks we perform, as important in acquiring beliefs as in defending and applying them.

But with this rough scheme of the virtues we have not yet analyzed any of these traits in detail. We have not explored, for instance, what makes something an instance of practical wisdom. What are the particular boundaries of this virtue? How does it differ, if at all, from discernment or insight? By what marks do we identify persons of practical wisdom? Each particular virtue constitutes a point of interest for anyone exploring the landscape of intellectual virtues.

The monumental task of exploring the scores of intellectual virtues that exist exceeds the scope of this introductory book. What follows, then, is a brief glance at a few virtues (as well as their corresponding vices) that bear on the four main types of intellectual activity.

3.1 Studiousness and Vicious Curiosity

Aristotle taught that we have a natural desire to know, a natural creaturely inquisitiveness that we admire and promote in our children. And we in philosophy, and in the tradition of liberal education in general, have indulged that natural desire, claiming that knowledge need not serve any practical or utilitarian interest but is its own end. Combine this with the high regard for free inquiry held in a democratic society, and we have some potent reasons for licensing a quest for truth unbounded in scope and subject matter.

Or do we? Should we indulge every desire to gain truth about a certain subject, regardless of what it is and how we attain it? For instance, suppose someone you consider reliable came to you offering to reveal some especially dark secret about one of your best friends. Would you accept their offer to expand the number of truths you know?

William James said there are two commandments that define our duty as knowers: we must know the truth and avoid error.[1] This account, however, offers too anemic a portrait of our lives as intellectual persons because it fails to integrate the task of discovering truth with other key intellectual and human concerns. To integrate our intellectual life within a whole life requires that we situate our intellectual pursuits within a broader motivational structure. We must monitor our *intentions* for seeking knowledge, the *methods* we employ and the *use* to which such knowledge is put, and we must evaluate the *relative importance* of the truths we do obtain.

Unless we are duly aware of how we employ our mental powers, we may find them serving pernicious ends. Truths we may uncover, knowledge we may obtain, but we risk exemplifying what Robert

Coles has called "immoral intelligence." In an address titled "Educating for a Moral Life," given on the occasion of the 350th birthday celebration of Harvard University, Coles argued that intellectuals, like the Nazi intelligentsia, sometimes exhibit a kind of "mischievous intelligence" or "wicked intelligence." Elsewhere Coles recounts a conversation with the poet William Carlos Williams:

> As Williams once reminded me about the Nazi Joseph Goebbels and Williams' own friend Ezra Pound: "Look at the two of them, one a Ph.D. and smart as they come, and the other, one of the twentieth century's most original poets, also as brilliant as they come in certain ways—and they both end up peddling hate, front men for the worst scum the world has ever seen."[2]

Doctors, lawyers, philosophers, literary critics, journalists, psychologists and scores of Germany's most highly educated people willingly turned their mental energies to the service of one of history's most malevolent causes. Notice, though, that one needn't behave as heinously as the Nazis to display wicked intelligence. "How many of us," writes Coles, "are all too smart, and yet also weird, snotty, and selfish?"

Virtue epistemologists like Augustine and Aquinas stress that we should situate the life of the mind within a larger framework of motives and ends. For them, as Christians, this meant kingdom ends: our zest for knowledge and information must, in the final analysis, be bounded by devotion to God and love of neighbor. These medieval thinkers called a properly situated intellectual life "studious," whereas knowledge sought outside a virtuous framework was dubbed "curiosity." For the moment the terms *curiosity* and *studiousness* must be wrested from their contemporary use. A studious person is not merely a bookworm or an intellectual "nerd," nor is curiosity the mere desire for more knowledge. In the writings of these Christian thinkers the meanings of these words are morally and religiously laden.

According to Augustine, the mind is subject to a form of craving not unlike the appetites of the body.

> The mind is also subject to a certain propensity to use the sense of the body, not for self-indulgence of a physical kind, but for satisfaction of its own inquisitiveness. This futile curiosity masquerades

under the name of science and learning, and since it derives from our thirst for knowledge and sight is the principal sense by which knowledge is acquired, in the Scriptures it is called *gratification of the eye.*[3]

This diagnosis seems to apply perfectly to Mrs. Snagsby, a character in Charles Dickens's *Bleak House.* Mr. Snagsby describes her to a lawyer acquaintance thus:

"Well, sir," returns Mr. Snagsby, "you see my little woman is—not to put too fine a point on it—inquisitive. She's inquisitive. Poor little thing, she's liable to spasms, and it's good for her to have her mind employed. In consequence of which she employs it—I should say on every individual thing she can lay hold of, whether it concerns her or not—especially not. My little woman has a very active mind, sir."[4]

Like so much of the virtuous life, seeking truth appropriately is a matter of seeking it in the right way, for the right reason, using the right methods and for the right purposes. A completely unbridled quest for truth, one indifferent to right motives and means, is degenerate from its inception. We must therefore differentiate between two goods arising from our search for knowledge. On the one hand there is the good consisting in our having successfully laid hold of the truth about a certain matter so as to have knowledge (setting aside for the moment what conditions constitute success). The other good, the one pertaining to virtue, stems from our having responsibly and appropriately employed our cognitive powers. Analogously, financial security is a good thing; financial security achieved through robbery or in order to launch a career as a slum lord is not. Knowledge, like wealth, cannot be sought at any cost but is subject to moral restraints.

Why do you desire to further your education? Is it because you wish to appear important to others? Will your education promote in you an arrogant and supercilious attitude toward less-educated persons? Do you seek knowledge about others to wield as a weapon against them, as a tool for dominating them?[5] Or is your intellectual life motivated by charity? Do you desire to know in order to promote your neighbor's as well as your own highest welfare? These questions demand that we consider not only our motives but the purposes our knowledge will serve. Knowledge of particle physics is a good thing, but if that knowledge is sought with the deliberate aim of building the most powerful engines of destruction the world has ever known, then we see an example of what medieval thinkers called "vicious curiosity." Today virtually everyone recognizes the many advantages stemming from being knowledgeable about computers. If we seek such knowledge with the intention of invading the privacy of others, we have once again succumbed to vicious curiosity.

Methods of gaining the truth are also potentially vicious. A blatant example of immoral knowledge is that obtained by Nazi scientists during World War II. At Dachau, Dr. Sigmund Rascher and others tested the effects of immersing humans into freezing cold water for extended periods in order to determine how quickly the subjects succumbed to hypothermia and death.[6] Other experiments involved breaking the bones of children repeatedly to ascertain rates of healing. Clearly in these instances the desire to know has been corrupted into something unspeakably horrible. There are many less horrific examples of knowledge improperly gained. Some forms of human subject research, cheating, corporate spying, eavesdropping and willingly entertaining gossip about someone else spring immediately to mind. In general, anytime we gain knowledge at the expense of what is good and right and just, we fall into vicious curiosity. As Samuel Johnson observed, "Integrity without knowledge is weak and useless, and knowledge without integrity is dangerous and dreadful."[7]

Not every quest for knowledge, even when the interests of others are uppermost in our minds, can be commended as virtuously studious. It is debatable whether, say, fetal tissue research or certain forms of genetic engineering escape altogether the charge of vicious curiosity. Should we try to perfect recombinant DNA research until we have the power to clone persons, choose the physical characteristics of our children or extend the human life span to four times its present length, even if the health of others is our goal?[8]

Most people are not unqualifiedly curious or studious; rather, we display these traits in degrees. A somewhat more benign form of curiosity than those mentioned occurs when we seek after knowledge of a trivial and insignificant sort when we could have applied our mind to genuinely important matters. Augustine laments in his *Confessions* that he sometimes elevated trivial pursuits (he mentions watching dogs chasing hares at the circus) to a place in his consciousness that ought to have been reserved for more weighty concerns (praise and contemplation of God). Think of all the truths you could amass by committing to memory the batting averages of all the players on your favorite team since 1900; think of all the important truths you might have mastered instead.[9]

The cases cited so far of failure to be properly studious center on errors of excess—cases requiring that we exercise an appropriate restraint of our desire to know. We can, of course, err in the opposite direction—by being insufficiently interested in the truth and unmotivated to expend the effort we need to attain it (as many a teacher can be heard to lament).

Rex Muttrum, the worldly rogue of Evelyn Waugh's *Brideshead Revisited*, illustrates this type of deficiency. His plans to wed the wealthy Julia Marchmain in a lavish church ceremony are thwarted when he discovers that theirs would be a religiously "mixed marriage." He offers to convert to Catholicism on the spot but learns that matters are not so easy. He must first undergo a period of catechetical instruction and so is sent to Father Mowbray, "a priest renowned for his triumphs with obdurate catechumens."[10]

After Father Mowbray's first session with Rex, Julia's mother questions him about Rex's progress. Father Mowbray laments that Rex is "the most difficult convert I've ever met. . . . He doesn't correspond to any degree of paganism known to missionaries."

He doesn't seem to have the least intellectual curiosity or natural piety. The first day I wanted to find out what sort of religious life he had had till now, so I asked him what he meant by prayer. He said: "*I* don't mean anything. *You* tell me." I tried to in a few words, and he said: "Right. So much for prayer. What's the next thing?" I gave him the catechism to take away. Yesterday I asked him whether Our Lord had more than one nature. He said: "Just as many

as you say, Father." . . . He was exceptionally docile, said he accepted
everything I told him, remembered bits of it, asked no questions.[11]
Clearly Rex's acceptance of Catholic teaching is superficial at best, a
case of mere cognitive idling; his beliefs make no inroads into the rest
of his thought life, his emotions or his behavior. His lack of native
curiosity and the shallowness of his convictions (if his attitude toward
the claims of the church can be called convictions) leave him powerless to discriminate between theological fact and fiction. This is
brought to light when Julia's younger sister, Cordelia, decides to have
some fun at Rex's expense by telling him that all faithful Catholics
sleep with their feet pointed to the east because that is the direction of
heaven, that the pope once made one of his horses a cardinal, and that
a pound note with someone's name on it, placed in the right box at
the church, consigns the named person to hell.

What a chump! Oh, mummy, what a glorious chump! . . . Oh
mummy, who could have dreamed he'd swallow it? I told him a lot
more besides, About the sacred monkeys in the Vatican—all kinds
of things.

"Well, you've certainly increased *my* work," said Father Mowbray.

"Poor Rex," said Lady Marchmain. . . . "You must treat him like
an idiot child, Father Mowbray."

We achieve studiousness and avoid curiosity when we properly situate our efforts to gain and use knowledge within a comprehensive
framework of concerns that includes a commitment to a particular
vision of the good life. This vision includes many elements, such as
beliefs about the ends of human beings, an awareness of the responsibilities one bears within a community, and a detailed understanding
of the elements that make up moral and intellectual character. Wisdom
lies in undertaking to discover the elements of this comprehensive
framework and appropriately orienting one's entire life (not just one's
intellectual or academic efforts) to this vision. Not only has Rex failed
to exert any effort to discover the truth and orient his life around it,
but he lacks even the desire that could motivate such effort. His
phlegmatic regard for the truth makes Rex not wise but a fool.

If we are characterized by the general quality of studiousness, then we will be properly motivated to seek truth and vigilant against whatever temptations might subvert our efforts to achieve it. To value truthfulness in oneself, in one's work and in others are marks of intellectual honesty. A key ingredient, then, in achieving a studious orientation to the intellectual life is that we be intellectually honest persons.

3.2 Intellectual Honesty and Dishonesty

All men are liable to error, and most men are in many points, by passion and interest, under temptation to it. If we could but see the secret motives that influenced the men of name and learning in the world, and the leaders of parties, we should not always find that it was the embracing of truth for its own sake, that made them espouse the doctrines they owned and maintained.

Let ever so much probability hang on one side of a covetous man's reasoning, and money on the other; it is easy to foresee which will outweigh. Earthly minds, like mud walls, resist the strongest batteries: and though, perhaps, sometimes the force of a clear argument may make some impression, yet they nevertheless stand firm, and keep out the enemy, truth, that would captivate or disturb them. . . . *Quod volumus, facile credimus;* what suits our wishes, is forwardly believed.[12]

John Locke's unflattering portrait of our lives as intellectual agents sounds again the pessimistic note heard in C. S. Lewis's story of Mark Studdock: that our believings are not always fruits born of intellectual virtue. Vice plays a powerful role in any complete account of the way we acquire and sustain belief. In particular, we observe how passions and self-interest of various sorts prevent us from being intellectually honest with ourselves (in the form of self-deception) and with others (in the form of various kinds of lies and misrepresentation). To feel the persuasive power of a colleague's criticism of our views and to pretend otherwise is a form of dishonesty toward others, a failure to be forthright. More blatant examples include falsifying data or deliberately ignoring counterevidence that might jeopardize hard-won funding for our research interests. Even more disturbing, perhaps, are the ways our failures at being self-transparent foster intellectual dishonesty. We ignore, inflate, discount or subtly shade the meaning of information unfavorable to our cherished opinions. We refuse to follow an argument wherever it leads because we see that its conclusion is unpalatable to beliefs we hold dear. It is what St. Paul calls in Romans our capacity for deliberately suppressing the truth (see again Rom 1:18) that makes intellectual honesty so difficult to detect and treat.

Even the sciences are vulnerable to dishonesty at precisely the point where one least expects it—quantitative analysis. For eleven years John Bailar (chair of the department of epidemiology and biostatistics at McGill University) served as statistics consultant to *The New England Journal of Medicine,* during which time he reviewed nearly four thousand articles. He chronicles how scientists practice deliberate deception through the selective reporting of data—their version of half-truths. They accomplish this, for example, by failing to inform readers of the weak spots in their data, selecting data in ways biased to their own interests, failing to give credit to earlier work or placing reliable data in a context that causes readers to draw misleading (usually optimistic) conclusions about the success and significance of the project being reported. "When it came to the statistical review," writes Bailar, "it was often clear that critical information was lacking, and the gaps nearly always had the practical effect of making the author's conclusions look stronger that they should have."[13]

Sometimes one kind of intellectual dishonesty leads to another. Outright, bold-faced lies may lead to self-deception. It is a common observation that people sometimes wind up believing lies when they repeat them often enough (or at least become incapable of distinguishing the lines separating the truth from exaggeration and plain prevarication). But it also happens that lies we tell ourselves about a particular matter bar us from dealing truthfully with others, even if at the point of interacting with others we are no longer fully aware that we are not telling the truth.

The errors to which Locke directs our attention are not the all-too-common errors resulting from finitude. True, we are persons of limited intellectual means and resources, and even our best efforts sometimes fail miserably because we lack crucial information or find our meager abilities taxed beyond limit. But Locke is underscoring something much darker than finitude. Though he does not call it by this name, it is *sin*. There resides in the interior of all reasoners hidden "passions" and "secret motives," as Locke dubs them, and vices like greed that affect our thought life, making us prone to err on subjects where our interests are most readily at stake. In cases like these, says Locke, quoting Francis Bacon, "because we wish, we easily believe."[14]

What makes "hidden passions" and "secret motives" such formidable barriers to intellectual honesty is that we may succumb to them unaware; they are "stealth sins" whose operations often go undetected due to self-deception and the powerful grip certain passions have over us.[15] Secretly we don't want to be reminded of personal interest's role in our thinking but would prefer to imagine all our deliberations to be coolly neutral and entirely dispassionate. We sometimes devolve into conditions like that of Richard Carstone, the ward of John Jarndyce in Dickens's *Bleak House.* Richard is consumed by the prospect of gaining instant wealth through an interminable lawsuit (Jarndyce and Jarndyce), to the point that he forsakes friends and benefactors and grows increasingly suspicious of others. "Jarndyce and Jarndyce had obtained such possession of his whole nature, that it was impossible to place any consideration before him which he did not—with a distorted kind of reason—make a new argument in favor of doing what he did."[16] Sometimes passions of one sort or another gain such a powerful hold on us that they reconfigure our thinking, making it appear more innocent than it is.

Notice the special targets of Locke's indictment: "men of name and learning," "leaders of parties" and, from his illustration, persons of wealth (sex figures into another of his illustrations). A university education no more inoculates us against reason's powers to distort our thinking than do the other qualities Locke cites (recall the case of the Nazis): fame, the power of leadership or wealth. It is precisely here that we may be most susceptible to becoming, as he says, enemies of the truth. The reason for this is not, I think, difficult to see. We fear whatever we perceive as jeopardizing matters of personal interest, be it our reputation or our pocketbook. Imagine, as Locke bids us, that you are a professor of forty years' standing and authority,

> wrought out of hard rock, Greek and Latin, with no small expense of time and candle, and confirmed by general tradition and reverend beard, in an instant overturned by an upstart novelist. . . . And who ever, by the most cogent arguments, will be prevailed with to disrobe himself at once of all his old opinions, and pretenses to knowledge and learning, which with hard study he hath all this time been laboring for; and turn himself out stark naked, in quest afresh of new notions.[17]

Recent philosophers following the tradition of Marx, Freud and Nietzsche ("masters of suspicion," as Paul Ricouer calls them) explore in detail the various ways our careers as cognitive agents are undermined by the corrupting powers of passion and self-interest. These writers are chiefly preoccupied not by how successful we are in finding the truth or in justifying our various beliefs—in fact, some of these writers disparage altogether the project of epistemology thus construed—but in the processes by which we acquire and sustain our beliefs, the various ways our beliefs function in society and the uses to which they are put. Michel Foucault, for example, has done significant work in bringing to our attention the ways our beliefs serve prevailing political interests.

> The important thing here, I believe, is that truth isn't outside power. . . . Truth is a thing of this world: it is produced only by virtue of multiple forms of constraint. And it induces regular effects of power. Each society had its regime of truth, its "general politics" of truth: that is, the types of discourse which it accepts and makes function as true; the mechanisms and instances which enable one to distinguish true and false statements, the means by which each is sanctioned; the techniques and procedures accorded value in the acquisition of truth; the status of those charged with saying what counts as true.[18]

Merold Westphal believes that the writings of these masters of suspicion can serve a therapeutic and even a spiritual function, by forcing us to confront the subterranean impulses and hidden motives that lead to intellectual dishonesty and self-deception. Religious persons, he writes, are no more immune from the effects of sin on the mind and its operations than are unbelievers; in fact, a person's religious beliefs make possible a peculiar kind of "epistemological Phariseeism" whereby our very religious convictions become instruments of invidious comparisons and discrimination. So impressed is Westphal by the inroads that sin and self-deception make into our thinking that he is prepared to abandon the idea that we naturally have innocent beliefs, opting instead for the principle that all our beliefs are guilty until proved innocent, especially where personal interest is at stake.[19]

Westphal qualifies his "guilt principle" in a crucial way, by insisting that it not be understood as a concluding doctrine condemning any belief one accepts in areas where self-interest is at stake. The principle should rather be taken as a "point of departure for a retail practice of seeking to expose the variety of particular ways in which we suppress the truth and to find ways to counteract these tendencies within ourselves, individually and corporately."[20]

Westphal does well to offer the epistemological principle of guilt not as a diagnosis of a terminal condition but as a therapeutic tool designed to foster intellectual health. If intellectual honesty is not possible, then the "principle of guilt" itself cannot possibly be satisfied, for all our efforts to "prove" the innocence of our beliefs are equally (maybe especially) susceptible to self-interest. Again, we must be careful about how much ground we yield to suspicion. After all, it is human reason that concocts theories about epistemic sin and blindness, reason that correctly diagnoses particular manifestations of self-interest and deception, and reason that sometimes holds forth a cure.

Locke and Westphal concur in their judgment that our thinking is sometimes grounded in personal dishonesty; their insights about the inroads that ignoble passions make in our thinking (however partial) constitute a genuine gain in the knowledge we have about ourselves. The sword of suspicion is double-edged, however, and must therefore be wielded with considerable care, lest it rebound on its user. Wielding it in a wholesale and indiscriminate manner against reason itself is a paradigm act of self-stultification. Reason not only can see errors; it must find some truths (innocently), or else it could not discover error.

Being intellectually honest involves more than simply telling the truth.[21] One might do this out of fear of being caught or, like Kant's honest shopkeeper, because it is good for business. To be honest requires that we *be* honest persons, that we inwardly prize the truth and set our minds on it as a motive and goal of our efforts as rational beings. And the honesty of which Christianity speaks is not skin deep but ought to be inherent in who we are as persons. The Christian tradition teaches that our capacity for discerning and conveying truth is a part of God's design; it is one of the ways we partake of the divine image. So insofar as we strive to become honest persons who represent ourselves and our ideas sincerely, we are living obediently with God's intentions for what sorts of persons we are to become.

3.3 Wisdom and Folly

Though philosophy is the discipline named for its study of wisdom, there is precious little said about wisdom in current philosophical circles, and what is said is the subject of enormous disagreement. One reason for the reticence as well as the disagreement is that wisdom is a complex notion whose precise contours are shaped significantly by the larger philosophical and religious traditions in which it is embedded. Both the content of wisdom and the most effective means to it are studied most accurately when viewed in the light of the philosophical and religious commitments that inform them. There is, accordingly, Buddhist wisdom, Hindu wisdom, Confucian wisdom, Christian wisdom, Stoic wisdom and so forth.

Of course it cannot follow that the philosophical and religious commitments of these traditions are equally correct, for some (though not all) of the claims they make are incompatible. Nor does it follow that polemical exchanges between different traditions are not possible and profitable. To say that there is Buddhist wisdom and Christian wisdom is simply to acknowledge that the truths deemed most worth securing and the life most worth living, as well as the best means for attaining them, will vary as one's views about the nature of humanity, God and the cosmos change. Christians will not regard Buddhist wisdom as true wisdom, and vice versa.

Nevertheless, at the risk of ignoring my own advice, I think one can trace a common concern throughout varying virtue traditions. Wisdom is generally never equated with mere possession of information, even lots of it. Nor is wisdom to be equated with shrewdness, cunning, cleverness or even the sort of intelligence measured by IQ tests. As Walker Percy writes, "One can get straight A's in school and flunk life." We generally regard as wise those persons whose lives are marked by deep and abiding meaningfulness, anchored in beliefs and purposes that offer lasting contentment. Wise persons, according to most wisdom traditions, deliberately seek knowledge of ultimate significance—knowledge that explains the most important features of our world, especially as they bear on human happiness.

What truths are most important for us to grasp, and what method is best for grasping them, varies between traditions. Some traditions teach that wisdom is within the grasp of any person dedicated to employing his or her natural faculties in a prescribed manner. Buddhists believe the wisdom that confers salvation is obtained through a special kind of meditation, as the Diamond Sutra explains, whereby we cease clinging to notions of the self and individual personhood. Aristotle thought natural wisdom lay within the grasp of good philosophers who dedicated themselves to the study of metaphysics, which explores the ultimate causes at work in the world. By contrast, other traditions deny that the most significant truths for humans to grasp, especially those most central to human well-being, are within our unassisted grasp; they must be revealed. Hindus, for example, claim that the knowledge most essential for securing wisdom was given by the ancient seers and conveyed through the Vedas; but we are left to our own initiative and resources to unearth these important truths and understand their true significance for our lives. The great monotheistic traditions of Judaism, Christianity and Islam are unique in claiming not only that humans are dependent on God to show us the most important truths but that we are likewise dependent on him to assist us in understanding and desiring them.

The great Christian philosopher and theologian Thomas Aquinas further divided Christian wisdom into three parts, metaphysical wisdom, theological wisdom and mystical wisdom. With Aristotle, Aquinas affirms that human reason can by dint of its native powers discover some of the deepest truths, the ultimate causes at work in the world. According to Aristotle, this is the knowledge we have of God as Prime Mover. But metaphysical wisdom is crucially deficient both in what it knows and in the means whereby it knows God. It is deficient in content because it fails to disclose deep knowledge of God's nature, will, intentions and purposes for human beings, especially in matters of salvation and Christian living. To judge rightly in these matters, we must be filled with the "gift of wisdom," which comes only through divine initiative. Moreover, the mode of metaphysical knowledge is restricted to grasping truths analogically, through reasoning on the basis of the objects in the world evident to sensation. Metaphysical wisdom is not false according to this portrait but incomplete, in need of being supplemented by theological wisdom. So Aquinas says, "If the only way open to us for the knowledge of God were solely that of the reason, the human race would remain in the blackest shadows of ignorance."[22]

Theological wisdom is that knowledge revealed directly by God through the Scriptures and the church, containing truths about God and his purposes essential to our ultimate happiness. According to Aquinas, not only do we depend on God's initiative to receive the needed knowledge, but we depend on him to understand it aright. So on the Christian scheme, wisdom is, in addition to a purely human virtue, also a divine gift. It is God who enables us to receive and understand theological wisdom. But even when God reveals knowledge to us, he must make use of particular linguistic frameworks and intellectual categories. If God wishes for his revelation to be intelligible to us, he must make use of the intellectual categories current in a particular cultural/linguistic context. So even with theological wisdom we do not know God as intimately as we might; there is, however, a more perfect way.

Mystical wisdom refers to the knowledge we will have of God when we see him "face to face" in the beatific vision, when we know as we have been known. Here at last we know God not by faith but by sight: by direct and immediate apprehension of the divine nature as it exists in itself. Such knowledge will not be mediated by linguistic or intellectual categories but will be intuitively immediate and nondiscursive. This is the wisdom reserved for the blessed, though the Christian tradition has held that God sometimes grants such mystical insight to persons yet in this life.

Acquiring wisdom (and any other virtue for that matter) is not simply a matter of grasping certain truths (though it certainly includes this); being wise is fundamentally a matter of being a certain kind of person. In discussing the gift of wisdom Thomas expounds on the passage in Wisdom (1:4) that states, "Wisdom will not enter into a malicious soul, nor dwell in a body subject to sins." Wise persons see the world from God's perspective and are thus able to make right judgments about matters of eternal significance. But an important part of judging correctly, Thomas reminds us, is that we be ourselves sympathetically constituted so as to have a natural affinity for the eternal matters that form the subject of our judgments. Our inner desires and motives and our wills must be naturally attuned with the matters about which we judge. On the Christian scheme, however, it is God who must accomplish the transformation of our inner selves, though not in a way that completely overrides the human will.[23] So whether or not we are growing in wisdom is a matter over which we have some voluntary control. As was stated earlier, intellectual virtues, no less than moral virtues, have to do with some human behavior that is subject to the human will and is affected by our choices. We see, then, that wise persons not only possess knowledge of eternal or ultimate significance but have undertaken to become the kinds of persons who naturally desire and pursue this knowledge.

Ancient and medieval thinkers make a further distinction between speculative and practical wisdom. The former has to do with contemplative truths such as those dealing with God's nature, which do not bear directly on human behavior. The latter, to which the name *prudence* is given, has to do with the wisdom that expresses itself in our day-to-day thinking and acting. With this distinction in mind, Aristotle writes: "We say Anaxagorous, Thales, and men like them, have a philosophic but not a practical wisdom, when we see them ignorant of what is to their own advantage. . . . They know things that are remarkable, admirable, difficult, and divine, but useless; *viz.*, because it is not human goods they seek." The integral connection between being wise and being good (living the good life) is captured in the classical doctrine of prudence. Prudence is an intellectual virtue from which we receive counsel regarding what is good for us. It is a special kind of wisdom permitting us to discern how to act so as to promote our highest welfare, and for this reason it is sometimes called "practical wisdom": reasoning that seeks to guide our behavior rather than furnish us with additional contemplative truths. So construed, prudence is a bridge virtue, with one foot in the camp of reason and the other in the camp of action.

Prudence is a complex trait according to many medieval analysts, including Aquinas. Prudent persons are distinguished, among other ways, by their ability to gain knowledge about themselves, their strengths and weaknesses, and the world in which their character formation is taking place. They estimate correctly their own moral merits and demerits and strategize appropriately about courses of self-improvement. They are also aware of their external circumstances and surroundings, judging how best to act in them so as to achieve their vision of the well-lived life. Prudent persons, in sum, have sufficient knowledge of themselves and their circumstances so as reliably to direct their behavior toward the goal of a well-lived life.

The good life that prudence makes known concerns human goodness in its totality, moral goodness strictly speaking, as well as nonmoral human goods. For example, a prudent person might be one who discerns what is good for human beings by way of diet and exercise and is able to give good counsel for how best to order that part of our lives. But prudence in an absolute or comprehensive sense must encompass the totality of human goods, especially those pertaining to the moral life. A person able to give valuable advice about exercise but not about justice would be deemed prudent in only a narrow and not an unqualified sense. So prudence in its fullest sense includes the intellectual capacity by which we discern what is virtuous and what specific actions are required of us in concrete circumstances to bring about a morally good end.

We cannot be good by having good intentions alone, though acting from the proper motives is an indispensable part of being prudent. If we are to be successful in our efforts at doing the right thing, we must also act in accordance with correct information. No military commander would undertake an attack against the enemy without "intelligence"—specific knowledge of terrain, enemy troop strength and positioning, the weapons at one's disposal and so forth. Our moral actions must similarly be grounded in the "moral intelligence" that prudence makes known. Because persons of prudence are thus gifted in identifying along which path justice lies, they are able to discern what would constitute excess and deficiency in one's behavior. One has to be wise to be good, and one cannot be good without likewise possessing a measure of wisdom.[24]

The vice traditionally opposed to wisdom is folly, which, like prudence, is a complex trait that manifests itself in various ways. If practical wisdom consists in the knowledge of self and world, together with the ability to orient our lives reliably toward the goal of lasting felicity, then one aspect of folly can be characterized as the habitual and willful forsaking or suppressing of what we believe to be true or adopting a manner of life incompatible with what we believe to be in our best interests. This definition is not adequate by itself, since it presupposes that we possess beliefs adequate for the task. So another form of folly consists in the persistent refusal to avail oneself of the knowledge of self and world that could lead to lasting felicity. In short, fools willfully think and act in ways that are likely to frustrate their own flourishing. Homer says, "Folly shuts men's eyes to their destruction. She walks delicately, not on solid earth, but hovers over the heads of men to make them stumble or to ensnare them" (*Iliad* 19.90-94).[25]

We all do foolish things from time to time, but we attribute the vice of folly to those in whom such patterns have taken up permanent residence. A single act of foolishness does not make one a fool any more than latching onto a single important truth affecting human happiness makes one wise. Consider Mildred, a middle-aged mother of dependent children, who is told by her doctor that if she doesn't give up cigarettes and unhealthy eating she is likely to die within two years. Despite her doctor's counsel, Mildred willfully persists in behavior that will lead to her premature death. She argues that the evidence supporting the carcinogenic effects of cigarettes is inconclusive; she offers anecdotal evidence of people she knows who lived to ripe old ages despite their bad habits; she persists in the adolescent attitude that she is somehow exempt from the normal course of events operating on the rest of humanity—"it won't happen to *me!*" But we tend to regard such responses as lame rationalizations, a thin tissue of excuses, not genuinely mitigating reasons.

I have included willfulness as a component part of folly. This vice does not overtake us like a disease but requires our complicity. For this reason we blame people who succumb to folly, whereas we don't blame people who catch the measles. Having said this, let me consider a possible counterexample. Suppose for the sake of argument that Christians are correct in believing that the only true, deep and lasting happiness is found in friendship with God. It would follow from the truth of Christianity that committed Buddhists are willfully thinking and acting in ways that will in fact frustrate their own best interests. Yet we don't call a committed Buddhist a fool. Why not? The answer, I suggest, is that the committed Buddhist sincerely believes that the cessation of all desires and the ultimate annihilation of the self is the path to happiness. Not only do committed Buddhists act in accordance with their best lights about the path to lasting felicity, they avail themselves of opportunities to refine their thinking about such matters. In the lives of devout Buddhists there is a consistency, and integrity if you will, between what they sincerely believe to be true and what they profess and do.

Of course there are any number of ways to be a fool; two examples follow. Aquinas draws our attention to a sort of folly that arises in persons who see the world topsy-turvy, accepting as highest and ultimate good some feature of the world that is only a limited and subordinate good. Mistaken judgments about ultimate goods might arise for a number of reasons, but we identify as folly those errors of judgment that owe to our own poor choices. Again, we blame fools, we hold them responsible for their condition, in a way we do not those who are merely mistaken. Sometimes we see the world from an inverted perspective when we, like Richard Carstone of *Bleak House*, immerse ourselves in the pursuit of subordinate goods such as wealth and pleasure; they so fill our field of vision as to blot out what is genuinely good and induce a sort of epistemic blindness.

A person can also be a fool by being indifferent to growth in wisdom and understanding. Thus the book of Proverbs identifies those who are indifferent to instruction as fools and says that "fools despise wisdom" (Prov 1:7). To be foolish in this sense is not primarily to lack information but to lack a certain passion or zeal for the truths that are essential to human happiness, or to lack incentive to cultivate traits that can help us discern such truths. Consider Michael, whose highest ambition is to be remembered by his fraternity brothers as a "party god." While college life offers plenty of opportunities for Michael to think about what constitutes the good life and how one might achieve it, he routinely avoids them. Sometimes he is stricken with the unbidden thought that his life is shallow and incomplete, but when such thoughts arise he cranks up the music and commences drinking until they go away. Such is the pattern of Michael's life; Michael is a fool. This species of foolishness usually has strong connections to the vice of sloth. And if we lack zeal for the truths essential to human happiness, we can expect mistaken judgments and false beliefs to follow.

The virtues discussed here represent merely a small sample of the traits of character directly relevant to our flourishing as intellectual beings. Wisdom, understanding, prudence, studiousness, intellectual honesty and love of truth are not the special province of philosophers but are especially interesting because of the attention paid them by many philosophical and religious traditions. Carving out an adequate account of these intellectual virtues offers a wonderful exercise in the integration of faith and reason.

3.4 The Relationship Between Ancient and Modern and Contemporary Epistemological Concerns

In the next chapter we will begin to examine some of the issues that have animated epistemologists in modern and contemporary thought—roughly the period from Descartes to the present. Those who review the literature, say, on the foundations of human knowledge, the debate between internalism and externalism in epistemology, or competing theories of justification will note the absence of an interest in intellectual virtues. Most epistemologists of this period do not write to augment our understanding of the virtues, and their work most certainly is not motivated by a desire to cultivate habits of mind that more closely accord with their understanding of the divine design. In fact, traits like wisdom, prudence and studiousness rarely arise in their discussions. In the main their sights are set on other quarry: defeating skepticism, identifying the necessary and sufficient conditions for knowledge, and offering an adequate account of philosophical justification.

These are worthy pursuits, and a commitment to intellectual virtues does not require that one abandon them; but it is obvious from what has been argued thus far that they do not exhaust our epistemological tasks. For situating these tasks within a framework that includes an appreciation for the intellectual virtues affects how we think about the very tasks dominating modern epistemology. It might occur to one to wonder, then, what implications a commitment to the intellectual virtues might have for some modern and contemporary epistemological projects.

While contemporary epistemologists may not work within a tradition dominated by notions of intellectual virtues, one can, with a bit of finessing, see a significant overlap in what are taken by the two traditions to be epistemological desiderata. The marks of good thinking have been fairly constant throughout the history of philosophy. Contemporary as well as ancient epistemologists are concerned, as

William James put it, to honor "the first and great commandments as would-be knowers": to seek truth and avoid error, and to identify what behaviors ought to be in evidence if our chief cognitive goal is to secure truth. Both virtue and nonvirtue approaches to epistemology are earnest in their efforts to figure out the nature and extent of human learning. Both are interested in what one must do to believe rationally, to avoid breaches in the canons of good intellectual conduct. There are goals held in common, though they may be pursued under different descriptions.

The goals of contemporary epistemology can, without too much difficulty, be integrated with the concern to pursue intellectual virtues. For example, the desire that one be justified in one's beliefs seems to indicate an aversion for folly, a wish to avoid the vice of gullibility. A concern to adjust one's level of assent according to the amount and quality of one's evidence might be viewed as intellectual humility—a desire not to make exaggerated claims for one's beliefs either to oneself or to others. Efforts to identify what contributes to a belief's being reliably produced or possessing warrant can, as Alvin Plantinga argues, be a way of talking about God's design for humans and the intellectual excellences that he intended for humans. Work on defeasibility provides still another possible point of intersection (if not overlap) between the issues pursued by contemporary and virtue epistemologists. In many cases what it means to be intellectually virtuous is closely linked with being philosophically justified or dealing conscientiously with criticism of one's beliefs.

The subject matter of much contemporary epistemology, then, overlaps or least parallels concerns arising in the study of the intellectual virtues. At the very least, studying contemporary accounts of subjects such as the foundations of knowledge and justification may contribute to our deeper understanding of the virtues, if not their cultivation. For example, I will argue later that the contemporary debate between foundationalism and coherentism contains important lessons about the limits of human understanding—lessons that can help us grow in intellectual humility. It will therefore be a motif of this book that study of some of the traditional concerns of contemporary epistemology illuminates powerfully our understanding of certain intellectual virtues, and vice versa. The old and the new thus complement one another.

Thinking long and hard about contemporary epistemological writing, with its characteristic rigor and precision, can deepen our analysis of the structure of intellectual virtues. And the benefits go both ways. If we are committed to cultivating a life of intellectual virtue, especially as this is conceived of in the Christian narrative, then we have a powerful motivation for pursuing epistemological themes that are absent in much contemporary writing. The philosophically isolated and aseptic manner in which many contemporary epistemological issues are discussed gives them all the lure of a good puzzle, with rewards commensurate to those that come from successfully tackling a tough brain-teaser. But seeing epistemological issues, and the academic life in general, as contributing factors to a well-lived virtuous life imbues them with much greater significance.

These many points of intersection should not mask the fact that intellectual virtues are largely alien to the concerns of most modern and contemporary epistemology. Virtue theorists insist that we situate our intellectual endeavors, as well as our thinking about how such endeavors might best be undertaken, within a broader philosophical framework. Essential to any such framework are beliefs about the nature of the person, what constitutes a good life, the responsibilities owed to the community of which one is a part, metaphysical beliefs about what sort of world we live in, beliefs about human ends and God, and much more. As was argued in the last chapter, many modern and contemporary approaches are deficient because in taking up the issues of epistemology they divorce the intellectual agent from these indispensable contexts.

Four

Foundationalism

W hat happens to unprofitable corporations? Sometimes they undergo "restructuring": experts carefully review and then recommend a rearrangement of the corporation's parts. Such reviews commonly reveal that the business labored with unclear lines of communication, illogical chains of command, attention and expense paid to one area of the business that ought to be shifted elsewhere, and so on. The rationale for such reviews is that with a clearer understanding of its parts and their interrelations, a corporation can be managed more efficiently and profitably.

Some of history's notable epistemologists have recommended that our "noetic structure," our beliefs and the relations between them, are no less in need of review and cognitive restructuring. The benefit of such restructuring is not monetary profits but *epistemic justification*.

4.1 The Motivation for Foundationalism
In the course of their studies, students of philosophy frequently

encounter advice not unlike what managers of businesses receive. If you want to increase your "intellectual profitability," so to speak—if you want to increase your chances of satisfying your epistemic goals, such as winning the truth, being justified and being intellectually virtuous—then you must carefully manage your beliefs by consciously organizing them into a structure that is most apt to win these goals. By structuring our beliefs we make clear, among other things, what are our most certain beliefs, the relationships of dependency and subordination among our beliefs, and the strength of the support for our beliefs. After all, since the right kind of organization is indispensable in realizing our goals in many other areas of our life (business, military, education and so on), doesn't it seem reasonable to suppose that the same holds true of our intellectual life?

Foundationalism stands historically as one of the most significant efforts at showing what an ideal ordering of one's cognitive life should be like, if we have a maximally justified set of beliefs as our goal. The root idea suggests that each of us holds some beliefs "basically" or "immediately," while we hold other beliefs "nonbasically" or "mediately." Nonbasic or mediate beliefs receive their support from other beliefs we hold. For example, I believe that insects attacked my garden during the night; this belief is based on my belief that there are holes in the leaves of the plants. Basic or immediate beliefs do not receive their support from other beliefs we hold but are based directly on experiences or the "self-evident deliverances of reason," to cite two commonly alleged sources of basic belief. I believe there is a chair under me, not on the basis of other beliefs but because of experiences I am having. So on the foundationalist view, some beliefs are justified even though they are not based on other beliefs we hold.[1]

Of course no one consciously begins their cognitive life with a foundationalist agenda. As children we take in a welter of beliefs indiscriminately; we accumulate beliefs rooted in perception, questioning them only rarely, if ever. We accept as true what we are told by various authorities within our traditions, such as parents, teachers and priests; and it is a good thing that we do, for we should surely perish as children if we had to confirm for ourselves, say, each parental warning that certain substances are poisonous and certain activities are dangerous. We require an initial deposit of beliefs before we begin thinking about our intellectual lives in a reflective way. Chronologically speaking, we accept inputs to our repertoire of beliefs as they come. Logically speaking, however, not all the beliefs we accept deserve to be accepted in the same way. Some are obviously pivotal, anchoring other beliefs we hold; others are subordinate. As we shall see, foundationalists believe there is advantage for our intellectual lives in getting clear about what logical ordering of our beliefs is ideal.

Our lives as intellectual beings begin and continue for some time (a very long time for some) without our actively reflecting on what we believe or the reasons we believe. For most of us there comes a time, however, when we start to assume greater responsibility for our careers as cognitive agents. Just as we "come of age" in our moral life by deliberately guiding our behavior in accordance with values we have internalized and claim as our own, so too there comes a time when most persons come of age intellectually. As we mature we become more discriminating in what we believe, less prone to gullibility, more discriminating regarding the testimony and counsel we accept from others, and more capable of recognizing some beliefs as better grounded than others. We come to recognize that wisdom, understanding, discernment, intellectual honesty, teachability and other intellectual virtues contribute to a well-lived intellectual life in a way that their vicious counterparts do not. We recognize that not everyone thinks the same way we do about lots of issues, and that persons holding views different from ours are not obviously irrational—perhaps they are no less intellectually virtuous than ourselves. We also awaken to the idea that we have a general responsibility to try to govern our intellectual lives with care.

What is there, though, about becoming more intellectually mature and independent that would prompt us to consider the recommendations of foundationalists? Why ever would one wish to participate in the kind of intellectual structuring they recommend? The case of René Descartes, the father of modern classical foundationalism (indeed the father of modern Western philosophy), offers some answers.

One noticeable feature of our mature intellectual lives is a new awareness of our liability to make mistakes in our believings. Descartes observed in his famous *Meditations* not only that he had made errors of judgment in accepting some of his beliefs but that he had in consequence compounded the problem by building on those errors.[2] The discovery that one's set of beliefs contains a few "bad apples" might prompt one to consider taking thorough inventory of what one believes to see how much of it passes muster. Imagine the kind of reshuffling of your beliefs that would ensue were you to discover as an adult that you were the biological child of someone other than the parents who raised you. Suppose that in taking stock of your thinking about religion or politics you became convinced you had made serious errors of judgment. Would this not result in some significant reordering of your system of beliefs (your "noetic structure," as epistemologists sometimes call it) like the corporate restructuring that takes place in an unprofitable business?

Descartes was, I think, motivated to embark on his program of rational reconstruction by something more troubling than occasional error—namely, pervasive and seemingly intractable disagreement about fundamental intellectual, religious, moral and political matters. Descartes was educated in Europe at a time when the scholastic paradigm that had dominated the university curriculum for centuries was in disarray. The burgeoning disciplines of science were revolutionizing the way people thought about the earth and its place in the universe. Various social and political events such as the religious wars following the Reformation jointly contributed to an atmosphere of intellectual uncertainty, whose disturbing effects were keenly felt by Descartes. No longer could questions about religion and morality and justice be settled by appealing to a tradition embraced by all. He complains in his *Discourse on Method* that his professors would argue earnestly and convincingly in support of diametrically opposite conclusions—an experience all too familiar, perhaps, to college students today. The discovery that trusted authorities whose judgments you are not competent to question disagree with one another on very fundamental intellectual matters can induce tremendous cognitive dissonance.

Matters grew worse for Descartes. He opted to skip graduate studies and see the world, courtesy of a stint in the army. But to his dismay he found that fundamental disagreements over matters moral, religious and political were not limited to academia but arose between different cultures as well. Not only is what we believe in large measure due to geographical and historical accident, observes Descartes, but persons from other cultures often have reasons in support of their convictions every bit as good or better than the reasons we have for our own.

> I further recognized in the course of my travels that all those whose sentiments are very contrary to ours are yet not necessarily barbarians or savages, but may be possessed of reason in as great or even a greater degree than ourselves. I also considered how very different the self-same man, identical in mind and spirit, may become, according as he is brought up from childhood amongst the French or Germans, or has passed his whole life amongst the Chinese or cannibals. . . . I could not, however, put my finger on a single person whose opinions seemed preferable to those of others, and I found that I was so to speak, constrained myself to undertake the direction of my procedure.[3]

There appears, then, a rather impressive list of reasons for thinking that our intellectual lives are in need of every bit of order and structure we can provide. We are liable to error in our various judgments and prone to build hastily upon what we had little reason to think was true in the first place. Many of our convictions about a wide range of subjects are due to accidents of birth, history and geography. Moreover, even the beliefs bequeathed to us by our culture and the intellectual traditions within it are subjects of discord among those we trust as authorities.

It is enough to produce a mild crisis in even the stoutest of intellects. Is there no way to sift and sort among this babble of competing claims so as to secure some certain truth? Is there not an ideal ordering of our intellectual lives that can stave off the skeptical conclusion that knowledge and certainty can't be had in this life? Descartes's response, which set the tone of modern philosophical inquiry, is to seek certainty not in the church or tradition, which no longer spoke with definitive finality, but within the mind of the knowing subject.

One winter Descartes sat alone in a stove-heated room and devised his foundationalist answer to an age of troubled reason. He resolved to "raze everything in my life, down to the very bottom, so as to begin again from the very foundations," treating as positively false any claim that was susceptible of even the slightest tincture of doubt (a most extreme cognitive restructuring). After applying himself to the "destruction" of his former opinions, he arrived at last at that one indubitable truth for which he will forever be remembered: *cogito ergo sum*, "I think, therefore I am."

From this meager deposit of foundational truth Descartes struggled to secure all that he had formerly believed, with this important difference: he was no longer content to have knowledge accidentally or unwittingly. He judged that if anyone genuinely knows a claim, then they are self-reflectively aware of the fact that they know it (mere hunches or surmises that one knows a claim won't suffice). There is no way a person might confuse a genuine article of knowledge with some lesser grade of belief. Moreover, he was prepared to demonstrate to anyone who might inquire that all his beliefs were firmly rooted on an unshakable foundation. Given Descartes's consternation over protracted disagreements, it doesn't seem unreasonable to think that knowledge claims should meet these additional conditions. After all, what kind of solace can one take from certainty one isn't even aware one has? And amid the clamor of competing voices can be heard many *assertions* that one has certainty, but how many can demonstrate it?[4]

Thus far I have mentioned a quasi-existential reason for thinking seriously about the project of rationally reconstructing one's noetic structure. There is also a famous philosophical reason, called the "regress argument," for thinking this ought to be accomplished along foundationalist lines. Suppose you were asked what your reasons are for believing that Chicago is in the state of Illinois. You might respond by saying that you had personally visited Chicago; you had seen it with your own eyes. What if someone were to call your perceptions into question? Suppose they asked what reasons you have for believing that your perceptual faculties are reliable. If you were inclined to answer the question at all, you might answer that you remember them to have worked reliably in the past. But if you were asked what reasons you have for thinking that your memory is reliable or that your conscious mind works correctly, you would be at a loss. How could you give a reason without presupposing the reliability of consciousness itself? It seems that you take for granted the general reliability of your conscious faculties, and indeed must take them for granted. There are no more basic, no more fundamental claims on which the general reliability of your conscious mind might be based. The buck stops here.

This example illustrates that there comes an end to the business of giving reasons for the things we believe. Eventually this process must terminate in a belief or set of beliefs that are immediately justified for us: beliefs it is appropriate to embrace without having first supplied independent reasons on their behalf. The task of offering reasons for our beliefs must terminate, then, in beliefs that are *epistemically basic.* It is the hallmark of foundationalism to affirm that the ideal logical ordering of our cognitive lives begins with foundationally basic beliefs.

One should be aware right off the bat, however, that there are multiple versions of foundationalism on the market. Just what beliefs are reckoned as properly basic, by what criteria they can be identified and just how they lend support to the other things we believe are, as we shall see, matters of significant dispute. The position that has come to be termed "strong foundationalism" or "classical foundationalism" attempts to meet the uncertainty generated by liability to error and disagreement in the strongest possible terms: by grounding our entire edifice of knowledge on invincible certainty. The best way of halting the regress of reason giving is to have it stop in beliefs about which it is impossible for us to be in error.

Perhaps it is also worth mentioning at the outset that since its inception, and for over three hundred years, the strong foundationalist program of Descartes and others has suffered from the unrelenting criticisms of a host of detractors, culminating in the twentieth century with the alleged death of the foundationalist enterprise.[5] To determine whether these obituaries are premature, and on what precisely they rest, we will need to explore the contours of the foundationalist project more deeply.

4.2 The Rudiments of Foundationalism

A geometric system and a building are useful metaphors as we consider the foundationalist's recommendations for an ideally structured cognitive life. There are three essential components in any sturdy building: a solid foundation, some means of imparting the strength of the foundation to the rest of the building (beams, buttresses, wires and the like) and, of course, the upper stories that rest on the foundations. As premier geometer of his day, Descartes may have had a mathematical rather than architectural model in mind in devising his version of foundationalism. In geometry we reason from a commonly agreed-upon set of foundational starting points, or axioms. There is a commonly agreed-upon procedure (rules of inference) for moving from one's axioms to additional knowledge (one's theorems). What Euclid did for geometry, Descartes wanted to do for all of human knowledge.

There are, then, three components to any foundationalist picture of knowledge. First, as was noted above, there are what are called "basic" or "immediate" beliefs; these form the bedrock of all that we believe, undergirding everything else we are justified in believing.[6] All of our "mediate" or "nonbasic beliefs" (everything else we believe) constitute the second element of the foundationalist model. Basic beliefs function like Aristotelian "unmoved movers." They are the epistemic engines of our noetic structures, imparting justification to all of our nonbasic beliefs while not themselves requiring justification from any other beliefs—the support goes just one way. Finally, there is some sort of connection between our epistemological starting points, our basic beliefs, and all that is based on them. This connection is generally referred to as the "basing relation"; it specifies how the epistemic merit of our basic beliefs is to be transferred to our nonbasic beliefs.

That there are basic beliefs and that they somehow lend support through an appropriate basing relation to nonbasic beliefs is where the agreement among foundationalists ends. What kinds of beliefs are properly basic, how many of them there are and the nature of the support they lend to nonbasic beliefs are subjects of ongoing disagreement. This has resulted in a rather dizzying array of permutations of the simple foundationalist account.[7] It may not be an exaggeration to say that there are as many different versions of foundationalism as there are foundationalists who have written on the subject. Because of the very nuanced differences that sometimes separate various versions, we will have to rest content exploring the theory along its major lineaments, forgoing many of the intricacies of variation and argument.[8]

4.3 Strong Foundationalism

Strong foundationalists severely restrict what can count as a basic belief, what kind of support it lends to the other beliefs we hold, and the manner in which this support is communicated to nonbasic beliefs. They claim that the foundations of human knowledge must be unshakably certain and that the only way this certainty is transferred to nonbasic beliefs is by the ordinary logical relations of deduction and induction. Nonbasic beliefs must either be deducible from the set of basic beliefs or be supported by one's foundations to a suitably high degree of probability. As we shall see, weak foundationalists (also called "soft," "modest," "minimal" and "mitigated" foundationalists) have good reasons for relaxing the standards of proper basicality and expanding the way in which basic beliefs lend support to nonbasic beliefs.

By what criteria shall we identify this privileged class of basic beliefs? Most strong foundationalists following Descartes offer three different conditions, the satisfaction of any one of which will qualify a belief as properly basic. First, a belief is properly basic if it is *self-evidently true*. Self-evidently true beliefs are those we see to be true immediately, without the benefit of deliberation or argument, merely when we understand the terms of the claim in question. If you know what the terms *whole* and *part* mean, for example, you see in an instant that the whole is greater than any of its parts. Candidates for self-evident status most often cited include the axioms of logic (e.g., that $A = A$, the law of identity) and mathematics (e.g., the trichotomy axiom: for every pair of real numbers a and b, exactly one of the following is true: $a< b$; $a = b$; or $a>b$) and other statements whose truth is a matter of logical necessity.[9]

A second criterion for a belief's being basic is that it be *incorrigible*. This means that the belief in question is one that it is impossible to believe and be mistaken about; simply having the belief is sufficient for its being true.[10] Examples might include beliefs such as "I exist" or "I am in pain." How could one possibly have beliefs such as these and be mistaken about them, since my belief does not extend beyond that of which I am fully aware?

Finally, and somewhat more controversially, a belief is properly basic if it is *evident to the senses*. John Locke, for example, called by the name "sensitive knowledge" those truths that we have as a result of our immediate commerce with the world of objects. That there is an external world, or that there is a hand in front of my face when I hold up my hand, are claims that, while not quite on a par with intuitive knowledge, nevertheless are certain enough to serve as epistemically basic starting points.[11] Basic beliefs, then, are not subject to proof or demonstration; they are instead the starting points of all our reasoning.

Foundationalists allied with the philosophical movement known as positivism offered a narrower interpretation of "evident to the senses." Ordinary claims about external objects can't be certain because, as happened to poor Lady Macbeth, there is always the possibility of discrepancy between my report that I am experiencing a particular object in the world and the actual existence of anything corresponding to my experience; the blood I see and feel staining my hands might be a hallucination. The starting points of all empirical knowledge, then, must be gleaned not from claims to be acquainted with objects in the world but from the immediate contents of my perceptual consciousness, a preconceptual sensory "given." I may be mistaken in my claim to see a tomato, but it is impossible, claimed these foundationalists, to be mistaken about my claim that "I *seem* to see a tomato," or, less elegantly, that "I am appeared to in a red, round, firm fashion." On this construal of "evident to the senses," certainty is thus restricted to the realm of sensory appearance; no undefeatable certainty is claimed for assertions made about the independent existence of the objects that appear to the senses. Such claims about the independent existence of physical objects are conclusions reached at the end of a process of inductive reasoning, not its proper starting points.[12]

Just how do basic beliefs support nonbasic beliefs? In the early phase of his project Descartes proposed the quite restrictive policy that only beliefs that can be deduced from our basic beliefs should be accepted. The reason for this is simple; entailment is the only logical relation that preserves certainty. If one starts with self-evidently true starting points and accepts only what can be validly derived from the same, one thereby ensures that one's entire set of beliefs is untainted and error-free. Other strong foundationalists (Locke, for example) permitted nonbasic beliefs to be justifiably grounded in basic beliefs inductively, supported in varying degrees of probability.

To this skeletal account of strong foundationalism we must add a few additional features often accompanying it that are the special targets of antifoundationalist criticism. As we have seen, Descartes's foundationalism seems to require that certifiable claims to knowledge must satisfy some very high "access requirements." That is, one cannot claim to have knowledge simply by asserting that one knows (any unreflective person of puny mind can do this); one must be inwardly cognizant that one's claims to knowledge are genuine, and one must be prepared to show that this is the case. Put briefly, in order to know, one must know that one knows and be able to show that one knows.[13]

Second, a strong element of individualism marks Descartes's program. He doesn't feel obliged to seek wise counsel from fellow academics, clerics, friends or a broader intellectual and cultural tradition to quell his doubts about whether we have knowledge of a mind-independent world. Indeed tradition, with its conflicting signals, was part of the problem, an obstacle to be overcome, not a voice to be indulged. Instead Descartes believed he had to free his thoughts from history's influence, endeavoring to accomplish his philosophical tasks alone. A solitary mind of sufficient acumen and penetration could accomplish the task of cognitive restructuring, thought Descartes. His was an epistemology of "pure reason," one which, as he put it, has "no need of any place, does not depend on any material thing ... [and] is entirely distinct from the body."

Third, and perhaps ironically, Descartes also held that his a priori account of the foundations of human knowledge was universal, a rational reconstruction of human knowledge fit for all people at all times and in all places. He never intimates that his foundationalism is fit only for local consumption.

Finally, Descartes believed that a noetic structure, properly ordered, reflects a mind-independent reality. There is thus an *isomorphism* between the things we believe, thoughts clearly and distinctly discerned, and the very structure of the universe.

We could undoubtedly add to the list of ingredients deemed constitutive of strong foundationalism. Whether these are the most important, or whether they are intrinsic to foundationalism at all, are themselves subjects of great debate in the literature of epistemology.

4.4 Problems with Strong Foundationalism

Virtually every element of Cartesian foundationalist theory, those central as well as those peripheral, has been the target of criticisms whose numbers are legion these days. These criticisms divide into two main classes: those attacking the notion of a basic belief and those attacking the way nonbasic beliefs receive their support from the foundations. Some criticisms are meant to undermine any version of the theory whatsoever, while others apply only to strong and not weak foundationalism. After rehearsing a few of the most commonly leveled objections against Cartesian-type foundationalism, we shall investigate whether a weak foundationalist approach fares any better.

The notion of basic beliefs is the heart and soul of foundationalism; as it goes, so goes the theory. Consequently, critics have posed what they deem to be devastating objections against human knowledge's being grounded in beliefs that are epistemically basic as described by the strong foundationalist. Why, critics ask, should we think that only beliefs that are self-evident or incorrigible or evident to the senses are properly basic? True, any belief meeting one or more of these standards is an ideal candidate for proper basicality, but is it *necessary* that a basic belief meet these standards? Should this list of criteria be considered exhaustive? These criteria alone appear much too restrictive, for they fail to encompass many beliefs we hold without the benefit of argumentative support. Consider one's beliefs in the reliability of one's senses or memory or consciousness; none of these beliefs is either self-evident or incorrigible or evident to the senses, yet they are held as properly basic by virtually everyone.

Alvin Plantinga has argued that the criteria offered for identifying genuine basic beliefs introduce a deeply self-destructive feature into the foundationalist account. If, as foundationalists claim, only beliefs that are self-evident or incorrigible or evident to the senses are properly basic, then it behooves us to ask about the epistemic status of this belief itself: that only beliefs that are self-evident or incorrigible or evident to the senses are properly basic. Is this belief *itself* self-evident or incorrigible or evident to the senses? No. Is it logically rooted in basic beliefs that meet these conditions? Again, the answer seems to be no. Strong foundationalism's acceptance of the criteria for proper basicality thus runs afoul of its own standards.[14]

One of foundationalism's vaunted benefits is its ability to halt the regress of reason giving. If called on to explain why we accept a certain conclusion, we might produce the premises. And if asked why we accept these premises, we might be able to produce premises for the premises. But since this process cannot continue indefinitely (and arguing in circles is frowned upon), we must halt the regress in beliefs that are epistemically basic. A major objection to strong foundationalism, however, is that it fails at precisely this point of alleged strength.

What the objection boils down to is this. Any acceptance of supposedly pure and certain basic beliefs in fact makes use of various background assumptions or information that compromises their certainty and undermines their "basicality." Even as primitive a claim as

"I think, therefore I am" turns out on closer inspection to rely on yet more fundamental beliefs. What is the "I" who thinks? Descartes tacitly assumes that he is a unified center of consciousness that perdures through time, a substantial self and not a series of discrete disconnected states of consciousness, as Buddhists believe, or an episode in the mind of some cosmic Absolute. There is also an implicit underlying commitment to the reliability of memory, for he must at least accept that the "I" who begins this simple argument is the same "I" who finishes it. Bertrand Russell once quipped that all Descartes was entitled to say is that "thoughts are being thunk!"

A similar fate befalls self-presenting states of one's perceptual consciousness: states such as "I seem to see a door" or "I seem to see a red patch," whose job is to undergird all our empirical knowledge. The belief that an epistemic regress can be halted in these self-authenticating nonverbal episodes of perceptual consciousness is what Wilfred Sellars calls the "Myth of the Given." The myth consists in thinking that perceptual states such as "this is red," and our powers of sensory discrimination in general, are pure and incorrigible, completely independent of any theoretical contribution or background beliefs. On the contrary, our perceptual beliefs depend for their being intelligible on our being able to connect them correctly with past experiences of redness. Being cognizant of my visual field as red tacitly requires a comparison to previous occasions of my having been appeared to in this way. Behind "this is red," then, lies the logically prior reliance on our recollection of previous red experiences as well as an awareness that our present state of perceptual consciousness betokens standard conditions for visual perceptions of a red sort. Sellars writes:

> For the point is specifically that observational knowledge of any particular fact, e.g. that this is green, presupposes that one knows general facts of the form X is a reliable symptom of Y. And to admit this requires an abandonment of the traditional empiricist idea that observational knowledge "stands on its own feet."[15]

The nonbasicality of immediate perceptual reports can be argued for not only by the way they depend on reliable memory but also by considering the role that concepts play in perception. Philosophers of science such as Stephen Toulmin, Thomas Kuhn, N. R. Hanson and others in the tradition of Kant have shown us that perceptual reports, even of so primitive a sort as "I see red," are embedded in larger theoretical and linguistic frameworks (language games, as Wittgenstein calls them) which invest them with the meaning they have for us. "All perception is theory-laden," as the old dictum states. Our cognitive experiences of color sensations (and other deliverances of the senses) are due in part to a contribution from a conceptual scheme whose status is anything but incorrigible, but is itself the subject of revisions over time.[16]

To the extent that basic beliefs are embedded in larger frameworks of belief, their status as invincibly certain will remain open to question. This will remain a problem as long as foundationalists maintain high access requirements. It is not enough to have basic beliefs, urge strong foundationalists (anybody could potentially claim that anything is basic for them); one must somehow also know that these stopping points are not arbitrary and that beginning with them will indeed confer the certainty one seeks. "A report must not only have authority, this authority must in some sense be recognized by the person whose report it is."[17] For Descartes, or anyone else, to declare that they, and not their intellectual competitors, have the right foundations for knowledge, they must be not only reflectively aware of their foundational beliefs but aware also of the properties or features making these and not some other foundational beliefs the ones by which certain knowledge is gained. Moreover, they must justifiably believe themselves to be competent to judge whether a belief possesses those features that make it basic. So accepting a certain claim B as basic requires that one also accept another claim K as basic: that B has whatever features are required to make it and not some alternative the proper foundation for knowledge. Thus the regress is not halted.[18]

So far, then, I have considered objections against just one aspect of the foundationalist program: the nature and status of basic beliefs. Strong foundationalists' claim to base all knowledge on beliefs about which it is logically impossible to be mistaken is excessive in the extreme. Not only is it logically possible that we might be in error (a point capable of being illustrated by any number of "science-fictiony" examples such as brains in a vat, evil demons, electroencephalograph scanners), but there are actual reasons for thinking that the likelihood of error with respect to foundational beliefs exceeds zero. To make matters worse, critics have been equally vociferous in objecting to the notion of basing relations contained in classical foundationalism—most notably the idea that all nonbasic beliefs can be inferred from basic beliefs via deduction or induction.

The logical relations of deduction and induction, however, don't exhaust the kinds of connections existing between a claim we accept and the beliefs that serve as its underlying support. Consider the oft-told story of the discovery of Neptune. Almost from the moment Uranus was discovered, astronomers were puzzled by peculiarities in its orbital behavior that could not be accounted for by current Newtonian models. Features of its movement could not be explained on the basis of the gravitational pull exerted by the sun and the planets then known to exist, nor was the variance between Newtonian theory and the behavior of Uranus attributable to miscalculation. So English astronomer J. C. Adams began to reason "backward": what would have to be true of our solar system to account for the behavior of Uranus? And as you've already surmised, he postulated and accepted the existence of a planet whose size and distance from Uranus precisely matched that of the planet Neptune. Yet independent empirical confirmation of Neptune's existence was not made until 1846 by the French astronomer Leverrier.

The case of Neptune's discovery illustrates that the support our beliefs receive is sometimes retrospective, a kind of reasoning from the best explanation. We infer that the planet Neptune exists from the fact that its existence best explains the data with which we are confronted. In fact, philosophers of science have aptly dubbed this kind of reasoning "retroduction," for it is reducible neither to induction nor to deduction.[19] It is a mistake, then, to suppose that all of our beliefs "fall out of" beliefs we already hold via induction or deduction. Instead the support sometimes adduced on behalf of claims we accept is a kind of inference from the best explanation.

If this is true, then the strong foundationalist's insistence on deduction and induction as the sole basing relations cannot be right, nor can many of our beliefs be grounded in anything remotely like the kind of certainty that strong foundationalists insist upon. So now it looks as though there is a possibility for a "slip 'twixt cup and lip" as the epistemic merit of our foundational beliefs gets transferred to nonbasic beliefs.

There is yet another kind of support a proposition may receive by virtue of its membership in a larger set of beliefs. "Sometimes," writes modest foundationalist Roderick Chisholm, "propositions mutually support one another. When this happens, each of the mutually supporting propositions may be said to add to the positive epistemic status of the other."[20] In other words, like the strands of a rope whose individual strength is increased when woven together with other strands, the support of a given belief is enhanced if it is included in a larger set of beliefs for which we already have some independent justification.

This type of support, which Chisholm, following the ancient philosopher Carneades, calls "concurrence," can be illustrated by a detective's observations which culminate in his belief that person A is a murderer. The detective has some, though not conclusive, evidence based on a pathology report for believing that victim X was murdered when she ingested an exotic poison. He also has some, though not conclusive, reason to accept that person A is knowledgeable about poisons (a trip to the library in X's town reveals that A checked out a book on poisonous frogs of the Amazon). The detective also has some reason for believing that A had a motive to kill X (the housekeeper claims she once observed A and X arguing vehemently). Like interlocking pieces of a puzzle, these bits of evidence achieve a strength when combined that exceeds what they have in isolation. The "supports" relation, then, is not always from the bottom up; sometimes the support we have for our beliefs is generated by the way they stand in relation to other beliefs we hold.

Even if the issue of the relationship between basic and nonbasic beliefs were unproblematic, we would still have to confront the fact that many of our perceptual beliefs are what Laurence Bonjour has dubbed "cognitively spontaneous": they are simply "injected" into our repertoire of beliefs without our having traced them back or inferred them from some basic beliefs. When you walk down the street, you are acquiring dozens of perceptual beliefs that at the time you are not overtly cognizant of acquiring. Maybe only through intense effort could you recall them even if asked to do so. (Eyewitnesses can sometimes recall events under expert questioning and hypnosis that they couldn't recover by themselves.) Nor do we claim any sort of infallibility for such beliefs. The reason for this is that we are psychologically so constituted that when confronted with a certain kind of perceptual display, we immediately and *noninferentially* form a corresponding belief. (Perhaps it would be more accurate to say that a corresponding belief is formed in us.) It is not a question of whether our perceptual beliefs are rooted in induction, deduction or even retroduction. The point is that they are not inferred at all; we hold them as basic.

It is simply false that we reason as follows:

I am experiencing thus and such a perceptual display.

When thus and such appeared to me in the past, it was a bird.

Therefore it is a bird now.

Thus the idea that a certain basing relation underlies all nonbasic beliefs fails to square with our best understanding of cognitive psychology.

The fact that we accept many beliefs without their having been inferred from a set of basic beliefs highlights the preposterous task of founding the vast quantity of beliefs we hold on such meager foundations as Descartes's *cogito*. We face what is called a security versus content problem. The strict demands for unimpeachable certainty leave one with so small a set of basic beliefs that they can't possibly bear the heavy weight of all that we believe. A moment's reflection shows that the thousands of beliefs we hold about matters aesthetic, moral, religious, political, economic, historical, scientific, philosophical and so on can't all be derived from the very small set of basic beliefs insisted on by strong foundationalists.

Finally, we must consider some objections to some of the peripheral elements often associated with classical foundationalism: the access requirements, the individualism, the alleged universality and the metaphysical realism. Critics have been especially scathing in their attack on foundationalism's individualism. There is, of course, something ironic about embarking on an intellectual endeavor that begins by divesting oneself of all one's former beliefs (as if this were possible), not to mention the very beliefs that led to the conclusion that such a project should be undertaken in the first place. In fact, quite a bit escaped Descartes's chopping block: his trust in the reliability of consciousness, such beliefs as were necessary for fashioning the criteria for a new foundation, as well as beliefs directly attributable to the traditions from which he sought to extricate himself, notably his moral beliefs. At no point does Descartes propose that we start anew with respect to them.

The hermeneutical philosopher Hans Georg Gadamer argues that it is hasty in the extreme to abandon all of reason's starting points (he calls them "prejudices") simply because they are bequeathed to us from a tradition; after all, they may very well be true. Moreover, reliance on authorities other than oneself (apart from evidencing the virtue Aquinas called docility, or teachableness) does not require that we abandon our own reason, but just the reverse. Acknowledging another's legitimate authority on intellectual and other matters represents a judgment of one's reason. According to Gadamer,

> the authority of persons is ultimately based not on the subjection and abdication of reason but in an act of acknowledgment and knowledge—the knowledge, namely, that the other is superior to oneself in judgment and insight and that for this reason his judgment takes precedence—i.e., it has authority over one's own. . . . It rests in acknowledgment and hence on an act of reason itself which, aware of its own limitations, trusts to the better insight of others. Authority in this sense, properly understood, has nothing to do with blind obedience to commands. Indeed, authority has to do not with obedience but rather with knowledge.[21]

How about strong foundationalism's high access requirements? Must one know the second-order belief that one knows, and be able to demonstrate that one knows, before one has knowledge? Descartes sought to rise above the competing claims of knowledge by using a method that would, as it were, allow him to climb outside his own skull, there achieving a kind of Archimedean standpoint (a God's-eye perspective, if you will) from which to conduct an internal audit of all he believed, ostensibly to settle once and for all the true relation between his claims and a mind-independent reality. Against the requirement that one satisfy second-order requirements, modest foundationalists have argued that knowledge of a claim P does not necessitate that one possess another belief Q, that one knows that one knows P. For if in order to know P it is necessary that I possess another belief Q, then in order to know Q I must possess still another belief— and we're caught in the very type of regress that foundationalism was meant to avoid. As we shall see below, Thomas Reid and others argue that one has knowledge not because one has additional beliefs *about* one's knowledge but because the items of one's knowledge stand in a certain relation to the world.[22] Thus efforts at achieving a kind of transcendence over one's knowledge are not essential aspects of foundationalism, and certainly not part of foundationalism in its more defensible forms.

The thinking of philosophers from diverse points of view has coalesced in the judgment that Descartes's efforts to ground philosophy in the thoughts of a solitary transcendental thinking subject is the result of an unnatural surgery separating body and mind. His artificially cerebral starting point belies the inescapable fact that we engage the world not as disembodied minds but as flesh-and-blood persons *with* minds, as whole persons enmeshed in life circumstances that mediate our experience of the world.[23] It is a modern gnosticism that would attempt to deny the fundamental fact that all of our thinking is situated socially, historically and linguistically.

When we think about matters of knowledge and justification, we do so as denizens of a particular time and place, with concrete aims and obstacles uppermost in mind. Kuhn's discussion of "paradigms,"

Wittgenstein's talk of "language games" and Dilthey's "life catego-ries," as well as Gadamer's discussion of "horizons," all underscore the essential embeddedness of our thinking in concrete historical/cul-tural situations, from which it is fantasy to suppose we can extricate ourselves. What this means is that strong foundationalists are wrong to suppose that they have demonstrated the norms on the basis of which all justified thinking takes place. And with the loss of a tran-scendental point of view ("a view from nowhere") there is no way to secure an ironclad guarantee that the rational standards one does invoke precisely mirror a mind-independent world.

Finally, we must consider that in addition to the philosophical lessons there is a moral or theological lesson (a lesson bearing on the virtue of intellectual humility) to be learned from foundationalism's failed program of self-transcendent noetic cleansing. Merold West-phal claims that not all of foundationalism's failings are philosophical; it evinces an attitude he deems morally vicious. For it depreciates, if not altogether ignores, he says, the Bible's doctrine of sin, and in particular St. Paul's teaching about the noetic effects of sin on our intellectual endeavors. As sinful humans we are prone to various kinds of self-deception, including, as we saw in the last chapter, the tendency to subordinate concerns for truth and rationality to personal gain, power, wealth and other passions.

But wouldn't efforts at self-purification of the sort recommended by Descartes be a perfect antidote against unbridled appetite? Where's the problem?

The foundationalist attempt to remedy our transcendental deprav-ity can only be problematic unless we are Pelagians. For it is, in effect, the claim that sin can be cured by our own unaided efforts, that epistemological sanctification requires nothing more that the epistemological asceticism of sound method, whether that method be syllogistic, Euclidean, experimental, transcendental, or what-ever. . . . Foundationalism itself is partly to be understood as a sinfully arrogant attempt at methodological self-purification, void of contrition, confession, or dependence upon divine grace.[24]

Westphal's objection is as much against the hubris evident in foundationalism's pursuit of self-reflective purity as it is that such efforts have failed. Gadamer says that "philosophy is the way not to forget that man is never God."[25] Westphal's point is that this is a lesson we must continue to recite.

The points offered by Westphal and Gadamer should be welcomed by those seeking intellectual virtue within the Christian context, for their insights are congruent with a number of core Christian teachings. At the very least, the doctrine of creation tells us we are not God but finite and contingent beings who do not see the world as God sees it, but as befits our creaturely status. Westphal's claims about the ways in which our lives as knowers are subverted by wayward passions and self-interest are anticipated by Christian teaching concerning sin. And the scriptural lessons concerning the body of Christ suggest that our aspirations as intellectual beings ought to be set within the context of a community of persons whose talents and insights complement and enlarge our own. Assuming, then, that intellectual virtue is a trait to be cultivated, we turn to an account that attempts to frame a more modest foundationalist's program.

4.5 Modest Foundationalism

Modest foundationalists advise that we not lament the loss of what could never be had. The fact that we cannot achieve the self-reflective infallibility sought by Descartes does not mean that skepticism prevails, nor that there are no important insights to retain from the foundationalist program. We simply need to be a little more modest about the powers of human reason. What do modest foundationalists retain of the classical foundationalist perspective? The chief claim retained is that there are basic beliefs that serve as a basis of support for nonbasic beliefs.[26] Modest foundationalists make no claims about the invincible certainty of one's basic beliefs or about a need to be reflectively aware of which beliefs have the status of basic. Instead of claiming that one's basic beliefs enjoy infallible certainty, modest foundationalists ascribe only prima facie certainty. That is, one's foundational beliefs are not necessarily immune to any conceivable doubt—they can be overridden—but they are perfectly acceptable unless one has good reason for thinking they have been undermined. They are innocent unless proven guilty. The views of Thomas Reid, the Scottish commonsense philosopher and one of Descartes's earliest critics, embody much that is typical of modest foundationalists.

Reid, no less than Descartes and Locke, is enamored by the goal of an axiomatic method for the moral sciences. All knowledge should rest, he believes, on certain foundational first principles of common sense; else we should have no way of halting an epistemic regress or combating skepticism. Reid divides up basic beliefs into necessary and contingent first principles. The former consist of necessary truths known a priori, of which the laws of logic and mathematics are chief examples. The latter consist of contingent truths such as the following:

1. The thoughts of which I am conscious are thoughts of a being I call myself.

2. Those things really happened which I distinctly remember.

3. Those things really do exist which we distinctly perceive by our senses, and are what we perceive them to be.

4. What is to be, will probably be like what has been in similar circumstances.[27]

Descartes's disastrous move was to suppose that these beliefs stood in need of argument, an effort that, as we now see, involves us in the circular enterprise of using the very faculties whose reliability is under question. So long as this requirement remains in force, the skeptic wins the day, as Hume so powerfully showed. Reid's genius lay in claiming that we are epistemically entitled to these first principles without having to supply inferential justification on their behalf. The first principles are self-evidently justified, being believed merely upon being understood. Beliefs for which Descartes felt obliged to offer arguments are, according to Reid, the very foundations of all our thinking.

In another crucial departure from Descartes, Reid denies that basic beliefs must be the objects of our reflective awareness. In rejecting higher-level access requirements he anticipates a late-twentieth-century epistemological theory called reliabilism. According to one version of reliabilism, process reliabilism, one is prima facie justified in believing *P* just so long as it is produced or sustained by a truth-conducive cognitive process. Beliefs are epistemically warranted, reliabilists argue, just so long as they are reliably produced. You don't need to be introspectively aware of this fact; still less must you be able to demonstrate to others that your beliefs are reliably produced. You need only be in the state of having a reliably produced belief; you need not also be aware that you are in such a state.

Reid's departure from his strong foundationalist predecessors, then, stems from his claim that we are irresistibly drawn to accept first principles as self-evident due to our psychological constitution—a matter of "hardwiring," one might say. But even this claim is not what makes Reid distinctive; Hume too acknowledges the force of psychology when he chides the Pyrrhonian skeptic by saying, "Nature is always too strong for principle." Though Hume acknowledges that our experience of sensations may lead us irresistibly to belief in external objects, he denies that this psychological force of our constitution (or habit) has any *epistemic* force. It is precisely here that Reid foreshadows the reliabilist: since we accept first principles spontaneously and noninferentially due to psychological processes that we have every reason to deem truth-conducive, and no reason to suspect as misleading, we are then *epistemically* entitled to accept them and employ them. Reid thus makes an epistemic virtue out of a psychological necessity.

One may ask why Reid was not a thoroughgoing reliabilist. That is, why are we entitled to accept basic beliefs in virtue of their having been reliably produced but not similarly entitled to accept beliefs elsewhere in the superstructure that rest on our first principles? Why is not the story of justification one tells on behalf of first principles invoked for all our beliefs? The answer is, I think, that only first principles, and not the beliefs we infer from them, are forced upon us by our very nature. Moreover, only first principles are matters of universal agreement. Not only are we not forced, say, with respect to our political or religious beliefs, but they are also notoriously subject to dispute. They are not universal, irresistible or self-evident, nor do they bear any of the other marks of a genuine first principle. If they are to be justifiably believed, then they must be inferred from what is properly basic.

One might criticize Reid's modest foundationalism (and all modest foundationalisms) as Keith Lehrer does. "A little more critical circumspection," he says, "shows that common sense should not be allowed to run unbridled in the epistemic field."[28] If among our goals as intellectual beings is to believe only what is true and to avoid falsehood, then can we rest content merely to embrace first principles of the sort accepted by Reid as truth-conducive without first offering some additional reasons for believing them to be appropriate epistemic self-starters and, while perhaps not guaranteeing their truth, at least showing them to be correlated with the truth? Too much is at stake to respond blithely to such demands, "Oh, my basic principles are innocent until proven guilty." Aren't some assurances on behalf of our basic beliefs required up front?

But of course any attempt to satisfy Lehrer's request spells the immediate demise of soft foundationalism. For any reasons given for accepting one's basic beliefs shows, ipso facto, that they were not really basic after all; the background information with which one validates the basic beliefs turns out to be more basic still. The regress is not halted, and the central plank in the soft foundationalist program is undermined.

Does Reid's refusal to offer guarantees of reliability on behalf of foundational first principles reduce to sheer dogmatism in the face of a legitimate demand? Three points can be made in Reid's defense.

First, we cannot offer guarantees of the reliability of "first principles." For our evidence concerning reliability would have to include deliverances of the faculties whose reliability we are accumulating evidence for.

Second, while Reid doesn't purport to offer arguments on behalf of his foundational principles, he nevertheless says that they can be correctly identified by their accompanying "marks" or "signs." Genuine foundational principles are, he says, the sort of convictions that are universally subscribed to, indispensable for living, beliefs to which we are irresistibly drawn from the earliest moments of our lives and which are rooted in our very psychological natures. Again, these marks are not meant to demonstrate the truth-conduciveness of the first principles of common sense so much as to help you know one when you see one.

Third, if someone persists in requesting additional assurances over and above the usual "marks" accompanying properly basic beliefs, then the person holding such beliefs can only respond with genuine bewilderment. What could possibly count as underlying assurance for my belief that things other than myself exist, or that I remember having had a cup of coffee earlier this morning? Beliefs like these are the very paradigms of certainty; what quality could the critic be seeking to add to such beliefs that they don't already possess? We derive our very understanding of the terms *justified* and *certain* from beliefs such as these. If someone demands additional validation of such beliefs, then you can only shrug your shoulders and say, "I don't know what you are asking for."

As we conclude this discussion of modest foundationalism, I wish to note two areas of potential weakness in Reid's position. I think, first of all, that Reid may have underestimated the capacity for thinkers of sound mind and sincere will to disagree about alleged philosophical first principles. To his credit, Reid purports to offer neither an exhaustive list of first principles nor one immune from any conceivable doubt; his is, after all, a fallibilist foundationalism. Nevertheless, I see the potential for disagreements to arise in at least two ways. First, there are thinkers who reject beliefs I think Reid would endorse as legitimate first principles, and second, there are thinkers who accept as akin to first principles beliefs Reid would not endorse as such. Let me illustrate each of these disagreements.

The first sort of disagreement can be illustrated by considering the status often attributed to the principle of sufficient reason. In short, the principle says that for any fact you'd care to mention, for any truth you'd care to cite, there is some underlying reason it is true. The principle is a way of denying that there are any such things as brute unintelligible facts in the world. Here's what Richard Taylor has to say about it:

If one were trying to prove it, he would sooner or later have to appeal to considerations that are less plausible than the principle itself. Indeed, it is hard to see how one could even make an argument for it, without already assuming it. For this reason it might properly be called a presupposition of reason itself. . . . We shall then treat it here as a datum . . . as something which all men, whether they reflect upon it or not, seem more or less to presuppose.[29]

Taylor attributes to the principle of sufficient reason the marks of a genuine first principle. Bertrand Russell, however, in his famous debate with Father Copleston, denied the principle of sufficient reason in the sense in which both Taylor and Copleston were wont to use it; instead he preferred to say of the universe, "It's just there, and that's all." Is it obvious that either Russell or Taylor is mistaken about the status of the principle of sufficient reason?

The second kind of disagreement can be illustrated by considering a claim of Alvin Plantinga (who himself holds Reid in high regard) that belief in God can be held as a basic belief. Plantinga doesn't say that belief in God is a first principle in the sense that it satisfies all the marks by which Reid thinks a genuine first principle is identified. But the belief, Plantinga claims, can be justifiably held in the manner of a first principle, that is, without the benefit of argumentative support. Some people, he says, just find themselves believing in God spontaneously and noninferentially in the face of certain kinds of experiences. We know, however, from the *Inquiry* and from his *Lectures in Natural Theology* that Reid thought belief in God to be the sort of conviction requiring argumentative support, and indeed he develops several proofs for God's existence.

Now we can imagine the sort of reply Reid would most likely give to the claim that belief in God is properly basic: that it satisfies none of the criteria by which we identify genuine first principles. It is not universal, irresistible or self-evidently true, nor is its denial a mark of insanity. We can also imagine the sort of response Plantinga would offer in return. What is the status of these criteria for genuine first principles? They are not themselves first principles, for they are surely not themselves self-evidently true, universal and so on. Why then should one feel duty-bound to restrict the scope of properly basic beliefs (or first principles) to beliefs satisfying just these criteria? The question is this: What resources does Reid have to resolve these kinds of disagreements?

A final concern I wish to raise is prompted by Reid's belief that a person "may have a clear and certain knowledge of the operations of his own mind; a knowledge no less clear and certain than that which he has of an external object when it is set before his eyes."[30] The issue of the mind's transparency is set in interesting tension by another of Reid's claims: "When a demonstration is short and plain; when the points to be proved do not touch our interest or our passions; when the faculty of judging in such cases, has acquired strength by much exercise, there is less danger of erring; when the contrary circumstances take place there is more."[31]

I wonder whether Reid did not underestimate the various ways that our passions and interests make our minds much less than completely transparent, perhaps even opaque to introspective analysis. It is, of course, quite fashionable these days to talk about the ways our "demonstrations" serve various subterranean impulses or hidden agendas, such as promoting the interests of our own socioeconomic class or solidifying our position of power. Here we confront the specter of a different kind of skepticism, not raised by the possibility of an evil demon, nor born of fatally flawed philosophical assumptions, but something more deeply essential to who we are as humans. Reid is right to think that passions and interests do indeed cloud our philosophical judgments, though there are only hints, and no sustained discussion, in his writings as to how this occurs. As an advocate of a virtues approach to epistemology, I believe that a sustained exploration of the role of passions and interests, of intellectual virtues and vices, sheds light on the issue of disagreement, as we saw in earlier chapters.

Five

Epistemic Justification

C hances are you don't believe that our personal destiny is determined by the stars, nor that crystals strategically arranged on one's torso by a witch doctor will ward off illness, nor that there are humans who have been abducted by aliens. But there are great numbers of people who do accept at least one of these beliefs. (If these examples seem far-fetched, then select from any number of political, religious, moral or aesthetic beliefs your own favorite examples of irrational belief.) You probably also think that some people who accept these claims ought not to accept them, that they are doing something that is, if not wrong, at least unfortunate by way of their minds. Most people, if they were as conscientious as they could be about the stewardship of their intellectual lives, would not embrace these beliefs. By believing these things, or by engaging in the intellectual practices that lead to these beliefs, people fail to orient themselves as well as they might toward the truth.

But it is not an easy task to explain why a person's beliefs are

intellectually unjustified, nor to give a precise account of the intellectual standards and belief policies that ought to govern the way we
accept, reject or maintain our various beliefs. As was noted in chapter
one, the rationality of our beliefs, together with the cluster of questions
to which this gives rise, falls under the topic of *epistemic justification*.
The focused attention given to this subject by contemporary
epistemologists has sparked a lively and interesting debate between
competing perspectives.

Most philosophers stress an additional reason for getting clear
about the nature and conditions for justification: without it you can't
have knowledge. Merely having a true belief is not enough. Suppose
my horoscope for today tells me I will one day be wealthy. In a
moment of weakness (no doubt aided by wish fulfillment) I believe
it. Suppose further that it is true—unbeknownst to me, I will one day
inherit the fortune of an unknown uncle. Did I *know* that what my
horoscope said was true? Obviously not. What I lacked was some
justification for thinking that what my horoscope said was true.
Justification, then, is generally thought to be indispensable to having
knowledge.[1] But which among the various accounts of justification on
the market should one embrace?

5.1 Evidentialism

Embedded within the foundationalist scheme, as was discussed in the
last chapter, is an account of the kind of support any justified belief should
receive. You will recall that all nonbasic beliefs are justified insofar as they
are appropriately supported by one's epistemically basic beliefs. Strong
foundationalists claim the only appropriate support is logical: nonbasic
beliefs must be inferable either deductively or inductively from our basic
beliefs. Weak foundationalists are more generous in recognizing other
kinds of basing relations. In either case, accepting just any old belief
willy-nilly, with no thought to its being suitably anchored by supporting
beliefs, is unacceptable. Herein lie the rudiments of a theory of epistemic
justification known as evidentialism, a theory that at one time exercised
considerable hold on the philosophical imagination and that continues
to hold sway in much popular thinking.

The notorious dictum of philosopher W. K. Clifford expresses succinctly, and as a rough first approximation, the evidentialist view: "To sum up: it is wrong always, everywhere, and for anyone to believe anything upon insufficient evidence."[2] Clifford defends the view that each of us (he makes no exceptions for age, level of education or social role) is obliged to adduce reasons for every belief we hold, no matter how seemingly insignificant the belief. Any belief, however trifling, embraced without sufficient evidence is "sinful, because it is stolen in defiance of our duty to mankind."[3]

In saying that we are duty-bound to offer evidential support for every belief we hold, without exception, Clifford is at odds with the larger epistemological framework within which his view of justification is most comfortably situated. For we already know from our study of foundationalism that such a position is impossible because it leads to an infinite regress. Eventually, says the foundationalist, the business of giving evidence must terminate in some belief or set of beliefs that we may acceptably hold without argumentative support. But aside from this problem, Clifford's dictum raises more serious questions.

Since, according to Clifford, every belief requires the support of evidence, one might naturally ask what reasons he offers in support of his own dictum. That is, why should we accept the claim that "it is wrong always, everywhere, and for anyone to believe anything upon insufficient evidence"? Clifford's reasons boil down to the following: Unless you adopt his principle, two adverse consequences will ensue. First, if you allow yourself to believe something without sufficient evidence, you will become gullible, a dupe, a sucker, someone unable to discern truth from falsehood. This, second, will result in society's "sinking back into savagery," as he says. A bit less dramatically, we might reasonably suppose that a society of dupes ill-equipped to discern truth from falsehood will make poor jurors, rotten teachers and miserable politicians, and consequently that the general condition of society must suffer.

Clifford's reasons for evidentialism are, as you have probably already noticed, *pragmatic.* He is urging us to accept his dictum not because it is entailed by incorrigible basic beliefs or inferable from such beliefs with an extremely high degree of probability. He is arguing, "Accept these beliefs or bad things are going to happen." But pragmatic reasons, however persuasive (and we can certainly debate the persuasiveness of Clifford's reasons), aren't considered good evidence for the *truth* of a belief. I might argue, "Believe in god X, or bad things are going to happen to you and to society." Despite whatever rhetorical value such a reason may have, it does not entail the truth of the god's existence nor raise the probability that the god's existence is true. Pragmatic reasons are indeed a basis on which people sometimes accept beliefs; but this type of reason is independent of the truth of the claim for which it is offered as support.[4] So Clifford hasn't actually supported his own dictum with evidence that bears on the truth of his claim, and for this reason he is guilty of a self-referential inconsistency, a serious failing indeed.

Suppose we interpret Clifford's dictum not as a belief itself but as a quasi-moral prescription or as a statement of a policy he intends to follow. On this reading Clifford's dictum could be construed to say implicitly: "This is the way I intend to govern my intellectual life. So should you." So construed, the dictum is not a belief like any other, needing evidential support, but merely a statement of a belief policy that he recommends we all follow. Let us set to one side questions about textual support for this reading. Does the theory fare any better on this understanding? I don't think so. For Clifford thinks that his policy, if ignored, will eventuate in social disaster, our "sinking back into savagery." This is slippery-slope reasoning at its most blatant. At the very least, Clifford owes us an explanation that shows the causal connections between ignoring his policy and our social ruin, and he offers no such support. And this is by no means the least of his difficulties.

Among the other failings plaguing Cliffordian evidentialism are those arising due to the vagueness of the notion of "evidence." Whether we construe Clifford's dictum as a policy or a belief, we still need to get clear as to what, exactly, evidence is, and how much is sufficient. Traditionally foundationalists argued that all evidence comes in propositional form—that is, only a belief can support another belief. The reason for this is easy to see. If the only kind of basing relations one allows are the logical relations of deduction or induction, then one's evidence must assume the form of another belief, for logical relations obtain only between propositions. From the claim "There are more than fifty people in this room" it follows deductively that "there are more than twenty-five people in this room." Also, from the claims "Nine out of ten philosophy graduates have taken a course in logic," and "Adam is a philosophy graduate," we have very strong inductive reasons for thinking that Adam has taken a course in logic. And because of strong foundationalism's influence, epistemologists like Clifford have assumed that the justification of a belief must be provided by another belief: what John Pollock calls "the doxastic assumption."[5]

While Clifford does not say so explicitly, we can infer several other requirements attaching to his brand of evidentialism. Not only must evidence for a given belief P assume a propositional form, but the beliefs on the basis of which P is believed must be occurrent in the thinking of the person employing them—that is, one must be cognizant of making use of the evidence one does. It's no good having evidence if one doesn't consciously make use of it. Would a savvy prosecutor accuse a defendant by withholding evidence essential to her case? Finally, the evidence I make use of must in fact provide the logical support I think it does if it is to serve as genuine evidence. If I mistakenly take a set of propositions as evidence for P, but in reality P is supported neither deductively nor inductively by this set of beliefs, then they are not genuine evidence. Thus it is possible that I cite beliefs x, y and z as my evidence for P and be in error that they are in fact evidence for P; they may have no logical connection to P whatsoever.

All this raises important questions. Must all evidence assume a propositional form? Must I be able to rehearse consciously the connection between beliefs serving as evidence and the belief they support?

Modest foundationalists like Reid answer both questions negatively. He argues that not all evidence must assume a propositional form; in fact this may not even be the dominant form that our evidence takes. Sometimes an experience, not a proposition, serves as evidence and is therefore what justifies me in believing a certain claim. This is particularly evident in the case of beliefs we hold as basic. The irresistibility and vividness of my experience of a world of independently existing objects is what constitutes my evidence for my belief in a mind-independent material world. My experience of remembering that I rode my bicycle an hour ago is evidence that I did indeed ride my bicycle. Of course, I believe that I rode my bicycle without rehearsing silently to myself the connection between my memory experience and my belief. The connection between experience and belief is much more automatic, a matter of how we as humans are psychologically constructed. If we are working properly, then in the face of certain kinds of experiences we immediately, spontaneously and noninferentially find ourselves believing the corresponding claim.[6]

If beliefs are formed in us immediately, spontaneously and noninferentially as a result of our having undergone certain kinds of experiences, then it is also not essential for justification that we must be able to rehearse consciously the line of inference between a given belief and some other beliefs that serve as its basis. In fact, more sophisticated versions of evidentialism share little in common with the cruder Cliffordian-style evidentialism that one sometimes hears voiced in popular and even professional discussions of religion. For example, consider the cruder form of evidentialism assumed by J. L. Mackie in his arguments that theism is improbable:

> The probabilities with which we shall be most concerned are epistemic ones: the epistemic probability of a certain statement relative to some body of information is a measure of the degree of support that that body of information gives to that statement or, equivalently, of the degree of belief that it is reasonable to give to that statement on the basis of that information.[7]

More sophisticated brands of evidentialism do not restrict evidence to propositional evidence, as does Mackie, nor do they require that one be able to rehearse to oneself, or to others, the connections between one's experiential grounds and the belief they support. Stephen Wykstra, for example, has argued for what he calls "sensible evidentialism." According to sensible evidentialism, epistemic agents do not have to be self-consciously aware of the evidence undergirding a particular belief. Nor should we require, even if the agent is so aware, that they be able to convey this information to others, still less persuade others to think the same way they do. Perhaps all you need to be justified in believing as you do is that someone in your community be capable of these higher-level requirements, and that you be aware of that.[8]

So far we have looked at criticisms of the ideas that all evidence must assume a propositional form and that each agent must have personal access to a body of beliefs serving as evidence for the claim in question. But what about sufficiency of evidence? How much is enough? Even more defensible versions of evidentialism struggle to answer this question. John Locke advises that "we proportion our belief to the evidence," and David Hume urges that we assess the amount and quality of our evidence by "weighing competing experiments."

What exactly is being recommended by Locke and Hume is not clear, but a reasonable interpretation might be as follows. Suppose an urn contains seventy white balls and thirty red balls (suitably mixed up), and I am asked whether I believe the first ball drawn from the urn will be white. Obviously there is a 70 percent chance that the first ball will be white, so I must proportion my belief to the evidence, where we might suppose *proportioning* to mean that I will assent to this belief in something less than an unconditional way. If I were forced to wager money that the first ball drawn will be white, I would hedge my bets somewhat.[9]

Or to take another case: Suppose archaeologists are divided as to the exact site of the ancient city of Jericho. The majority believes the site to be in one location, whereas a small minority (including some of the leading experts in such matters) believes the location to be somewhere else. If I "weigh competing experiments"—that is, if I balance off the opposing testimonies of the two groups of archaeologists—then I will not give decisive, unconditional assent to either view. If I side with the majority I will presumably accommodate my behavior to reflect the fact that I have something less than apodictic knowledge. I will not profess publicly to have invincible knowledge of the whereabouts of ancient Jericho. (This is consistent with arguing that we locate our research efforts in one place rather than another.)

These examples raise many difficult but relevant questions. Must all evidence be of the public sort cited by the archaeologists? How will I proportion my assent if, for various reasons, I think that the archaeologists for the minority view are better archaeologists (perhaps I admire their college degrees and think more highly of the journals they publish in)? Is all evidence quantifiable? Can we even make sense of the notion that all beliefs can be proportioned? Might it not be that different kinds of beliefs admit of different kinds of evidence? For as Aristotle says, "It is the mark of an educated man to look for precision in each class of things just so far as the nature of the subject admits; it is evidently equally foolish to accept probable reasoning from a mathematician and to demand from a rhetorician scientific proofs."[10] If this is correct, then what constitutes "sufficient" evidence is inescapably ambiguous; it must be indexed to a particular subject matter. Sufficiency of evidence in the domain of physical chemistry, and therefore what constitutes justified belief, will be altogether different from sufficiency in the domain of history, archaeology, ethics or economics. Indeed, not only must sufficiency of evidence be indexed to a particular subject matter, it must be indexed to persons as well.

The inescapable ambiguity of "sufficiency of evidence" can be further illustrated by considering another example. Suppose I cite as evidence for my belief in God a numinous encounter, a mystical experience in which I felt as though I had directly confronted the holiness and power of God. This experience, I claim, makes it evident to me that there is a God. Do I have sufficient evidence for belief that God exists, and am I justified?

This question cannot be answered in the abstract, for it all depends on what else I think I know. If, for example, you are a committed metaphysical materialist, you will assess the amount and quality of my evidence differently from the way you would if you were a theist. If you were personally acquainted with me, if you knew me to be a person in whom the intellectual virtues had taken deep root, then you would likely appraise the sufficiency of my evidence differently from the way you would were I a complete stranger. Or, to turn things around, if *you* are a person in whom the intellectual virtues have taken deep root, it is reasonable to think you would assess the sufficiency of my evidence differently from the way you would if you were a person in whom there was much intellectual vice.

In other words, the standpoint from which you appraise the amount and quality of my evidence, the particular scales on which my evidence is weighed (your *inductive standards*, as we sometimes call them), will emerge amid a host of background claims you already think you know or justifiably believe. It will also turn on more personal variables such as what kind of training you have undergone and what kind of person you are—whether, say, you are morally and intellectually virtuous—and so on.[11]

A personal story illustrates this last point. I had a friend in graduate school who was doing pioneering work in cancer research. One evening I went to his lab, where I found him exultant about having received experimental confirmation of one of his hypotheses. In fact, he invited me to see it for myself, motioning me over to a very sophisticated-looking microscope. I peered into the lens, only to discover that I was looking at my eyelash. Once past this embarrassment, I saw what appeared to be a mass of little squiggles, not unlike what you would see if you stared into a plate of finely chopped spaghetti noodles. It meant nothing to me. Did my friend have sufficient evidence for his scientific belief? Obviously, not being a scientific peer, I was in no position to say. Do religious experiences provide sufficient evidence for the beliefs of theists? Here too, it seems that not just anyone is in a position to answer.[12]

5.2 Coherentism
Due to the weaknesses of classical foundationalism and the evidentialist theories of justification embedded in it, coherentism has become

a dominant alternative. Coherence theories can be studied both as accounts of the general structure of our beliefs and as theories of epistemic justification. The two notions are related, for the core idea of coherence theories is that we are justified in believing a claim just so long as it fits in (or coheres) with the rest of what we believe. On this view all the things we believe form a vast interconnected web or network. Whether some new belief candidate gains acceptance into our network of beliefs is determined by how well it fits in with the rest of what we believe.

Indeed there is something very intuitively right and prephilosophically natural about coherence theories of justification. As was noted in the last chapter, as children we accumulate thousands of beliefs from a variety of sources long before there is a philosophical bone in our body. And long before we consciously think about matters of philosophical justification, we can see that considerations of coherence are already at work in our intellectual lives.

One day an argument breaks out among the friends you play with. Billy accuses Brendan of stealing one of his baseball cards, and because of this urges that he be banished from your group. But you hesitate to accept Billy's accusation. To your knowledge, Brendan has always been impeccably honest; in fact you recall the time he returned Mrs. Jenkins's wallet, which had accidentally fallen from her purse. Moreover, you know Billy is prone to jealousy, and you wouldn't put it past him to say this about Brendan as a way of jockeying for favor from the group. Besides, Brendan's grandparents always take him to the baseball card shop whenever they visit. Why would he steal what he could so easily have been given? All in all, the claim that Brendan is a thief doesn't fit with everything else you believe, and so you don't accept the claim.

Of course we seldom reason this explicitly as children; a child's reasoning is more a kind of information processing that goes on in a fragmentary or perhaps even subconscious level. But this example shows how considerations of coherence govern the way one should accept beliefs.

Of course it could turn out, contrary to all expectations, that Brendan did steal the card. People do occasionally act out of character, after all. And should this be the case, it would call for a bit of readjustment in your network of beliefs, at least as far as Brendan is concerned. The relevant segment of your web of beliefs would need to be modified to take account of this corrective.

And so it goes our whole lives. We navigate our way in the world on the strength of our respective webs of belief, patching, revising or perhaps even undertaking major overhauls as life's experiences dictate. It may be that the network of beliefs by which you presently operate looks dramatically different from the one you had as a kid, with very few overlapping beliefs. Our repertoire of beliefs has been likened to a raft on which we find ourselves adrift, undertaking such repairs and making such improvements as are necessary to stay afloat.[13]

It remains to be seen, however, whether coherentism can be developed beyond whatever prephilosophical plausibility it may have into a full-orbed and completely adequate account of epistemic justification. To ascertain whether coherentism is merely an aspect of being justified or the whole show, or whether one of the versions of coherentism is more defensible than another, requires that we expand on the very sketchy account thus far given.

The example of Billy and Brendan shows how considerations of coherence pose a negative constraint on belief: if a belief I am wondering whether to accept fails to cohere with the rest of what I believe, then I have a sufficient reason to reject the belief candidate. Failure to cohere is also one of the chief grounds we have for revising beliefs we already hold. If my long-standing belief in the tooth fairy runs afoul of an ever-expanding set of beliefs with which it fails to cohere (the testimony of my pals, the strong resemblance between by mother's writing and the note from the tooth fairy, and so on), then I will abandon my belief in favor of the claim that there is no tooth fairy—a belief that better coheres with the rest of what I now accept.

But in addition to acting as a barrier to belief, coherence is often a positive basis for accepting a belief. Perhaps the story of Neptune's discovery in the last chapter is a good example. We might embrace a belief precisely because it coheres so well with the rest of what we believe, and in fact by accepting it, we find that the overall level of coherence within our system of beliefs is raised. Sometimes we accept a belief not because we have compelling independent reasons for thinking the claim true but because of its capacity to make sense of so much else we believe. It imparts a strong measure of explanatory power to all the rest of what we believe; it unifies and makes the best sense out of all that we already accept.

I have so far assumed that we have a rough-and-ready idea of the concept of coherence. Improving on that rough-and-ready concept, however, is not so easy. Whatever else coherence may be, it has something to do with the way my beliefs are related to each other; but what is the nature of this relation? Since logical inconsistency is the most obvious way two or more beliefs can fail to cohere, one might think that coherence amounts to no more than logical consistency. We can, however, imagine systems of belief that are free of contradiction but have nothing else to recommend them. Suppose my system of beliefs consisted only of the five following beliefs:

{2 + 2 = 4; grass is green; Sacramento is the capital of California; World War II ended in 1945; Elvis is alive and working at a laundromat in Atlanta.}

Though this set is logically consistent and 80 percent true, that is about all there is to recommend it. One could have as large and as perfectly coherent a system of beliefs as one wishes, yet it could be a system of disjointed, discrete members that have nothing whatsoever to do with one another. Whatever coherence is, it must be more than freedom from inconsistency.

Not only will a coherent set of beliefs be free of logical contradiction, but its members (or relevant subsets thereof) must be interconnected in some way. The set above displays nothing like what Chisholm calls "concurrence." The reasonableness of its members is not enhanced by virtue of their being held in combination. They neither explain nor are explained by each other, or by any new candidate for adoption into the system. What else, then, must be added to freedom from contradiction to form an adequate account of coherence? Alan White describes what is needed as follows:

> According to the coherentist theory, to say that a statement (usually called a judgment) is true or false is to say that it coheres or fails to cohere with a system of other statements; that it is a member of a system whose elements are related to each other by ties of logical implication as the elements in a system of pure mathematics are related. Many proponents of the theory hold, indeed, that each member of the system implies every other member.[14]

This passage from White suggests that a coherent set of beliefs will contain only members related by ties of logical implication—that is, by being deductively inferable from each other.

Other coherentists see explanatory power rather than logical implication as the ingredient over and above absence of contradiction that makes a system of beliefs coherent. To see this, consider the debate concerning the authorship of Hebrews. Whoever wrote the book was obviously knowledgeable of Jewish thought and customs. The author was also familiar with the writings of St. Paul, for Hebrews repeats many of the theological themes of the Pauline corpus and displays a similarity of grammatical style. The claim that St. Paul is its author explains all this interconnected data (or so claim its proponents) in a way that no alternative claim does that is incompatible with it.

Critics argue that the Greek prose style in Hebrews is arguably the most sophisticated of the New Testament and must therefore have been penned by a native Greek speaker. They suggest that authorship by Apollos of Alexandria, a Christian familiar with the work of Paul and also knowledgeable of the large community of Diaspora Jews residing in Alexandria, best explains the full range of data, including the discrepancy in the Greek prose style between the book of Hebrews and the rest of the Pauline corpus.

Advocates of Paul counter that Paul customarily dictated his writings in general outline to an amanuensis, who in turn exercised a bit of stylistic freedom. This latter claim, in conjunction with the claim of Paul's authorship, most satisfactorily accounts for the full range of data.

And the debate goes on. What this example illustrates is that the coherence of a belief turns on how well it either accounts for a set of beliefs we already accept or is itself explained by that set. Therefore coherence is best understood as equivalent to *explanatory power.*

A number of objections confront the claim that either logical entailment or explanatory power is by itself sufficient to elucidate the notion of coherence. First of all, rival systems of belief may be mutually exclusive yet equally coherent. Two sets of beliefs that shared all necessary truths in common but contained the contradictories of all contingent truths could tie for coherence if logical implication were all that mattered. Moreover, it is possible for logically incompatible systems to tie in their explanatory power. Suppose theism and naturalism are equals in explanatory power, and no third system explains more about the world than they do. Each explains as much data as the other, and no alternative system explains as much as they do. Considerations of coherence alone cannot help us to adjudicate between them as to which is the better justified.

Another example reveals a further weakness of coherence construed simply as explanatory power. Consider a rich old recluse with a penchant for Cold War–style conspiratorial thinking (the recluse would not, of course, describe his intellectual habits as conspiratorial). Tucked away on his estate, he is isolated from the full range of experiences that might alter his beliefs about covert undertakings by the government. And whatever counterevidence to his pet theories manages to penetrate the physical barriers he has erected cannot bypass his mental barriers. He discounts objections by claiming that they are the work of crafty propagandists, clever maneuvers to throw him off their trail. In this way the recluse is able to construct and preserve a coherent set of beliefs that explains all that comes within its web. This illustration calls to mind the words of W. V. O. Quine: "Any statement can be held true come what may, if we make drastic enough adjustments elsewhere in the system."[15] The recluse achieves coherence and explanatory power by the unacceptable ploy of limiting the number of beliefs he has to handle and by failing to allow the fresh winds of experience to blow through his system.

As Alvin Plantinga points out, a belief system that is suitably unresponsive to changes in our experience may be coherent, but this of itself is not sufficient for our being justified. A true account from Oliver Sacks's book *An Anthropologist on Mars* shows that coherence isn't a sufficient characteristic of an ideal intellectual agent. In his chapter "The Last Hippie" Sacks recounts the story of Greg F., a 1960s acid freak and Grateful Dead fan who joined the Hare Krishnas. He grew increasingly spiritual, so much so that the swami of the order declared that Greg had achieved the state of enlightenment known as "Krishna consciousness." What was mistakenly diagnosed as spiritual insight was in fact a brain tumor the size of a small grapefruit extending on both sides of Greg's frontal lobes. Sacks describes his first encounter with Greg as follows:

> Questioning him about current events and people, I found the depths of his disorientation and confusion. When I asked him who was the president, he said "Lyndon," then, "the one who got shot." I prompted "Jimmy . . . ," and he said, "Jimi Hendrix," and when I roared with laughter, he said maybe a musical White House would be a good idea. A few more questions convinced me that Greg had virtually no coherent memory of events much past 1970. . . . He seemed to have been left marooned in the sixties—his memory, his development, his inner life since then had come to a stop.[16]

Through several examples, Plantinga generalizes that a person's having a coherent set of beliefs may be attributable to some pathological condition from which he or she suffers, some kind of "cognitive malfunction." The conclusion obviously is that coherence, considered by itself, does not exhaust the list of desiderata characterizing an optimally ordered cognitive life.

5.3 Keith Lehrer's Coherence Theory

Keith Lehrer offers an account of personal justification that relies on our understanding the concept of coherence as *competition*, which may surmount the aforementioned problems.[17] An account of personal justification attempts to set down the requirements that you, the individual, must satisfy in order for one of your beliefs to be rationally acceptable in *your* web. Being justified in accepting a belief does not require your determining how it fits into everyone else's web; your set of beliefs is the ultimate arbiter of whether you are entitled to accept some belief candidate.

Two features of Lehrer's account are crucial. First, Lehrer says that any justified belief you have must be accepted in the interests of gaining the truth. We may suppose that Greg F. does not accept his belief that Lyndon Johnson is president out of a concern for securing the truth; his belief is owing more to a tumorous brain than to an appreciation of the truth. That the recluse was motivated by the interests of truth rather than by fear is also open to doubt. Lehrer, however, doesn't require that we put ourselves in a position to judge others' motives. He says we must use a principle of charity, taking people at their word when they say that they accept a belief in the interest of gaining truth.

Second, Lehrer's theory elucidates the nature of coherence through the notion of competition. That beliefs compete for entrance into what Lehrer calls our "acceptance system" (the body of beliefs we have embraced in the interests of gaining the truth and avoiding error) is a phenomenon familiar to most of us.[18] Politician A urges passage of a bill affecting reform of the health care system, arguing that it will not result in a tax hike and may even save the taxpayers millions of dollars. Politician B argues that the bill in question will have the effect of raising our taxes. These arguments cannot both be true, and each politician wants you to believe the way they do. These beliefs about health care reform are in competition; which belief wins the competition is a matter of which would be most reasonable for you to believe, given the system of beliefs you already have. Perhaps you already believe, based on past experience with education and other entitlement programs, that a government's efforts at social reform generally result in higher taxes. Your colleague at the university who is expert in economics, and whose track record of judgments in such matters is highly reliable, and whose opinions you have always trusted, believes that the bill will raise taxes. Your existing repertoire of beliefs obviously favors the claims of politician B.

It may also happen that the arrival of a belief candidate leads us to revamp some part of our system of beliefs rather than reject the candidate that competes with it. On the basis of elementary studies in biology, I accept that all reptiles are cold-blooded. Since I also accept that dinosaurs were reptiles, I believe that dinosaurs were cold-blooded. Some paleontologists claim, however, that dinosaurs were in fact warm-blooded. As my acceptance system presently stands, the belief should be rejected. But further thinking about the matter causes me to hesitate in rejecting the claim. I also believe, based on my elemental training in the sciences, that scientific theories are subject to change; we certainly don't think of matter, time and space today in the way scientists did hundreds of years ago. Moreover, the claims serving as evidence in support of the warm-blooded theory appear to me, especially when presented by colleagues whose work I have good inductive reasons for trusting, highly plausible: beliefs about the bone structure and bone density of dinosaurs, the length and speed of their strides, their migratory patterns and so on. It now appears to me more reasonable to accept this evidence and the theory about warm-bloodedness it supports than to retain my old belief that all dinosaurs were cold-blooded.

Might there not be occasions, you object, in which a belief proposed for my acceptance has no competition, with no rivals either inside or outside my system of beliefs? And since any belief is coherent with itself, won't I be justified in believing it merely by virtue of embracing it? No, says Lehrer; mere acceptance is not enough for you to be justified. You must have some reasons to think that accepting this seemingly isolated belief serves the interests of truth. In order for you to think reasonably that you have the interests of truth in mind, you must be able to counter possible objections a skeptic might pose against the belief candidate. Suppose while channel surfing past a television documentary, I just manage to hear the claim, before zipping on, that the average person in Thailand consumes seventy-five pounds of rice a year. Should I believe this? Well, it isn't accompanied by any rivals, as in the case with the health bill. Nor does it compete with any of my preexisting beliefs. As far as I can tell, I have never had a single thought in my entire life about the amount of rice consumption in Thailand. Even now as I attend to the belief, I can discover no rival beliefs, no other considerations that would bar me from accepting it. Would I be justified in accepting it on Lehrer's view? He responds:

> It is not enough that one accept something for it to be more reasonable than its competitors on the basis of one's acceptance system. One must have some information that such acceptance is a trustworthy guide to truth. The objective of acceptance is to obtain truth and avoid error in the specific thing accepted. For it to be reasonable to think one has succeeded, one must have information to meet the objections of a skeptic in the justification game.[19]

Lehrer has here added an important new requirement for my being within my rights in accepting that persons in Thailand consume, on average, seventy-five pounds of rice annually: that I be able to rebut the objections of a skeptic bent on showing me that I am not entitled to this belief. It is not necessary to itemize the many different skeptical objections that might be posed in order to see that Lehrer has set down an impossibly stringent demand, one leading to an infinite regress. For now it is not enough that a belief cohere with the rest of what I believe for me to be personally justified; it is also necessary that I have additional information that would enable me to rebut various objections that a skeptic might pose against my belief. The difficulty is that whatever additional information I invoke to combat the skeptic's attack on my original belief might itself become fodder for a renewed round of objections; "Well, how do you know that you are not mistaken with respect to this additional information?" Must I then come up with still more additional information to defend against the skeptic? There is no way off this merry-go-round.[20]

What this criticism reveals is that Lehrer's coherentist account of justification contains an unduly high access requirement. It is not enough that a given belief cohere with the larger body of my beliefs *simplicter*. In addition to a belief's cohering with my initial acceptance system, I must have beliefs *about* the fact that it so coheres; I must be reflectively aware of the fact that a given belief coheres with the rest of what I believe. I do not gain personal justification for a belief of mine, on the coherentist view, if the belief coheres perfectly with the rest of what I believe, yet I remain oblivious to the fact of its so cohering. It seems, then, that for every belief of mine that I am justified in holding on coherence considerations, I must also have a metalevel belief about the fact that it so coheres. But if I am to be justified in this metalevel belief, I must be aware that it too coheres with the rest of what I believe—and so on ad infinitum. The most obvious lesson to draw from this objection is that we must reject any condition requiring that I have additional beliefs about how a belief candidate stands with respect to the rest of what I believe before I can be justified in accepting it.[21]

But matters are still worse for the coherence theory. It's not even clear that a person can satisfy the conditions necessary to form the *first* of an infinite string of metalevel beliefs about my beliefs. In a nutshell, Lehrer's theory of justification boils down to saying that I am justified in believing a certain claim P just so long as P does a better job than any of the beliefs with which it may compete in assisting me in getting in touch with the truth. So my belief that I see an Australian shepherd puppy standing before me is justified for me, if it coheres better than the claim that I am seeing a stuffed replica of an Australian shepherd, that I see only a holographic projection of a dog, that I am having a drug-induced hallucination of a dog, that it is really a German shepherd but wish-fulfillment mechanisms have caused me to believe it is an Australian shepherd, and so on. Each of these latter beliefs competes with P; which one I am justified in accepting depends on which one would yield the coherent system most likely to put me in touch with the truth.

How fair is this competition, someone might ask? Every belief I accept must compete not only with all the other rival claims simultaneously vying for entrance into my acceptance system (as with the rival bills on health care) but also against all the beliefs that I already have in place. But who really thinks that every belief candidate passes before the bar of everything we already believe? For we literally hold thousands of beliefs, most of which we can't dredge up at the moment some new claim comes knocking at the door of our acceptance system.

As I entertain some belief, I have to ask myself whether it or some rival competes most favorably with my overall web of beliefs. But how much of my web do I have access to? How many beliefs will I summon up as I make this determination—three or four perhaps? The fact is, we cannot conjure up all the beliefs we hold when we check for coherence, but only a significantly reduced subset. So any given belief candidate must pass muster with the three or four beliefs I can consciously recall that I believe are relevant to accepting the candidate. And this is a far cry from coherence with the overall system. Belief candidates compete only with beliefs I can consciously recall, what are termed "occurrent" beliefs, not with "nonoccurrent" beliefs, which most likely constitute the bulk of what I believe in each case of competition. So one might legitimately wonder whether the competition was fair, whether the strongest competitors to the candidate belief were in fact the ones I consciously recalled.

Lehrer, or some other coherentist, might respond that the beliefs that in fact come to mind for the purposes of the competition just are the relevant beliefs needed for assessing a belief candidate's overall coherence. After all, a chess master (unlike IBM's Deep Blue) does not entertain every possible response to his opponent's last move: inwardly he preselects only the four or five possibilities viable, given the particular configuration of pieces before him. Perhaps something analogous to this happens every time we entertain a candidate belief.

This claim cannot, it seems to me, remain at the level of hopeful assertion; by the coherentist's own requirements it is itself in need of justification. The hermeneutics of suspicion might prompt us to ask whether the process of competition is not subtly and imperceptibly rigged by various subconscious impulses. Lehrer's response, I believe, would be to say that insofar as a belief is included in one's acceptance system as a result, say, of wish-fulfillment mechanisms, one hasn't accepted the belief in the interests of truth. But now it seems that in order to be justified, I have to have additional knowledge about myself: that no considerations other than those oriented toward the truth were in play at the time I accepted the belief in question. The trouble is that here we again have the makings of another regress, since the justification of this new belief about the fairness of the competition process must be made with reference to the whole body of what I already believe.

This survey of the coherentist account of justification shows that while considerations of coherence constitute an important strand in an overall account of justification, coherence does not suffice alone. Part of its difficulties stem from difficulties surrounding the very idea of coherence. It's like the idea of "simplicity": not a simple matter at all. Graver difficulties arise because of the "access requirements" each agent must satisfy.

Any account of justification that can avoid my having to preside consciously over each and every belief I accept will escape many of the difficulties plaguing coherentism. *Reliabilism* is just such a theory. We turn now to see if it fares better than its evidentialist and coherentist accounts.

Six

Reliabilism

Despite their many contrasts, evidentialism and coherentism share several important assumptions about the nature of justification. As portrayed in the last chapter, each maintains that my being justified in holding a belief depends crucially on what and how I think about it. According to evidentialism, not only must I have evidence for my beliefs, but I must also see and appreciate the way the evidence supports my beliefs. Similarly with coherentism: in order to be justified, not only must a given belief in fact cohere with the rest of what I believe, but I must see and appreciate the way it coheres. In each case justification requires my having (or at the very least my being capable of acquiring through introspection) metalevel beliefs *about* my justified beliefs. Each view requires as a condition of believing justifiably that agents satisfy what are often called "accessibility requirements"—that is, by "looking" inward they must be able to discern within themselves the ground and strength of their justified beliefs.

Evidentialism and coherentism can also be viewed as sharing a normative conception of justification.[1] My holding a belief justifiably follows as a consequence of my having acted responsibly to satisfy whatever duties or rules or practices I deem essential for justification. These rules can be variously stated, for instance: "Never believe anything without evidence, and never believe to a degree greater than the evidence allows," or "Only accept those beliefs that contribute most to the coherence of your web of beliefs." Being justified, then, is a matter of my having fulfilled my epistemic duty, of having done my best to honor what I regard as its requirements. Thus evidentialists and coherentists regard the mind as analogous to the conscience; its status is something you yourself are best situated to determine, and you are chiefly responsible to preside over its care.

As if with this analogy in mind, W. K. Clifford urges: "Whoso would deserve well of his fellows in this matter will guard the purity of his belief with a very fanaticism of jealous care, lest at any time it should rest on a an unworthy object, and catch a stain which can never be wiped away."[2] Unfortunately, these requirements are simultaneously too stringent and too lax. To insist that we satisfy high accessibility requirements for all of our beliefs is surely excessive. For as we saw earlier, we consider ourselves to be perfectly justified in believing lots of things, such as immediate reports of perceptual experience, that we do not make the subject of reflective meditation. Moreover, formidable problems in the form of possible vicious regresses await anyone who makes the attempt. On the other hand, though we may strive to the best of our ability to discharge our epistemic duties, we might still fall short of the mark. Being conscientious to satisfy the demands of justification does not guarantee that we will satisfy those demands, or even if satisfying them, that we will light upon the truth. Poor Christopher Columbus went to his grave believing that he had indeed discovered the Far East, and given the geographical and cartographic evidence of his day this belief may have been not only amply supported but most coherent with the rest of what he believed. As we know, of course, he was wrong; his best efforts epistemically did not result in his securing the truth.

An account of justification known as *reliabilism* has more recently emerged that deftly avoids both these problems and tightens the connection between justification and truth. Reliabilism shifts our thinking about justification from a subjective or first-person perspective to an objective or third-person perspective. Instead of depending on something like duty satisfaction, justification depends on whether I acquired the belief in a way that makes it highly likely that I have gained the truth.

This distinction is easily captured if we consider its moral analogue. We all recognize the difference between striving to be good and actually succeeding in being good. Actions that I might sincerely consider innocent might nevertheless be wrong from a "God's-eye perspective." Though I may be deserving of an A for effort, though I may not suffer any pangs of conscience, I may nevertheless fail to achieve the highest standards of moral excellence. Similarly, beliefs I sincerely think cohere or take to be adequately supported by evidence might nevertheless be deficient in these respects and unlikely to lead to the truth. For this reason, reliabilists claim that my being justified in a belief is not a reward based on effort and good intentions but a consequence of my cognitive state's being in right relation to the world, whether or not I am so aware. Justification is a state or condition that accrues by virtue of having one's cognitive faculties working *reliably*.[3]

Just what is the "right" relation between my cognitive states and the world that is essential for justification? Reliabilists differ here.[4] D. M. Armstrong suggests as a fitting analogy the relationship between a thermometer and the world. We can account for the rise and fall of mercury in a properly working thermometer *nomologically*, that is, by referring to laws of nature. There is a lawlike relation that links the position of the mercury in a glass tube and the surrounding air temperature. Analogously, we can account for an agent's having justified beliefs nomologically; justification occurs when my cognitive state is linked to the world by the appropriate laws of nature.

Robert Nozick says the link between justified belief and the world is best thought of counterfactually: "If p weren't true, S wouldn't believe that p."[5] I am justified in accepting a certain belief p if my believing p is due to factors that wouldn't occur if p were not true. When I hallucinate a pink elephant, my belief that I see a pink elephant is not due to the truth of there being a pink elephant before me. Since a belief induced by hallucination would persist even though no pink elephant is in view, my belief is not justified. But if my belief that I see a pink elephant is such that I would not have had it had there been no pink elephant present to me, then my belief is justified.

Think of our cognitive equipment as similar to a radar. In a reliable radar, no blips would appear on the screen if there were no objects being scanned. So it is with justified beliefs; as Nozick says, they result from our cognitive faculties' having successfully "tracked the truth." We would not believe as we do if the world were not just as we believe.

Perhaps the most widely discussed effort to strengthen the link between having a justified belief and having a true belief is Alvin Goldman's "process reliabilism." The central claim of process reliabilism is that I am justified in my beliefs when they have the right *causal history*, when they have been produced in me by a reliable cognitive process. Vision is a paradigm reliable cognitive process: it takes inputs in the form of visual stimuli and, by way of properly working cognitive equipment, produces as outputs beliefs about material objects. Reliable cognitive processes, Goldman explains, are those whose belief outputs have a high ratio of truths to falsehoods. Beliefs formed by sensation and introspection have a high truth ratio, unlike beliefs formed by wish fulfillment or random guessing.

Some reliable belief-producing processes, such as deductive reasoning, take other beliefs as inputs. But flawless inferences done on false input beliefs will not yield justified beliefs. Thus we must differentiate, says Goldman, between cognitive processes that are belief dependent and those that are belief independent. Belief-dependent processes, such as logical inference, are "conditionally reliable" so long as the input beliefs were themselves true and a sufficiently high number of its output beliefs are true. Belief-independent processes are based on no inputs that are belief states.

Of course psychological processes vary in their degrees of reliability. Testimony, though reliable, is generally thought to be less reliable than seeing for oneself. Even the reliability of seeing for oneself will vary as conditions change—seeing up close in broad daylight, for example, as opposed to seeing at a distance in twilight.

Suppose my neighbor informs me that a skunk has taken up residence in my garage. Am I justified in believing it? That depends, says Goldman, on whether I might have employed a more reliable process that would have led to a different belief. Suppose a visual inspection, were I to have conducted it, would have revealed that my garage is free of skunks. Then the belief grounded in testimony, though coming from a generally reliable process, is unjustified in this case. So Goldman states the reliabilist condition for justification as follows:

> If S's belief in p at t results from a reliable cognitive process, and there is no reliable or conditionally reliable process available to S which, had it been used by S in addition to the process actually used, would have resulted in S's not believing p at t, then S's belief in p at t is justified.[6]

Many questions of detail remain concerning the crucial notion of reliability. How reliable does a belief-producing process have to be in order to yield justified beliefs? Will a ratio of 90 percent true beliefs to 10 percent false beliefs do? Goldman demurs rather than specifying any exact ratio, but he does say that perfect reliability isn't necessary. This means that a reliable process can have a rare false belief as its output, thereby making it possible for me to be justified in holding a false belief.

What is it exactly whose reliability is crucial to my being justified? Is it my retina, my neural circuitry, the v-4 color receptors of my frontal lobes? Goldman doesn't wish to tie reliability to any specific mechanism per se, but rather to the entire cluster of psychological and physiological mechanisms at work in those processes that permit us to remember, to see, to infer and so on.

Are the processes involved in *my* acts of memory what are central to judgments about memory's overall reliability? No, because the outputs of my memory fluctuate in their reliability, depending on whether they are recent or distant, distinct or hazy. Are we to calculate an average reliability of all my memories and assign to each memory output just the degree of justification that befits their average reliability? Surely not, for doing so would blur the evident disparity in justification between recent memories and those fragmentary pictures of early childhood. Goldman anticipates this concern, claiming that our judgments as to memory's reliability are not grounded in a particular dated sequence of events resulting in a memory belief in the mind of a particular person. Rather, it is memory as such—that is, memory as a general *type* of process occurring in the human race—and not any particular embodiment (or *token*) of this process as occurs in this or that person.

Even so, doesn't the reliability of, say, the visual process as a general type vary relative to circumstances? Presumably not any output of the visual process is justified; suppose we do live in a world where our thoughts are manipulated by a Cartesian evil demon. In this case beliefs arising from vision could not be considered reliable. Goldman's answer appears ad hoc. He requires that reliable outputs be restricted to what he calls a "non-manipulated environment," one in which "there is no purposeful arrangement of the world either to accord with or conflict with the beliefs that are formed."[7]

Two important contrasts separate reliabilism from the views of justification we have already examined. First, being justified does not require that agents be aware of their cognitive faculties' having worked in a reliable way. Just as my bodily organs can function properly without my being aware of it, thereby making me healthy, so too I can be justified if my mental faculties—my sensory faculties, my brain—are working properly without my being self-reflectively aware of this fact. It is enough that they are so working; I needn't also have beliefs about their working the way they do.

Second, reliabilism differs from coherentism and evidentialism by depreciating, if not in many instances altogether eliminating as an ingredient for justification, the role of personal responsibility and effort, in the normative sense spoken of earlier. In evidentialism and coherentism, my being justified requires that I expend effort to gather evidence or to assess how a belief candidate coheres with the rest of what I believe. No such expenditure of effort is needed to be completely justified on the reliabilist view.[8] Either it is or is not a fact about me that reliable cognitive processes were causally responsible for my believing as I do. If so, then my beliefs are justified; if not, then they are unjustified; and what I think about the status of my beliefs is immaterial.

Reliabilism offers tremendous advantages, not the least of which is that persons other than philosophers—children and uneducated persons—wind up being justified in many of their beliefs. Since lack of years and philosophical training doesn't keep one's cognitive equipment from functioning reliably, such a lack poses no barrier to justification. Don't we wish to say that when a child is stimulated by the appropriate visual display and spontaneously believes she sees her brother riding his bike, she is justified? The child is not required to reason about this belief in any particular way in order to be justified. This view accords much more closely with our commonsense conviction that most people are, by and large, justified in most of what they believe. Clifford's evidentialism suggests that the opposite is true.

Second, reliabilism supplies a ready rejoinder to the perennial attacks of skeptics about justification.[9] Epistemologists have devoted considerable effort to crafting accounts of justification to address the problem posed by the possibility that some evil demons or malevolent scientists are manipulating our beliefs. Many epistemologists who accept some form of high-accessibility requirement have thought that being justified requires that we know and perhaps even show that this is not the case. But here's the rub: If your thoughts were being so manipulated, they'd look no different to you than if they were not. And since you can't know that your beliefs are not being tampered with, you cannot be justified in your ordinary beliefs. Reliabilists respond simply: To be fully justified we don't have to know that our beliefs are free from demonic tampering. Being justified requires only that we are not in fact so manipulated—not that we are aware of this, and still less that we are able to show this.

Another advantage is that our concept of epistemic justification gets empirical anchorage by being defined in something other than the closed circle of normative terms. We don't make much headway in our efforts to understand the nature of justification if it is always explained in cognate terms like "doing your epistemic *duty*" or "being *entitled* to your beliefs" or "believing *rationally*." Reliabilism permits us to explain the nature of justification by appealing to concrete empirical processes and states of affairs. Interestingly, by rooting justification in reliable psychological processes like perception and memory, reliabilism displaces philosophers from whatever privileged position they may have enjoyed to decide on matters of epistemic justification. On this view, perhaps cognitive psychologists and neurophysiologists are equally if not more qualified to judge what constitutes reliably functioning perceptual faculties.[10]

6.1 Objections to Reliabilism

Despite these impressive advantages, reliabilism suffers from sustained criticism. Problems inherent in details of the theory, as well as competing intuitions about the very nature of justification itself, form the basis of ongoing attacks. One of the gravest problems besetting this view (a problem some epistemologists consider decisive) is called the "problem of generality," advanced to powerful effect by Richard Feldman.[11] The problem can best be explained by way of example. Suppose I am gazing out my kitchen window and see a cardinal eating at the bird feeder. On the reliabilist view, am I justified in believing that I see a cardinal? That depends on whether my seeing exemplifies a reliable belief-producing process. Herein lies the problem, for my belief that I see a cardinal is an instance of any number of different types of processes: perception, vision, color vision, vision at dawn, vision on a Monday, vision of a bird, vision of the type that results in my believing that I see a cardinal, and so on. Which process should we select as the relevant one in judging whether my belief has been reliably produced? Since these processes differ so obviously in their degrees of reliability, the reliabilist owes it to us to specify which process we should invoke in determining whether my "cardinal belief" is justified.

To specify precisely the belief-producing process that is relevant to the evaluation of my belief, the reliabilist must steer between the two extremes of delineating the process too widely and too narrowly. Suppose we subsume my belief that I see a cardinal under the process type "visual beliefs." This designation of the relevant process is obviously too wide, for it includes "seeing in the dark," "seeing through a fog," "seeing a very tiny object," "seeing in a fleeting glance" and so forth. Since reliabilism assigns to all outputs of the process type called "vision" the same degree of justification, we are stuck with the undesirable consequence of having to regard my belief that I see a cardinal at the bird feeder as on a par with my belief that I see a gnat on the bird feeder. Obviously the two beliefs are not equally well justified. But if we subsume both under the broad category "beliefs resulting from the vision process," then we must judge them to be equally well justified—an infelicitous consequence indeed.

Specifying the relevant process too narrowly leads to equally unpalatable results. Suppose I characterize the process resulting in my belief that I see a cardinal as follows: it is an instance of the type "seeing a cardinal while seated in my kitchen on August 7 at 5:32 a.m. with atmospheric conditions [fill in the blanks] at my precise age and physiological statistics [fill in some more blanks] all on a Monday morning!" Though this process certainly doesn't lack specificity, it is so narrow that it can happen only once, producing one and only one output. This means that if it is true that I see a cardinal, my belief-producing process has a reliability of 1.0, and if false its reliability is 0![12] This untoward result conflicts with the obvious fact that causal processes of the sort resulting in beliefs about ordinary physical objects yield varying degrees of justification.

Let's suppose the problem of generality can somehow be met. Even so, we can identify belief-producing mechanisms that are reliable in the requisite sense but that nevertheless fail to produce justified beliefs. The problem is due to mechanisms that are *accidentally* reliable. Another true story from Oliver Sacks illustrates this point.

Franco is a painter obsessed with just one subject: his boyhood home, Pontito, Italy. While in his early thirties Franco undergoes an illness marked by high fever, weight loss and delirium. Precisely what illness affected Franco is never conclusively settled. What is clear, writes Sacks, is that while ill Franco began having uncannily vivid dreams about Pontito, dreams whose images would remain with him after he was awake, "dreams with the most microscopic, veridical detail, a detail beyond anything he could consciously remember." Sacks speculates that these dreams were Franco's peculiar way of coping with a psychologically traumatic departure from Pontito during childhood.

> What seems to have occurred, by singular fortuity, was the co-occurrence, the concurrence, of an acute need and a physiological state. For if his sense of exile and loss and nostalgia demanded a sort of world, a substitute for the real world he had lost, his experiential seizures now supplied what he needed, an endless supply of images from the past—or rather, an almost infinitely detailed, three-dimensional "model" of Pontito, an entire theater or simulacrum he could mentally walk about and explore.[13]

This account illustrates that Franco's "experiential seizures" leave him not just with a reliable memory but with an astounding capacity to recall in three-dimensional detail scenes so complex that they exceed by far anything normal memory can reproduce. Franco's memory isn't just reliable, it's "super-reliable." It seems that Franco's beliefs are justified par excellence, according to reliabilist criteria. Yet we hesitate to accept this judgment, however, because of the accidental, even pathological, way his memorial beliefs were produced.

Whatever other problems may beset reliabilism, these examples suggest that reliability cannot be a sufficient condition for justification. Something more than merely having been reliably produced is necessary—something Alvin Plantinga calls "proper function." Not only does the justification that knowledge requires involve cognitive faculties that work properly, but they must work properly in the right environments and in the way they were intended by God to function, says Plantinga.

So far reliabilism's difficulties stem from efforts to work out the theory in sufficient detail. Some philosophers, however, oppose not just efforts to supply needed details; they resist the very idea that justification might be developed along reliabilist lines. In particular they attack the theory at one of its alleged points of strength: its rejection of first-person, subjective elements in justification.

An oft-cited example developed by Laurence Bonjour illustrates this point.[14] Imagine that Norman possesses reliable clairvoyant powers, though he does not know this. In fact, he even takes himself to have good evidence that no such powers exist. One day his reliably functioning clairvoyant capacities produce in him the true belief that the president is in New York City, though he has no evidence that this is true. Is Norman's belief justified? Not if you think something more than being the output of a reliable mechanism is necessary for justification. Norman's belief concerning the president's whereabouts comes to him as a bolt out of the blue, so to speak. He had no evidence on its behalf and doesn't even believe that the faculty responsible for its production exists. Surely something more than reliable production is needed for Norman to be justified.

What does Norman lack? Bonjour is quite plain that being justified epistemically requires that we pursue the truth *responsibly*.[15] We have a duty, he says, to orient our cognitive lives so that we deliberately accept only those beliefs we have adequate reason to think are true. This kind of reflective awareness of what one accepts and rejects is conspicuously absent from the cases of Norman and Franco. Their beliefs, though true and reliably produced, come to them in entirely serendipitous fashion, disconnected from their conscious, responsible intention.

Keith Lehrer's imaginative example of "Mr. Truetemp" highlights what is lacking in reliabilist accounts of justification. Without his knowing it, Mr. Truetemp has been surgically fitted with a "tempucomp," a computational device whose undetectable sensor lies implanted beneath his scalp. The tempucomp functions by recording the surrounding air temperature and relaying signals to Mr. Truetemp's brain, causing him to form reliable beliefs about the temperature. Though Mr. Truetemp is puzzled by the frequent turn of his thoughts to the weather, he accepts without question the beliefs the tempucomp generates. Lehrer's point is that while the requisite nomological, counterfactual or causal relationship between world and belief may be satisfied, Truetemp does not have the kind of personal justification Lehrer thinks essential to knowledge. Truetemp merely accepts true information. To convert this information into the complete justification necessary for knowledge requires that Truetemp accept the background claim that his beliefs about the temperature are being produced and sustained by a reliable process.

> The conversion of mere acceptance into personal justification depends on my accepting the things about myself whose bare existence the externalist [reliabilist] mistakenly assumes to be sufficient to convert true belief into knowledge. . . . The error of externalism [reliabilism] is to fail to notice that the subject of knowledge must accept that the externalist conditions hold true. The insight of externalism is the claim that the conditions must, indeed, hold true.[16]

The discussion of justification in this chapter and the preceding ones has uncovered deep and abiding disagreements about the very nature of justification and the distinctive epistemic merits that it captures. On one side are philosophers like Lehrer and Bonjour, who insist that agents possess a degree of reflective awareness about what they believe and why they believe it; these philosophers and their ilk are called "internalists," for reasons that are probably apparent by now. They think that justification requires that we be able to discern inwardly the reasons that support our beliefs. On the other side are thinkers such as Goldman and Armstrong, who argue that having our beliefs connected in a reliable way to the world is all we need for justification; we needn't also be reflectively aware of this fact. These philosophers are called "externalists": what counts for justification is a relation I bear to states of affairs in the world that are external to me.

Both views capture elements one would expect a fully virtuous agent to possess. Is there some way to reconcile these competing intuitions? Some philosophers urge that we keep the epistemic merits of each side distinct by differentiating between strong justification, which strongly ties justified beliefs to the world, and weak justification, which requires only that the agent do her best to secure the truth.

Plantinga, as I note below, recommends a linguistic division of labor, with the term *warrant* designating the ingredient that turns true belief into knowledge and *justification* designating the normative concerns of an agent doing her best to secure the truth. I will argue in the next section that a virtue epistemology has the best resources for accommodating the important insights of both camps.

6.2 Virtue Epistemology and the Internalism-Externalism Debate

As we have seen, epistemologists have argued themselves into a virtual stalemate over the nature of epistemic justification, throwing into sharp relief the competing intuitions dividing internalists, externalists and those opting for a mixed view. In this section I will draw on a virtues approach to epistemology to argue for a mixed view. The virtue tradition contains resources for mediating this dispute quite naturally from within its comprehensive picture of the knowing enterprise, while accommodating satisfactorily the insights of both internalists and externalists. I will argue that some kinds of knowledge require that we be justified in a way that stems from our embodying intellectual virtues of the requisite sort.

The crux of the debate between internalists and externalists concerns the nature and extent of the personal access, or oversight, each of us must have to the factors contributing to our justified beliefs. Internalists, among whom are many evidentialists and coherentists, insist that the grounds of our justified beliefs be something to which we have (or could have) introspective access. "It must consist," says William Alston, "of something like a belief or experience, something that the subject can typically spot by turning her attention to the matter."[17] The evidentialist John Locke, for instance, requires that all justified beliefs be supported by evidence whose probative force the agent sees and appreciates, and so Locke speaks of knowledge—and by extension justification—as "the view the mind has of its own ideas." If I ask you why you believe that the planet Mars once had vast reserves of water, you might appeal to long-standing theories about canals on Mars in addition to all the recent information supplied by the Mars Pathfinder mission. In this case you have a belief as well as a clear grasp of what underwrites it. Only by so "seeing" can the agent adjust the level of her assent to the amount and quality of her evidence as Locke's theory requires her to do. Coherentists such as Keith Lehrer require that we monitor the way candidate beliefs cohere with our "verific acceptance system." For internalists, then, justification has an "inspectionist character": that a given belief of yours is justified and how it is justified are features of your cognitive life available to your mind's eye.

Why, you might ask, should we place so much importance on cognitive agents' having access to the grounds of their belief? Why should this be considered a necessary condition for justification? At bottom, the issue of personal responsibility does much to motivate internalism. Laurence Bonjour's critical comments about externalism reveal intuitions typical of internalists here: "The fact that a given sort of belief is objectively reliable, and thus that accepting it is in fact conducive to arriving at the truth, need not prevent our judging that the epistemic agent who accepts it without any inkling that this is the case violates his epistemic duty and is epistemically irresponsible and unjustified in doing so."[18] The underlying assumptions here are (1) we accept the beliefs we do out of an interest in gaining the truth; (2) in order to accept beliefs for this reason, we must have some sense of the grounds that provide support for the belief in question; and (3) to accept a belief without any sense of its grounds is to act in a manner that is "epistemically irresponsible." These sentiments are summed up in John Greco's claim "Although there are many different versions of internalism, almost all internalists agree that their general position is supported by a 'responsibilist' conception of epistemic justification, or a conception of justification which takes epistemic responsibility to be central to justified belief."[19]

Internalism can be formulated in varying degrees of strength, and no consensus has formed as to how internalism is best portrayed. Strong versions of internalism, such as Locke's, not only require that the agent have grounds for her belief that are introspectible but require still further that she "see" the way her grounds support her belief. We could ratchet up the stringency of the demand to another level by requiring not only that the justifying factors be within the agent's perspective but also that the agent be justified in believing that they are so. Weaker versions will obviously not impose these higher-level requirements. Indeed, some versions don't require that you actually fulfill these various demands but only that you be able to meet them should you be called upon to do so.

It is not necessary to rehearse internalism's various permutations, however, to see that they are at root motivated by a common conviction: cognitive agents of good standing ought to be responsibly invested in overseeing their intellectual lives, accepting beliefs only because they believe that they are sufficiently likely to be true.[20]

As was noted earlier, one can attend scrupulously to the way one accepts and maintains beliefs, having in full view the grounds for one's beliefs, and still fall short of cognitive excellence. A person can be conscientious to a fault in the way he marshals and makes use of information and in the way he applies considered epistemic principle in attempting to secure justification for his beliefs, yet run seriously afoul of the truth. For example, one might have evidence and see how it supports a candidate belief, yet all the while be employing eccentric principles of evidence or bizarre inductive standards. One can imagine children of a primitive tribe being taught principles of evidence such as "Accept only the testimony of those with sufficiently strong witch aura," or "When predicting the future, rely more heavily on chicken entrails than tea leaves." Though a young epistemologist from this tribe is dutiful in conforming to principles he thinks are truth conducive, he fails to track the truth and, we are inclined to say, fails to embody much of the intellectual life we desire despite the introspective access he has to his beliefs and their grounds.

Internalists traditionally insist that one cannot accidentally employ the right inductive standards and be justified; one must at least justifiably believe that one has the right standards. This insistence makes the requirements for justification so stringent, however, that only philosophers (if even they) wind up being justified in their beliefs. This grates against our commonsense conviction that most people are justified in most of what they believe. Moreover, many doubt that it is even possible to argue on behalf of all our principles of evidence, even should we be so inclined. This is because we would perforce make use of such principles in offering any argument whatsoever. If we argue for a certain principle of testimonial evidence, we will invoke other principles of evidence in so doing. But we can't argue for every principle of evidence we employ, so that unless we claim that our standards are self-evidently obvious, there remain beliefs to which internalists are committed that never satisfy their own standards.

Earlier we saw that the potential gap between justification and truth on the internalist account has prompted externalists (such as Goldman) to tighten the connection—to make sure that when we believe justifiably we are highly likely to believe truthfully. Externalists deny, however, that individual cognitive agents must have personal access to all the elements contributing to a belief's being justified. The agent isn't responsible for personally overseeing that the right sort of connection between belief and the world obtains; either it does or it doesn't, but this is not a fact of which the agent need be aware in order for her beliefs to be justified. Externalists deny that we earn justification by correctly reasoning on behalf of a belief; rather, justification is something that happens to us. According to one version of externalism, a belief has *positive epistemic status* (hereafter PES) based on the reliability of the causal processes leading to its formation. Other externalists (notably D. M. Armstrong) maintain that if I have PES for a belief *P*, then a law of nature must support the connection between my believing *P* for the reasons I do and the world being the way it is.

Externalist theories seem to offer a particularly apt way of describing the way PES attaches to beliefs formed by sense perception. The great bulk of what we believe is injected into our body of beliefs in a spontaneous manner. They are formed in us immediately and noninferentially by the circumstances in which we find ourselves, not typically through deliberation and conscious inference. When I have experiences characteristic of seeing a dog, the belief that I see a dog is immediately made a part of my network of beliefs. The sheer volume

of information we take in makes it impossible to monitor self-reflectively all our beliefs, or perhaps even a small portion of them. In
driving my car across town I am deep in thought. I unconsciously
brake, shift gears, change lanes, negotiate my way through traffic and
fiddle with the radio until I pull into my driveway. Later you ask if I
saw any fire trucks along the way, and I respond that I did, though I
hadn't thought of it till I was asked.

Externalist theories yield the counterintuitive result, however, that
I can be maximally justified in holding beliefs even if I think that I
ought not to hold them. The example of Norman in the last section
illustrates this point, as do the recent views of Alvin Plantinga. *Warrant* is a term Plantinga uses to connote positive epistemic status for
a belief. It is the quality that, when it is sufficiently present, turns true
beliefs into instances of knowledge.[21] Roughly, warrant accrues to a
belief just in case it has been formed by that segment of my cognitive
apparatus given to putting me in touch with the world, functioning
in the right way and in the right environment. These conditions, thinks
Plantinga, can be satisfied even when the agent thinks she ought not
to believe as she does. Consider his example: I take it into my head
that I have an epistemic duty not to trust my "red beliefs." I work
strenuously to avoid letting myself form any beliefs that I see red
things, but in the process I become exhausted and resentful of having
to do my duty. "Finally, I am appeared to redly in a particularly
flagrant and insistent fashion by a large red London bus. 'To hell with
epistemic duty' I say, and relax blissfully into the belief that I am now
perceiving something red."[22] According to Plantinga, even though I
think I ought not to hold the belief in question, I can nevertheless have
warrant and thus have the epistemic merit that is essential to knowledge. "A person can know," he writes, "even when flouting intellectual duties."[23]

So consider two persons A and B, standing shoulder to shoulder as
they gaze upon the same visual field. A lets in an appropriately
formed red belief and thinks himself perfectly correct to do so. B lets
in an appropriately formed red belief and thinks she ought not to have
done so. Let us suppose she believes herself to be acting irresponsibly

in accepting the belief—that it is wrong of her to do so. On Plantinga's view this difference is insignificant as far as the requirements for warrant go: B's belief can have PES sufficient for knowledge even if she thinks otherwise.

How can we understand Plantinga's claim that a person can have warrant sufficient to turn true belief into knowledge even when she thinks otherwise? Perhaps he is trading on a parallel distinction made in moral philosophy between first-person and third-person perspectives in assessing moral acts. For the purposes of illustration, let's recall Huckleberry Finn's famous struggle with conscience over whether or not to return Jim, a runaway slave he has helped to escape.

Jim said it made him all over trembly and feverish to be so close to freedom. Well, I can tell you it made me all over trembly and feverish, too, to hear him, because I begun to get it through my head that he *was* most free—and who was to blame for it? Why, *me*. I couldn't get it out of my conscience, no how no way. It got to troubling me so I couldn't rest; I couldn't stay still in one place. It hadn't ever come over me before, what this thing was that I was doing. But now it did; and it staid with me, and scorched me more and more. I tried to make out to myself that I warn't to blame, because I didn't run Jim off from his rightful owner; but it warn't no use, conscience up and says, every time, "But you knowed he was running for his freedom, and you could a paddled ashore and told somebody." ... My conscience got to stirring me up hotter than ever, until at last I says to it, "Let up on me—it ain't too late, yet—I'll paddle ashore at the first light, and tell." I felt easy, and happy, and light as a feather, right off. All my troubles was gone.[24]

As it happens, however, when white slavers in search of runaway slaves ask Huck if he knows the whereabouts of any runaway slaves, he lies, leading them away from Jim. From a first-person perspective, Huck's actions, though commendable from our standpoint, might have been occasions of sin for him, since he thought he was violating his conscience in doing them. From a third-person perspective, however, one could say that Huck's act of compassion was a good thing; after all, slavery was an evil institution, and it wasn't just that Jim should never have been enslaved in the first place. Plantinga clearly thinks that just as I can do good all the while thinking that I am doing something forbidden, so I can have warrant for my beliefs even if I think I am flouting my epistemic duty. What I *think* about my beliefs and their formation is irrelevant to their having warrant.

Virtue epistemology, on the other hand, holds that just as an ideally integrated moral agent successfully unites a pure conscience with right behavior, so too an ideally integrated cognitive agent blends doing one's intellectual duty with successfully tracking the truth. A strong intuition discourages us from looking favorably on situations in which we do what is morally right but are racked by guilt, or occasions in which we successfully track the truth but inwardly feel as though we have done something intellectually disreputable. A virtuous agent is not fragmented by the demands of virtue.

So a virtue epistemology will insist that externalism and internalism both capture important intuitions about justification. One requires that our justified beliefs be strongly tied to the truth, and the other requires that we bear some responsibility for overseeing our interior intellectual lives. Obviously, the way to get the best of both worlds is to craft an account of justification that combines features of each. My claim is that an account of justification derived from the broader tradition of virtue epistemology captures the key insights of both internalists and externalists. As we shall see, it insists on a strong connection between my beliefs' being justified and their being true, while continuing to assign to individual agents a responsible role contributing to their cognitive successes and failures.

Let's call to mind a few important features about intellectual virtues. They are, as we have already seen, well-anchored, abiding dispositions persons acquire over time that enable them to think in ways that contribute to their fulfillment as persons. Intellectual vices, by contrast, are settled traits of character that undermine human flourishing. Whether we are virtuous- or vicious-thinking persons depends in some measure on our deliberative will. No doubt I could have taken steps to thwart the growth of the traits that characterize, and I have likewise made choices contributing to their development.

Similarly, there are belief-forming practices of a positive and negative sort over which we have a measure of voluntary control. And it is for this reason that we are proper objects of praise or blame insofar as we are virtuous or vicious persons. Recall also that one must be reliably successful in acting out of a virtue, though we do not require that one act infallibly out of the virtue.[25] If I can be counted on to exercise patience amidst vexatious circumstances, then even if I lose my patience on some rare occasion, I might be properly deemed a patient person. The same point holds for vices. Even a predictably gullible person may display rare moments of critical awareness without thereby ceasing to be gullible.

The situations that occasion these rare lapses permit us to explore the workings of virtues more deeply. Sometimes we fail to act virtuously due to causes outside our control. I might fail intellectually because unbeknownst to me I am suffering from the onslaught of Alzheimer's disease. Sometimes we fail to be virtuous not as a result of any internal failing, culpable or nonculpable, but because the world doesn't cooperate in the right way. Let me illustrate: A few years ago the psychology majors at my school staged an experiment of dubious propriety. They dressed people up to look as though they had been injured, plopped them down in various locations around town, and then watched to monitor bystander response. Suppose my virtuous powers of moral discernment tell me, *There lies a person in great need*, and I act compassionately on that person's behalf. In reality, however, I am being cleverly conned, so that my efforts at being virtuous are, in some measure, not ideally realized. For one thing, I will not in fact have come to the aid of anyone, since no one actually needs my help. Also, my having acted out of the virtue of compassion will result in my forming false beliefs about my behavior, among them that I have just assisted a person in genuine need. What shall we say about such cases?

I am dependably virtuous when I can be counted on to act or otherwise function in a way characteristic of a virtue that genuinely fosters human flourishing, intellectual or moral. But being virtuous has implications for how a person relates to his or her environment.

We must therefore index these human traits to *normal environments* in which by acting out of the virtue I genuinely promote moral and intellectual flourishing. The example above is anything but normal. Typically when I see persons who appear injured and I help them, they are indeed injured and in need of help.

Take another example: I form the true belief that Bob was at the dance hall last night, but in reality the person I saw was Rob, his identical twin brother. Bob was in fact at the dance hall, but not during the time I was there. I was dependably virtuous; typically when I have an experience of what I perceive to be Bob, I do indeed see Bob. But owing to my eccentric circumstances, my path to true belief is not ideal. I don't think such eccentric circumstances undermine my having acted virtuously. Thus while my beliefs are justified because I have acted or functioned in a manner characteristic of virtue, the justification is defeasible and is thus only prima facie justification.

Now we have the rudiments to appreciate how a virtue epistemology can capture the twin concerns of externalists and internalists. A moral analogy will help. We can, I take it, be moral agents in good standing by acting from virtuous habits while at the same time not being self-reflectively aware of the conditions grounding our moral actions. That our powers of moral perception were in play and that we correctly identified and assisted someone in need are behaviors that can occur automatically. In fact, we think it is a desirable trait of deeply moral agents that virtuous deeds issue forth from them spontaneously. Their moral sensibilities are so finely developed that they respond to moral situations in appropriate ways without necessarily thinking of themselves as acting morally; virtue constitutes for them a kind of "default mode" of behaving. No doubt upon seeing a child in need, Mother Teresa was the sort of person who responded with immediate compassion; her thought was for the child, not for herself and how dutiful she was for tending to the child. Her desire to ameliorate a child's suffering arose immediately and unreflectively. Years and years of compassionate behavior habituated her emotions and thinking to the point where she was able to act in what might be said reflex manner.

One cannot grow in the moral life, however, without making one's status as a moral agent a matter of conscious reflection. For this reason practical wisdom bulks large among the virtues. Prudence is that virtue whereby we think well to act well. (We should understand the thinking characteristic of practical wisdom to include moral perception and other noninferential noetic acts.) Adherents of the virtue tradition recognize that moral maturity seldom occurs—and probably never occurs in any sustained way—accidentally. Generally we mature in the moral life to the extent that we periodically monitor our interior lives, our motives, our strengths and weaknesses, and devise appropriate strategies of self-management. We need to occasionally take accurate stock of the general tenor of our moral lives if we wish to be successful in working to improve them.

The parallels between the moral and the intellectual life are, I'm sure, easy to see. For much of what we justifiably believe we accept by virtuously employing our natural cognitive powers such as memory, perception and inferential reasoning. These powers, together with the virtuous dispositions to employ them rightly, are indispensable to our efforts to obtain true beliefs about the world. Such powers vary both in their degree of excellence and in the extent to which they are capable of cultivation. I might display refined powers of understanding of a certain subject without being aware of myself as exhibiting such powers. I might grasp immediately a complicated mathematical axiom and be unconscious of the fact that I am exemplifying virtuous understanding; I may be conscious of no more than the axiom itself. In this way I am like the agent who acts morally on autopilot: I display these traits spontaneously and unreflectively. Here, then, is the externalist side of a virtuous epistemic life. A virtuous intellectual agent believes justifiably and tracks the truth without necessarily being cognizant at the time of the grounds of the belief.

But the model of the virtuous agent who acts spontaneously and unreflectively in accordance with virtue cannot be a sufficient model for all beliefs and actions. Some traits of intellectual excellence require that we be successfully introspectively aware. This is especially evident in the domain of self-knowledge, which is by its very nature reflexive. For some types of self-knowledge our own selves and our own thoughts not only form the content of our believing but become the focus of our philosophical inquiry. One side of the virtue of practical wisdom illustrates this paradigmatically.

Two important components mark the critical thinking of practically wise persons. First is self-knowledge, the ability to diagnose accurately one's epistemic condition. For example, you might think yourself credulous, or prone to hasty generalization, or less than fully intellectually honest when engaged in argument with peers about certain subjects. How you diagnose yourself will stem not just from your powers of introspection but also from your broader philosophical commitments.

A second component of the practically wise person is the capacity to embark on personal management strategies to rectify the shortcomings that are revealed through introspection. Say you diagnose your thinking in a certain area to be unduly biased by your desires for wealth; you can set about to correct this deficiency by practicing certain techniques of self-management to loosen the desire's hold on you. When thinking about financial matters you might, for example, remind yourself that when you die you aren't taking anything with you, or that lots of people with money are nonetheless miserably unhappy; in this way you reconceptualize the nature of wealth. By exercising the virtue of practical wisdom in this deliberate way, you lessen the likelihood that your epistemic goals will be frustrated. So the virtue of practical wisdom plays a pivotal role in accommodating the internalist requirements for justification.

It should be obvious why a purely externalist account of knowledge fails to account satisfactorily for the self-knowledge that practical wisdom makes available. By its very logic, self-knowledge is not the sort of thing that I can know and not be aware of. I cannot have self-knowledge of the sort characteristic of practical wisdom and not, from time to time at any rate, be occurrently aware of it. Practically wise persons characteristically have a certain level of access to their own thoughts, their grounds and some ideas of the adequacy of these grounds. Of course, the amount of access a person has will vary. People vary in the degree of practical wisdom they embody just as they vary in the extent to which they display patience and compassion.

On Plantinga's view, a belief of mine can have warrant sufficient for knowledge even if I believe that I am flouting my epistemic duty in believing it. But this can't be true of self-knowledge that arises out of accurate inspection of my own intellectual character. How can I diagnose myself as virtuously prudent and simultaneously think that I am not? For prudence, by its very nature, requires that we accurately, consciously and honestly assess our noetic character.

Internalists err in supposing that for a belief to be justified, I must be reflectively aware of its justifying conditions. On a virtue account, I need only be occasionally aware of these conditions. Externalists are right to hold that justification requires that we be more or less successful in our cognitive endeavors; but virtue theorists think externalists err in thinking that justification never requires reflective access to our beliefs and their grounds. I have argued that internal access is indispensable for some types of knowledge, most notably self-knowledge.

We turn now to a potential difficulty in my position. Does attention to intellectual virtues completely satisfy the intuitions of internalists? Inasmuch as it is consistent to say that a person is virtuous in some respect while sometimes failing to act out of the virtue, it is reasonable to think that persons of practical wisdom could misdiagnose their epistemic condition, mistakenly giving themselves clean bills of epistemic health or self-diagnosing a problem that does not exist.

Suppose that upon conducting the kind of personal inventory practiced by persons of practical wisdom, I mistakenly deem myself prone to hasty generalization. In fact, I display the requisite amount of care in forming beliefs, but owing to some deep-seated fears or insecurities, the normal length of time I spend investigating appears to me too short. As a result, I deem myself unjustified in some perfectly acceptable belief because I mistakenly think that I formed it on the strength of a hasty generalization.

Consider another example in which I take myself to be justified in a belief we would consider unacceptable. My son is failing in school and experimenting with drugs. Friends have kindly hinted that I ought to investigate these matters, but because I find the subject very painful and the prospect of confronting my son wrenching, I suppress this information, rationalizing instead that his behavior is nothing but what is typical of teenagers and thus that he is normal. So in the kinds of personal inventories characteristic of practical wisdom, there is the possibility for self-deception and thus culpably flawed diagnoses.

Why is the possibility of self-deception a problem, and why would someone's falling prey to it mean that they fail to meet the internalist's requirements? So long as a person acknowledges the possibility of self-deception, she has grounds for doubting that she has correctly diagnosed her intellectual condition. Doubting that one is justified works to undermine one's being practically wise, as well as the self-knowledge it generates, just as much as actively believing oneself to be unjustified. One cannot be practically wise and simultaneously doubt that one is. So, one might argue, unless a person knows that she is not self-deceived, she cannot have practical wisdom, and without practical wisdom the virtue account cannot meet the internalist's requirements.

But self-deception is notoriously difficult to detect. Merely believing oneself free of self-deception isn't sufficient for being practically wise, for being self-deceived is quite consistent with believing that one is not; in fact, that is its usual form. We cannot, unfortunately, step outside our own skulls so as to confirm the accuracy of our introspective analyses. Since there is no way of being justifiably confident that one isn't a victim of self-deception, there isn't an adequate basis for thinking oneself practically wise. So, one could argue, the requirements of internalism are not satisfied by the resources of virtue epistemology.

It is true not only that we err occasionally in our self-diagnoses but that we err *culpably*. The reasons are various, but such errors are frequently linked to inordinate passions. As Thomas Hobbes writes: "For the thoughts, are to the desires, as scouts and spies, to range abroad and find the way to the things desired: all steadiness of the mind's motions, and all quickness of the same, proceeding from thence" (*Leviathan* 8). That our minds are so subject to the passions is a feature of ourselves of which we can become aware and so undertake corrective measures. In fact, part of being practically wise is being aware of the power of the passions to subvert our quest for truth. It is the fool and not the person of practical wisdom who fails to be cognizant of the possibility of self-deception.

The question, then, boils down to the requirements for practical wisdom. If to be practically wise I must be invincibly justified in believing that I'm not self-deceived, then the standard is impossibly high. Guarantees of this sort, while a part of the Cartesian tradition, are no part of the virtue tradition, and for good reason. Guarantees of immunity to error are no more available here than against the work of evil demons or evil brain scientists. Thomas Reid was right when he wrote:

> Can any man prove that his consciousness may not deceive him? No man can; nor can we give a better reason for trusting it, than that every man, while his mind is sound, is determined, by the constitution of his nature, to give implicit belief to it, and to laugh at or pity the man who doubts its testimony.[26]

When it comes to the reliability of consciousness, virtue epistemologists show their externalist colors. I have to exercise charity toward myself and trust that, in the last analysis, when I sincerely endeavor to assess my epistemic condition I am not deceiving myself but seeing accurately enough to be called practically wise. Practical wisdom requires only that I be prima facie justified in believing myself free of deception.

While there is nothing in my virtue solution that necessitates our being free of self-deception to be practically wise, three additional features of taking the virtues seriously noted in earlier chapters help to ensure that our internal audits are accurate. First, recall the distinction in the first chapter between "snapshot" and "career" assessments of our standing in the virtues. Our judgments about our excellence as cognitive beings can be grounded in both a momentary time-slice of our intellectual life (a snapshot, if you will) and in our reflection about our intellectual career. A single instance of self-deception within a career of otherwise flawless self-knowledge would not mean you could not justly be called a person of practical wisdom. Whether or not we are living successfully as cognitive beings must be determined by a long-term inspection of our believings, denials, withholdings and other noetic acts. A momentary cross-section carved out of our career at a particular moment doesn't provide enough information for a definitive judgment. Viewing epistemological questions in career terms, as the concerns of a lifetime, lessens the burden of getting every judgment right.

Second, cognitive agents pursuing intellectual virtue are bound up together in a community. We depend on a community of knowers in a number of ways. I have already alluded to the important role played by the community in shaping our initial orientations to intellectual and moral concerns. Communities can also reinforce existing virtuous behavior, such as being practically wise, in such a way as to help check self-deception. Working with peers who are intellectually honest, who admit their mistakes, will likely assist my efforts at intellectual honesty. In fact, some intellectual virtues require as a part of their internal grammar that we be interacting with other members of the community. The medieval virtue of docility, for example, is teachableness, a trait displayed in interactions with others. I mention the role of the community because interacting with the community is a safeguard against long-term, systematic self-deception. My intellectual career is lived out among people who, if they are virtuous in their behavior toward me, will say and do things that militate against long-term self-deception on my part.

Finally, it should be pointed out that the grammar of a virtue is partially determined by the broader theoretical tradition to which one is committed. So, for example, we speak of the differences between Buddhist, Christian and Stoic accounts of compassion. This is significant because the broader tradition specifies long-term goals that being virtuous is supposed to help us realize. Christians are attempting to "put on Christ" (with all that that entails), Stoics to become impassive, and Buddhists to cease craving. Truly virtuous behavior is that which aids my pursuit of goals I think are essential to genuine human flourishing. I will have the virtue only insofar as the overarching goals I have set for myself are being achieved. If I fail to see these goals materializing in my life, I have good reason for doubting that my internal audits are accurate.

Suppose I set for myself the goal of obtaining the truth about a wide range of important matters. A Stoic who is self-deceived about his being virtuous in the ways demanded by his tradition will have a difficult time suppressing his anxieties over an extended period of time. So the larger tradition within which virtues are being cultivated sets before us concrete goals that operate as a system of checks and balances against self-deception.

Seven

Epistemology & Religious Belief

We have surveyed several accounts describing the contours of the excellent intellectual life. Some accounts depict epistemic success in terms of reliably tracking the truth, while others require that our beliefs be supported by adequate evidence, cohere with each other in an appropriate way or stem from intellectual virtues. As one might expect, this contrariety of views surfaces anew when we ask whether believing in God is compatible with an excellent intellectual life.

Disagreements about the epistemic status of religious belief can arise in at least two ways. We might, first of all, agree on the standards any justified belief must satisfy but disagree about whether believing in God satisfies the standards; or we could disagree over the very standards themselves, irrespective of the type of belief in question. The purpose of this chapter is to bring many of the insights and distinctions we have learned thus far to bear on religious belief. I will again contrast internalist and externalist requirements for justification, showing how the competing intuitions that divide epistemology in general surface anew with respect to religious belief. I will defend the claim that believing in God is intellectually virtuous, and I will argue that thinking of the status of religious belief in this way not only integrates internalist and externalist concerns but also captures some important features of religious belief often ignored by other perspectives.

7.1 Internalism and the Justification of Theism

The famous atheist Bertrand Russell was once asked what he would do if, after dying, he were to find himself face to face before God for the final judgment. Russell, perhaps enamored with Hume's epistemology, quipped: "I'll tell him 'Not enough evidence, God, not enough evidence!' " Russell's bravado underscores one long-standing objection to believing in God: that in this life we lack sufficient evidence for justifiably believing that he exists.

As we saw earlier, evidentialists claim that the canons of good intellectual conduct require that we have and make use of evidence adequate to underwrite each belief we hold, and this goes for theistic beliefs as well. Stated this way, evidentialism embodies the demands of internalism, because it insists, as do all types of internalism, that agents have cognitive access to what justifies their beliefs. To believe in God justifiably requires not just that we have evidence but also that we see and appreciate its sufficiency to underwrite our beliefs.

Let us be clear here; while evidentialists are internalists, the converse is not necessarily true; one could be a coherentist, for instance. Evidentialism is, however, one of the most common forms in which internalist views find expression, since having evidence and appreciating the way it supports one's belief represents one obvious way of meeting internalism's demands. So while I use evidentialism to illustrate how one variety of internalism bears on religious belief, keep in mind that we could consider other forms of internalism.

Historically many philosophers have expressed robust confidence in reason's power to meet the demands of internalism, notably by securing adequate evidence in support of theism. Indeed, the venerable tradition of natural theology has long taught that we can, by dint of our native intellectual powers, marshal evidence so powerful as to prove decisively that God exists. Somewhat more modest estimates of reason's powers claim that we can construct an overwhelmingly convincing case for the likelihood of God's existence or, at the very least, an argument showing that God's existence is more probable than not. A typical course in the philosophy of religion will not only familiarize one with such arguments but show some of the subsidiary benefits (in many cases, a refinement in one's thinking about metaphysics and epistemology) generated by efforts to construct them. Of course, if someone truly had a proof for God's existence whose steps she had rehearsed, she would by that very fact meet the internalist's requirements.

Our task, however, is not to rehearse the merits and demerits of specific arguments attempting to prove theism but to reflect instead on the very suitability of striving to meet internalism's demands. Again, the internalist requirement for all justified belief is that before we can hold a belief rationally we must, in principle at any rate, have cognitive access (typically through introspection) to the grounds of our belief. We saw in earlier chapters, however, that internalism in general and evidentialism in particular face formidable difficulties, several of which bear repeating. If, however, this general account of rational belief is flawed, the enterprise of showing that religious beliefs must meet its demands is of dubious merit. Let us consider again, then, some limitations of internalism and evidentialism that bear on religious belief.

Even natural theology's most ardent supporters have acknowledged its severe limitations. Philosophers such as St. Thomas Aquinas and Richard Swinburne note that our evidence-gathering skills cannot possibly support all the claims that religious believers accept and hold dear, not even all that Christians say is required for a complete account of God. Christians believe not just that God exists but also that he is triune, was incarnate in Christ reconciling the world to himself, and that we shall all appear before him in the general resurrection of the dead. We do not embrace such beliefs because they are self-evidently obvious or because we see and appreciate the way some body of evidence confirms them. They are articles of faith, accepted because God has revealed them. Thus our chief reason for thinking such beliefs to be true is indirect; we accept them not on account of evidence that directly confirms their truth but because we trust the testimony of someone (a prophet, for instance) who assures us that they are true.

Not only does seeking to secure justification for religious belief through argument limit the number of beliefs we can be said justifiably to believe, but it also severely restricts the number of people who can actively participate in the task of justifying even minimal theism. As we saw in our earlier discussion of internalism, if before we can justifiably believe even mundane claims about the existence and nature of material objects we must first cognitively apprehend the grounds of their justification, then most of us are not justified in most of what we believe. Perhaps a few epistemologists are up to this task—and that is a claim on which reasonable minds differ—but the rest of us are left in the lurch. How much more then, when we enter the realm of supernatural belief, shall ordinary believers be deprived of rational belief, if before they can be said to believe justifiably in God's existence they must first successfully see and appreciate the grounds of their belief. Even if it is possible to prove God's existence—and this too is roundly disputed—it is not a task to which most persons are suited by aptitude, training or leisure time. Again the words of Aquinas are apropos: "If the only way open to us for the knowledge of God were solely that of the reason, the human race would remain in the blackest shadows of ignorance."[1] The seeming impossibility of meeting internalism's demands with respect to our religious beliefs parallels the concerns expressed by critics of internalism over ordinary beliefs about the world.

We noted earlier that whereas internalism requires justified believers to have access of some sort to the grounds of their beliefs, it does not always require that they have justifiable beliefs about the adequacy of those grounds. But it is precisely over the adequacy of grounds that battles about justification are often waged. Suppose I believe the stock market is going to crash, and I believe this on the strength of detailed astrological data: star charts, graphs, tables and all the subtleties of the craft. When questioned about my pessimism concerning the market, I cite this welter of data as confirmatory. Although one could say I have satisfied the demands of internalism—I have grounds whose probative force I see and appreciate—not many will suppose that I have justified beliefs about the stock market. This is because most people will not countenance as evidence what I regard as acceptable evidence.

An analogous difficulty arises in the religious arena. Religious believers often cite as evidence for their belief in God experiences and other beliefs that simply aren't acknowledged in some circles as acceptable evidence. If I claimed that theism is massively confirmed and cited as my grounds for this belief the experiences of believers all over the world as they communed with God in prayer, in secular circles I'll still be thought to believe unjustifiably. This is because what I cite as grounds, what I bring before the bar of reason as evidence, isn't acknowledged by everyone as admissible evidence.

Not only do people disagree over what they are willing to acknowledge as acceptable grounds, they disagree over the "weightiness" or significance we should attribute to what we do acknowledge as grounds. Two doctors diagnose a patient's symptoms differently. They don't disagree, let us suppose, as to the relevance of an elevated white blood cell count, but they disagree about *how* significant an indicator this is; one doctor weights this symptom more heavily than the other. Similarly, jurors disagree about the guilt of a defendant. They disagree not at all about the relevance of the testimony given by the prosecution's star witness; they disagree instead as to its significance, some investing it with tremendous import, others with less. Two art critics dispute the authenticity of an alleged masterpiece. Their disagreement doesn't turn on what should be counted as relevant evidence: watermarks on the paper, x-ray and infrared photography to reveal layers of pigment, chemical analysis of canvas and wood to fix chronology, compositional elements, brushstroke technique and so forth. Instead they disagree over *saliency*, over what significance should be accorded to the evidence. Such disagreements are legion, arising in debates about history, aesthetics, exegesis, morals, law, the natural sciences, even a boxing match, and indeed anywhere that interpretive judgment is called for.

How are disagreements about saliency settled? Unfortunately, epistemologists lack the equivalent of an umpire's rulebook or the impeccable judgments of a perfect referee. Typically we invite our disputant to look again and see whether he or she is not as impressed as we are by the artist's use of light and shadow. Sometimes our views will be indisputably confirmed; a bear market does emerge, thereby lending credence now and in the future to my interpretive judgments of the market. Such confirmation, however, is rare, since the subjects of our disagreements often revolve around issues buried in the past, for which we cannot reasonably expect dramatic new evidence to emerge.

We puzzle not only over how disagreements over saliency are settled but over why they occur at all. Why should our standards of evidence be so variable? The reasons are numerous and complex. No doubt our finitude and the limitations imposed by our cultural, historical and linguistic perspectives play a large part. Epistemologists interested in matters of virtue, however, will want to accent another reason: issues of character. I want to mention now, and explore in more detail below, the idea that our powers to perceive our circumstances rightly and invest them with the significance they deserve stems in part from our having cultivated appropriate moral and intellectual virtues, along with a suitably developed affective (emotional) nature that contributes to such virtues.

How are we to account for the fact that two highly intelligent philosophers, acquainted with the same body of evidence in support of God's existence, can nevertheless come to opposing conclusions about the force of the evidence? One answer derives from a long-standing tradition reaching as far back as Plato and Aristotle, which argues that our cognitive powers cannot function as they ought if they are not appropriately connected with emotions and concerns that have been trained to virtue.

7.2 Externalism and the Justification of Theism
It is not difficult to see why the problems besetting internalism and

evidentialism have prompted some thinkers to claim that the prospects for justifying religious belief look brighter if we embrace some form of externalism. Externalist accounts of justification, you will recall, waive the access requirement that constitutes the distinguishing feature of internalist views. They deny as a necessary condition of justification that I be able to introspect and "see" the grounds of my justification. It is necessary only that I have grounds, and that the appropriate relationship exists between my belief and its grounds; I need not be aware of all this.

Again, perceptual beliefs are among the paradigm examples of beliefs so justified. Suppose I stroll through the woods, taking in the sights, sounds and smells. I see a squirrel scamper in front of me and race in winding fashion up the trunk of a tree, there to scold me with loud chirruping and vigorous shakes of the tail. My sensory and cognitive equipment faithfully record all this, and the belief that I saw a squirrel on my walk today is formed within me. Notice, I do not reason to this conclusion; I do not rehearse a series of inferences beginning with "I had squirrel-like perceptions" to the conclusion that indeed I saw a squirrel. The process of acquiring this belief was much more automatic than that of, say, a detective piecing together clues en route to his conclusion that "the butler did it." The belief is "basic," to invoke the language of chapter four; it is justifiably believed without the benefit of argumentative support, but no less reasonable for that.

Beliefs grounded in the immediate reports of perception are not all we take as basic; we also accept the deliverances of memory, rational intuition and testimony in this immediate way. I believe that my keys are lying on my dresser immediately upon recollecting that I placed them there. I accede to the trichotomy axiom immediately upon understanding what it says. I ask a student in the hallway for directions to the bathroom, and he tells me that I will find it down the stairs and to the left. I straightforwardly head down the stairs, believing the bathroom to be where I was told it would be. In none of these cases is my belief the result of deliberation or inference. I do not reason as follows: That student has an honest-looking face—no mischievous grin accompanied his instructions; it is not April Fool's Day, and I can think of no other reason he might have for tricking me as to the bathroom's location; on past occasions when I have asked for directions, I have been told the truth; thus it is probable that the bathroom is where the student has directed me. Rather, our beliefs in such cases are immediately consequent upon our having undergone a corresponding experience.

Thomas Reid, the modest foundationalist philosopher whose ideas were discussed in chapter four, was a forerunner of thinking about justification in externalist terms, and he developed a rudimentary cognitive psychology of belief formation to explain how certain experiential circumstances produce beliefs in us immediately and noninferentially. A large part of the cognitive equipment we routinely use to acquire beliefs consists of what Nicholas Wolterstorff, in writing about Reid, has dubbed "belief dispositions."[2] The human mind is so constituted, argued Reid, that a cognitive response is naturally and noninferentially elicited in us by the various experiences we undergo. In other words, our native cognitive equipment is such that when we are experientially stimulated in certain ways, there forms within us an automatic noetic response, typically a belief. Reid takes "the principles of common sense" for granted: "When I hear a certain sound, I conclude immediately, without reasoning, that a coach passes by. There are no premises from which this conclusion is inferred by any rules of logic. It is the effect of a principle of our nature, common to us and the brutes."[3]

Our faculties of sight, smell, taste and feeling are no less capable of triggering in us a belief response upon being activated: "I know this also, that the perception of an object implies both a conception of its form, and a belief of its present existence. I know, moreover, that this belief is not the effect of argumentation and reasoning; it is the immediate effect of my constitution."[4]

According to Reid, the grounds of our beliefs go beyond sensation to include memory, testimony, reasoning and self-evident deliverances of consciousness. And Reid makes similar remarks about the immediacy with which these faculties produce belief in us. Of memory, for example, he says, "I have a distinct conception and a firm belief of this past event; not by reasoning; not by testimony, but immediately from my constitution: and I give the name of memory to that part of my constitution, by which I have this kind of conviction of past events."[5]

Of course these grounds of our beliefs vary in the kind of support and the degree of justification they confer, says Reid. But in no case are we able to demonstrate independently the truth-conduciveness of these grounds, however much we are naturally led to accept their reliability. It is sufficient for being justified that my cognitive faculties reliably inform me about the world; it is not necessary that I know this introspectively, and still less that I be able to prove this to the skeptic. Internalists err, therefore, in thinking that justification requires either that we be reflectively aware of the grounds of our beliefs every time belief is engendered in us or that we be able to show that our faculties, which along with the experiential circumstances are the causes of our beliefs, are reliable. The deliverances of our powers of reason are thought by Reid to be innocent unless proved guilty—a marked contrast to Cliffordian skeptics, who hold that our beliefs should be considered guilty until cleared before the bar of reason.[6]

7.3 Reformed Epistemology

Some theists who are externalists claim that believing in God parallels perceptual beliefs more than it does beliefs gained through painstaking processes of reasoning. Perhaps our conviction that God exists arises in us automatically when we have certain kinds of experiences, just as my belief that I saw a squirrel arises within me when I have had appropriate sensory experiences. This claim is in fact defended by a number of philosophers, most notably Alvin Plantinga and Nicholas Wolterstorff.[7] Plantinga claims to be following the lead of various thinkers in the Reformed theological tradition—Hermann Bavinck, Abraham Kuyper and of course John Calvin—who teach that humans are psychologically so constructed by their Maker that when they undergo certain kinds of experiences, a belief in God is naturally and noninferentially the result. A natural tendency to believe in God, a *sensus divinitatus* as Calvin calls it, is part of the natural noetic equipment with which all humans are endowed. When suitably stimulated by experience, this *sensus divinitatus* gives rise to belief in God just as naturally as our perceptual faculties, properly stimulated, give rise to our belief that there is an external world.[8]

That some persons respond to their environment by immediately and noninferentially believing that God exists does indeed seem borne out in our experience. Consider the experience of Charlotte Brontë's Jane Eyre:

> Night was come, and her planets were risen: a safe, still night; too serene for the companionship of fear. We know that God is everywhere; but certainly we feel His presence most when His works are on the grandest scale spread before us: and it is in the unclouded night sky, where His worlds wheel their silent course, that we read His infinitude, His omnipotence, His omnipresence. I had risen to my knees to pray for Mr. Rochester. Looking up, I, with tear-dimmed eyes, saw the mighty Milky Way. Remembering what it was—what countless systems there swept space like a soft trace of light—I felt the might and strength of God.

On Plantinga's view (and Calvin's), an experience of the starry heavens above might very well serve as the catalyst that activates our natural belief-producing processes. Notice that the experience of the starry heavens is not being used as a premise for the construction of a design argument (though it no doubt could and has been used in this way); that would duplicate the inferential reasoning of the natural theologian. Instead the experience is being invoked for its emotive and psychological power to trigger an immediate response of belief; the experience of nature provides *nonpropositional* support for theism. Even Immanuel Kant, credited by many as one of natural theology's greatest foes, acknowledged the *psychological* force of the experiences on which such arguments are based. So in the *Critique of Pure Reason* he writes:

> This knowledge [of nature] again reacts on its cause, namely, upon the idea which has led to it, and so strengthens the belief in a supreme Author [of nature] that the belief acquires the force of an *irresistible conviction*.

It would therefore be not only uncomforting but utterly vain to attempt to diminish in any way the authority of this argument. Reason, constantly upheld by this ever-increasing evidence, which, though empirical, is yet so powerful, cannot be so depressed through doubts suggested by subtle and abstruse speculations, that it is not at once aroused from the indecision of all melancholy reflection, as from a dream, by one glance at the wonder of nature and the majesty of the universe—ascending from height to height up to the all-highest, from the conditioned to its conditions, up to the supreme and unconditioned Author [of all conditioned being].[9]
Though Kant still speaks of the heavens as offering evidence, he also seems aware of the power of such experiences to produce belief with "the force of an irresistible conviction . . . by one glance at the wonder of nature." Nature here serves not as evidence for an extended process of inference but as an experiential ground prompting in us belief that is spontaneous, immediate and noninferential.

Reformed epistemologists claim that more often than not we come to religious belief through the stimulation of our cognitive faculties by certain kinds of experience rather than by way of argument or inferential reasoning. An obvious advantage to construing the justification of religious beliefs in this way is that justification in one's belief that God exists is now readily accessible to persons altogether untutored in the ways of philosophy or, for that matter, those who lack any formal education whatsoever. Your epistemic state regarding belief in God as a student of philosophy may be no better—and could be worse!—than your pious grandmother's.

Plantinga and others in the Reformed tradition do not say that you cannot be justified in believing in God on the strength of inferential reasoning and argument. They prefer, however, that belief in God be held as basic, for then, among other possible benefits, you are freed from the anxiety of wondering whether some clever atheist has attacked your argument in some manner to which you are unable to respond.

Of course not every belief aroused in us by experiential circumstances is justified, nor does every belief that is held as basic necessarily remain so forever. It's possible that we could hold beliefs that were produced in us by experiences we later discovered were unveridical or deceptive in some way; but this is no less true of ordinary perceptual experience. I might, for instance, think that I saw a car parked in the middle of the quad but later discover that the world's largest hologram projector was being tested in the quad at just the time I perceived the car. Upon being so informed, I would likely acknowledge that the justification for my belief that a car was parked in the quad was undermined—undermined by my becoming aware that an alternative explanation for my perception was more likely. That is why Plantinga says that the justification attributable to our belief that there is a God, believed in this basic way, is prima facie only—that is, it is the sort of justification that could be defeated or undermined by additional information.

The justification-conferring conditions mentioned above must be seen as conferring *prima facie* rather than *ultima facie* or all-things-considered justification. This justification can be overridden. My being appeared to treely gives me a *prima facie* right to take as basic the proposition that I see a tree. But of course this right can be overridden; I might know, for example, that I suffer from the dreaded dendrological disorder, whose victims are appeared to treely only when there are no trees present. If I do know that, then I am not within my rights in taking as basic the *proposition I see a tree* when I am appeared to treely. The same goes for the conditions that confer justification on belief in God.[10]

How might a defeater arise to undermine my justification for believing that there is a God? Suppose I have long believed in God; moreover, my belief does not rest on arguments I have amassed but arises from my immediate response to what I take to be God's craftsmanship in nature and the uniform testimony of the devout community in which I reside. I go to college, and in an introductory class in psychology I am introduced to Sigmund Freud's claim that people believe in God as the result of a psychological wish-fulfillment mechanism. A common characteristic of human psychology, I am told, is to believe something to be true because one wishes it were so, or to disbelieve a claim because believing it would be too unsettling. We are terrified by nature's power and seeming indifference to our welfare, so Freud's theory goes, and because we have learned that our earthly fathers are not up to the task of controlling nature, we convince ourselves that a heavenly father exists who is.[11] Could it be, I wonder, that my viewing nature as God's handiwork is really a neurotic effort to tame what would otherwise be an intolerably brutal nature?

Of course, not only do beliefs we hold as basic sometimes get defeated, but sometimes the beliefs we thought had defeating power themselves go down in defeat. Suppose, to continue the example, I express my doubts to my philosophy-major roommate. He is not overly impressed by Freud's account and is not in the least inclined to think it shows that there is no God. Not only does he doubt whether any mechanism exists such as Freud describes, but even if it did, we might suppose that God implanted it in us to draw us to himself. He challenges me further by asking how I or anyone else could detect the workings of the wish-fulfillment mechanism and on what basis I could identify some specific belief as its output. Even if I have good reason for thinking such mechanisms exist, he argues, we cannot observe such mechanisms in operation and thus cannot be confident in picking out each and only those beliefs that are its products. If we *knew* there is no God, and if I knew that I had long desired that there be a God, then we would perhaps have good reasons for thinking that my newly acquired belief was attributable to the wish-fulfillment mechanism. But we do not know that God does not exist, and thus we have no way of knowing that my belief in God was the result of wish fulfillment.

As I consider the challenge, I come to believe that the very platform from which Freud's objection is launched is itself unsteady, and thus the salvos sent my way fall far wide of the mark. My confidence that my or anybody else's belief in God is due to wish fulfillment is undermined, and thus I come to think that the defeater to theism is itself defeated.

One might object that once I have made use of an elaborate defense against the charge of wish fulfillment (and lots of other objections besides), my belief in God is no longer held as basic; it now rests on all the reasons I put forward to defend my belief against this and other charges. According to Phillip Quinn, this is precisely the predicament of most sophisticated adult believers in our culture; they are all too painfully aware of a raft of potential defeaters of theism, among them the problem of evil, Marxist critiques of religion, and objections stemming from some evolutionary theorists. Quinn doubts that any theists are so favorably situated as to defeat all the objections arrayed against theism. And even if they were, their defensive efforts would show that the status of their belief in God has shifted; instead of being taken as basic, it would now be based on the host of arguments and defenses used to defend theism.

> I would insist . . . that many, perhaps most, intellectually sophisticated adult theists in our culture must, if their belief in God is to be rational, have a total case for the rationality of theistic belief which includes defenses against defeaters which have very substantial support.[12]

Does it follow, though, that if I offer reasons to counter the objections posed against my belief in God, it is no longer basic for me? As Plantinga points out, parrying criticisms against one's faith is not the same thing as offering evidence for the faith. One could engage in the task of *negative apologetics*, as it is sometimes called—the task of defeating objections posed against the justifiability of religious belief—and still not base one's own belief on argument.

Note the way that belief in God can itself sometimes play the role of defeating objections that might override theism's status as prima facie justified. Let us look first at a nonreligious example. Suppose I am an avid bird watcher, engaged in my favorite pastime of traipsing about some wetlands, knee-deep in muck, with binoculars and notebook close at hand. One day fortune smiles on me, and I spot an extremely rare species of bird long thought to have disappeared from the area where I am observing. I manage to creep within yards of the bird and gain a long and clear inspection, on the strength of which I take it in the basic way that

1. I saw the rare bird.

My buddies back at the bird-watching club meet my report with unrepressed skepticism. Their doubts turn on a raft of defeating evidence, the force of which I painfully acknowledge: no one has spotted this bird in this area for decades; the loss of wetlands has both diminished the supply of insects which constitute its main diet and caused its migratory pattern to veer far west of the place I claim to have seen it; such a bird typically travels accompanied by others of its kind, and the fact that I saw just one bird also counts against the veracity of my sighting. My buddies thus hold:

2. It is most likely that I did not see the rare bird I claim to have seen.

I am in an interesting predicament. On the strength of my perceptual experience I take it as basic that I saw the bird, and my belief enjoys a level of positive epistemic support in light of my experience. I also have defeating evidence against my perceptual belief, consisting of all the counterclaims of my colleagues, which also have a certain measure of positive epistemic support for me. But suppose I should decide that the degree of epistemic support, or warrant, possessed by my experience outweighs that of its potential defeaters. Might I not be reasonable in believing what seems to me to have the greater warrant? My acceptance of 1 is what Plantinga calls an "intrinsic defeater-defeater": it has more warrant for me than 2.[13]

Critic's of Plantinga's externalistic justification of theism have voiced a variety of objections. Let us consider a persistent objection that Plantinga himself anticipates and calls "the Great Pumpkin Objection." As noted in the chapter on foundationalism, Plantinga argues that the criteria for basicality insisted upon by classical foundationalists are both too restrictive and self-defeating. Foundationalists have no transcendental arguments establishing self-evidence, incorrigibility and being evident to the senses as the sole bases for arbitrating legitimate versus illegitimate basic beliefs. Hence, argues Plantinga, foundationalists cannot condemn as irrational theists who take their belief in God as basic. Against this latitudinarian approach to holding basic beliefs, critics charge that latitude has slipped into utter license. Does the theist's right to believe in God in a basic manner mean that epistemic permission is granted to anyone to take *anything* as basic no matter how absurd it may seem? Can we any longer reproach the intellectual conduct of someone wanting to take as basic a belief in the Great Pumpkin, who visits good girls and boys every Halloween?

Plantinga's first response, in the spirit of Thomas Reid, is illuminating. Reid says: "A man who knows nothing of a theory of vision, may have a good eye; and a man who never speculated about evidence in the abstract, may have a good judgment."[14] Similarly, writes Plantinga, a person without a formal theory of meaning can still spot gibberish, just as someone without criteria of proper basicality can nevertheless discriminate between appropriate and inappropriate basic beliefs. We accomplish this task (as Reid did) by identifying a set of paradigm examples that pair up certain kinds of experiential circumstances and their appropriate cognitive output. The beliefs we countenance as basic will be those most closely resembling the set of exemplary cases with which we start. Any criterion of proper basicality we may make use of is thus subsequent to our examples; theory must accommodate itself to our practical judgments, not the other way around.[15]

The proper way to arrive at such a criterion is, broadly speaking, inductive. We must assemble examples of beliefs and conditions such that the former are obviously properly basic in the latter, and examples of belief and conditions such that the former are obviously not properly basic in the latter. We must then frame hypotheses as to the necessary and sufficient conditions of proper basicality and test these hypotheses by reference to those examples.[16]

And where do we get the initial stockpile of examples by which to test new claims? In short, from our respective communities and traditions—where else could we start? Not only does Plantinga recognize the inevitability of our being situated in a particular community and the indispensable role it plays in shaping our conceptions of rationality, but he also recognizes that not all communities will necessarily agree as to the relevant set of paradigm instances of basic belief.

While Plantinga's rebuttal to the Great Pumpkin Objection may show that he is within his epistemic rights in taking belief in God as

basic, it also shows that someone from a different community, someone with a dramatically different set of paradigm instances of basic
belief, may very well be rational in not taking belief in God as basic.
In fact, if this quasi-inductive procedure for identifying basic beliefs
is correct, then atheists, polytheists and theists of various kinds might
with equal propriety claim that their central beliefs about religion are
also basic. This too Plantinga acknowledges: "Calvinists, Moonies,
Great Pumpkinites—all can follow my prescription; and probably no
two will arrive at the same criteria."[17]

Plainly, Plantinga's antifoundationalist account of basic beliefs represents a significant departure from the Enlightenment effort to find
one universal set of criteria that would judge definitively the
epistemic status of all beliefs. Because of the way basic beliefs are
grounded in the standards of a particular community, we shouldn't
expect that being rational in our belief in God gives us any polemical
advantage in showing that the basic beliefs held by persons of other
communities are unjustified. As Plantinga notes:

> This point is indeed correct, and one I meant to emphasize in
> R&BG:
>
> ". . . there is no reason to assume in advance that everyone will
> agree on the examples" (77). But is there a difficulty here? I accept,
> indeed, insist upon this consequence, but fail to see that it is
> legitimate grounds for complaint. Different philosophers employ-
> ing this method may arrive at different conclusions, true enough,
> but do we know of some viable philosophical method (for reaching
> criteria) of which this is not true? That's just life in philosophy.[18]

Being justified in holding a certain belief as basic may thus leave one
"toothless" in the debates that rage between members of competing
traditions.

Though the Moonie and Great Pumpkinite may be *justified* in
taking belief in God as basic, it doesn't follow that their respective
beliefs are *true* or *warranted*. Consider Mary, Martha and Miriam,
members of different belief communities, as they stand shoulder to
shoulder gazing up into the star-studded sky. The experience of
beholding the heavens instantaneously and noninferentially gives rise

to different beliefs in each. Mary is prompted to believe "God made all this"; Martha is prompted to believe "All is Void"; and Miriam is prompted to believe "All is one with the Tao." While their respective traditions and the paradigm instances of basic belief accepted in each may mean each woman is within her epistemic rights in taking what she does as basic, it is obvious that they cannot all have true beliefs. Perhaps one or all of them come from communities whose initial set of paradigmatic basic beliefs is wildly in error, thereby leading them to respond to their world in misleading ways; perhaps one or all of them have cognitive faculties that malfunctioned during the experience. We see that something more than being within one's epistemic rights is desirable; we want to be justified *and* get it right!

In addition to being justified in the sense of being entitled to what we believe, we prize the quality of having our cognitive faculties work in such a way that our experiences and thinking lead to true beliefs about the world. As noted in the last chapter, Plantinga applies the term *warrant* to that quality of our beliefs which when present in sufficient degree makes our true beliefs instances of knowledge. True belief by itself is not enough for knowledge. If someone whacks me upside the head with a polo mallet, simultaneously scrambling my brains and producing in me a true belief about the temperature in Bangkok, no one is tempted to call my newfound belief knowledge. Nor is justification in the deontological sense sufficient to turn our true beliefs into knowledge. I may faultlessly strive to satisfy what I consider to be the standards of justified belief, yet still fail to secure knowledge. A night watchman at a car dealership in a rough end of town listens attentively for sounds of prowlers; he doesn't realize that his hearing is impaired. He ends his shift in the serene confidence that nothing on the lot is amiss, and as luck would have it, he is right. The watchman may be justified in his belief, but we hesitate to say he has knowledge. The missing ingredient in each of these cases is warrant.

What is warrant, and how does it come to characterize our beliefs? Unfortunately, I cannot rehearse Plantinga's elaborate and nuanced account with all the care it deserves; we must rest content with a survey of the highlights.[19] According to Plantinga, warrant is a complex quality that comes in degrees; some beliefs have more of it than others. In *Warrant and Proper Function* Plantinga specifies a number of conditions that we must satisfy before our beliefs can be said to possess warrant. First, a belief has warrant insofar as it is the product of my cognitive faculties' having functioned properly, which is to say free of malfunction. Second, my cognitive faculties must also be functioning in an environment suitable for them. A perfectly functioning radio will not play in unsuitable environments (e.g., under water, or remote regions of space that are beyond the reach of any transmitter). Nor will our properly working cognitive equipment (eyes, ears, powers of judgment and so on) work well in a funhouse whose mirrors, deceptive lights, out-of-square rooms and trompe l'oeil façades leave us baffled and disoriented.

Even when these first two conditions are satisfied, we notice that we are inclined to accept some beliefs more readily than others. My memory, at work in a suitable environment, inclines me much more strongly to accept beliefs about what I had for lunch this afternoon than beliefs about what I had for lunch a month ago. We are more inclined to believe the sum of a simple two-digit addition problem than a sum made up of twenty ten-digit numbers, even though the faculties leading to each conclusion functioned properly in a suitable environment. Plantinga conjectures that when our faculties are functioning properly, the degree of warrant a belief has for us is proportional to the degree of inclination we have to accept the belief. We "feel" a stronger tug to accept the results of simple addition problems than of extremely complex ones.

Plantinga appreciates that our cognitive faculties are complex and that they may sometimes function properly (in their divinely intended sense) and yet not be working so as to secure truths about the world. It may very well be a part of the divine design that the mind dulls or suppresses from consciousness the memory of experiences that are too painful for us to bear or, as medical studies confirm, that sometimes we are optimistically inclined to think we will recover from illness just at the time our immune systems are most in need of the boost that positive thinking can provide. These "modules" of our cognitive powers have tasks other than putting us in touch with the truth. This being so, Plantinga restricts warrant to the proper functioning in a congenial environment of just that segment of our cognitive apparatus whose task is to secure the truth. Finally, we must add the proviso that when this segment functions properly it is highly likely that it latches onto the truth. Warrant would not attach to our beliefs if our cognitive powers, though properly functioning, were so pathetically poor that their proper deployment was more likely to yield falsehood than truth.

Why is Plantinga's account of warrant externalistic? The reason is plain to see. My beliefs can have warrant, even to a degree sufficient for knowledge, without my being aware that this is so. Being warranted in a belief doesn't carry with it the requirement that I am introspectively aware of the grounds of my belief, still less that I am aware of the adequacy of those grounds. And contrary to internalist claims, even if I base a belief in evidence I not only am aware of but whose probative force I properly appreciate, I may still fail to secure warrant. Suppose you glance at the clock tower to find out what time it is, and seeing that it reads twelve o'clock, you justifiably form the belief that it is twelve o'clock. Let us even add that you rehearse inwardly the propriety of your forming a belief about the time in the manner you are now doing. Unfortunately, the clock is broken; but fortuitously, the moment you glance at the clock just happens to be twelve o'clock sharp. In this admittedly contrived situation, you satisfy all the requirements for internalistic justification but fail to win warrant, for your environment was, in this instance, deceptive. So, then, on Plantinga's view, meeting the demands of internalistic justification proves to be neither necessary nor sufficient for warrant.

Finally, let's draw from Plantinga's account of warrant some lessons for religious belief by returning to Mary, Martha and Miriam. For the sake of the example, let us suppose it is Mary whose cognitive faculties have functioned properly; her noetic response to the star-filled sky and not those of her companions enjoys warrant. This shows, among other things, that Mary can be warranted in believing that God exists, even know that God exists, on Plantinga's view, without the benefit of argument, without seeing and appreciating the way some body of evidence supports her religious belief. But what are we to say about Martha and Miriam? Why do they lack warrant? It can't be because their environment is deceptive, for that would preclude Mary's having warrant. It must be, then, that their cognitive faculties have failed to function as they ought. But how shall we understand this? Are we to suppose that both Martha and Miriam suffer from malfunctioning visual or neurological equipment? Suppose not. Perhaps there are other ways to malfunction cognitively.

In the next chapter I wish to explore some aspects of cognitive functioning that supplement Plantinga's account. In particular I want to develop, in a way he does not, the idea that our concerns, and the emotions and virtues they inform, constitute a part of our cognitive equipment. My claim will be that proper cognitive functioning (and ultimately intellectual virtue) requires that we function properly on a moral and emotional level as well. In order to function properly in the sense necessary for warrant, we must pay attention to our emotions and other facets of our interior life, such as the disposition of our wills and moral character.

Eight

The Role of Emotions & Virtues in Proper Cognitive Functioning

I magine for a moment your ideal of an optimally functioning cognitive agent. What qualities would mark this person—extraordinarily acute perceptual faculties, remarkable capacities for abstract reasoning, and a fast and flawless ability to infer deductively and inductively in a cool and dispassionate manner on the basis of the data of experience? If you stopped here, you just described Mr. Spock, the famous Vulcan of *Star Trek*. Spock is the logician par excellence, whose sole concern as a thinker is to infer from the "facts" all and only what logic will allow. There is no room in Spock's mental life for cares and passions to interfere. Yet as anyone familiar with the character knows, Spock's lack of an affective nature makes him at times a deficient reasoner.

I wish to argue, against Descartes, that a properly functioning mind is not one that, as he puts it, has been "liberated from all cares" and "happily agitated by no passions," but one that has been suitably trained to care about the right things. I will propose that for many types of knowledge our emotions are not mere hindrances but indispensable aspects of proper reasoning itself. Contrary to the advocates of "pure reason," emotions constitute a chief means by which we gain, modify and sometimes reject important beliefs bearing on our well-being as humans: matters such as interpersonal relations, self-knowledge, issues of social justice, aesthetics and more.

Of course, on some occasions and for some subjects we should separate ideal cognitive functioning from certain expressions of our affective nature. For we all know how emotions such as fear, grief, intense anger and jealousy can cause reasoning to go off the rails. Who wants to be entrusted to the deliberations of a hate-filled judge or to the care of a visibly angry surgeon?

Such cases notwithstanding, a mind devoid of appropriate passions will, for some subjects and on some occasions, reason in a defective manner. But surely Luther's contemporary Erasmus errs in his overly pessimistic account of the relation between reason and emotion:

> Jupiter has bestowed far more passion that reason—you could calculate the ratio as 24 to one. He set up two raging tyrants in opposition to Reason's solitary power: anger and lust. How far Reason can prevail against the combined forces of the two the common life of man makes quite clear. Reason does the only thing she can and shouts herself hoarse, repeating formulas of virtue, while the other two bid her go hang herself, and are increasingly noisy and offensive, until at last their Ruler is exhausted, gives up, and surrenders.[1]

Against Erasmus, we shall see that for some types of knowledge our emotions are not mere hindrances but indispensable aspects of reason itself. I don't mean that emotions are merely ancillary helps to cognitive functioning but that they are partly constitutive of cognitive functioning. My claim is that emotions and moral virtues are to our cognitive life what rudders are to an airplane: they are *part of the thinking apparatus itself*. If they don't function properly, our cognitive life doesn't function properly. So whether or not we function intellectually in as complete a way as we generally think desirable hinges on whether our emotional and moral natures are mature.

8.1 How Emotions Assist Good Thinking

What are emotions, and why are they indispensable for certain kinds of understanding and knowing?[2] I have already discussed briefly in the second chapter how emotions motivate, sustain and come about as a consequence of our intellectual endeavors. But we need to consider this further. The paradigm human emotions are special modes of cognition whereby we perceive the world in the light of our concerns. They are a way of seeing or construing the things in our world (people, places, states of affairs and so on) beyond their surface appearances, as saturated by or conditioned by our concerns and values.

Two aspects, then, constitute paradigm human emotions: a *propositional grasp* of some situation in the world—there is something that emotions are about that can, in principle at least, be described—and some *concerns* these cognitions touch upon. Our concerns consist of our desires and attachments and touch upon many things of importance to us: we are concerned about the welfare of our families, our success in school, our success on a particular paper, our career, our ultimate destiny and many other matters. Our concerns can thus be general or specific, present to our thought or tucked away in our memory, oriented to goals proximate or remote, and so forth.

Suppose I am an ardent conservationist devoted to exercising careful stewardship of the earth's resources. I discover that a wildlife sanctuary I have worked hard to preserve is threatened by the chemical runoff of a nearby factory. My concern for the environment in conjunction with my awareness of the harm being done to it combine in my anger at the polluters.

Now, alter either aspect of the emotion—either the propositional content or the concern—and the complexion of the emotion changes. Suppose I could not care less about the environment and I want industry to prosper at any cost. Now if I discover that the environment is being polluted, my emotional state will no longer be anger; the character of my construal shifts with the changing concern. Or suppose I care deeply but I don't know what effect the chemicals may have on the environment. Again, my emotional state won't be as before; perhaps I will merely be apprehensive, for I may think the effect produced by these chemicals needs further study.

I am suggesting that anger is not an inference or mental state that comes on the heels of my having a certain belief and concern; the emotion of anger simply *is* a complex perception, a kind of value-laden seeing, consisting *all at once* of my perceiving the devastation to the environment in the light of my concern. Put this way, emotions such as gratitude, joy, compassion, anger, jealousy and so on are not opposed to reason—irrational juices swishing in our viscera—but rather among reason's regular modes of operation.[3]

How do emotions assist us in our cognitive tasks? This is a complex matter for which no single explanation seems adequate. As the example above suggests, emotions sometimes put us in touch with the world in a direct, quasi-perceptual fashion; we simply construe our world in terms of the emotion. Consider an illustration of Gilbert Harman: if "you round a corner and see a group of hoodlums pour gasoline on a cat and ignite it, you do not need to *conclude* that what they are doing is wrong; you do not need to figure anything out; you can see that it is wrong."[4]

At other times emotions connect us with the world indirectly, by making salient certain features of our experiences from which we then reason to particular conclusions. I am committed to the general moral belief that children should not suffer exploitation. A news story about children forced into slave labor to pay off debts incurred by their parents arouses in me shock and outrage. My emotional experience in this case makes salient morally relevant considerations from which I reason to particular and perhaps refined judgments about the injustice of any legal system that would permit such transfers of economic liability.

Antonio D'Amasio argues in his book *Descartes' Error* that emotions assist reason in at least three ways: they preselect options for reasoning, focus our attention on the items we reason about, and aid the memory in holding on to the things we're reasoning about. Fear, for example, keeps us alert to the tiger's whereabouts and prevents our thoughts from fixing on the jungle fauna. Emotions not only fix our attention but also serve as a catalyst for redirecting our thinking from one subject to another. Whereas deeply apathetic persons may sit listlessly for hours in front of a television set, persons with normal concerns of self-regard, self-love, will direct their thinking from one subject to another as befits their long-term goals of self-improvement.

To explore in more detail the role of emotions in proper cognitive functioning, let's turn to an extended, real-life example from Oliver Sacks's *An Anthropologist on Mars*.[5] Temple Grandin is a highly intelligent animal scientist who suffers from autism, a neurological disorder with wide-ranging symptoms. In Temple's case, the cognitive impairment prevents her from experiencing the same range of emotions normal people enjoy. Because she does not experience many emotions that arise in everyday human interactions, she fails to acquire a catalog of the emotional memories that are vital to empathic understanding, and consequently she fails to glean from her experiences lessons that strike most of us as obvious. Among other limitations, she is utterly unable to "read" people, to detect the nuances of vocal inflection, the ironies in people's conversation, the variations and reasons for their emotional displays, and the subtle social cues that tone of voice and gesture convey. The power to perceive these features of our interpersonal experience and to reason correctly from them is what allows us to learn that X is bored by my conversation, Y is merely flirting with me, Z is "pulling my leg" and so on. Temple, by contrast, describes her own mental life and thought processes as utterly computational, "lacking some of the subjectivity, the inwardness that others seem to have," due to the fact, as she puts it, that "the emotional circuit's not hooked up."[6]

Temple's impairment, and the unfortunately circumscribed life to which it gives rise, often displays itself in poignant ways. Watching Shakespeare's *Romeo and Juliet* left her bewildered because she was unable to empathize with the characters—unable, as Sacks puts it, "to follow the intricate play of motive and intention." Music, art and sunsets are all powerless to evoke in Temple any deep emotional response, demonstrating once again that there's more to seeing than meets the eye. When asked by Sacks whether she ever cared for another person, she responded, "I think lots of times there are things that are missing from my life."

Sacks eloquently recounts a spectacular drive that he and Grandin took through the Rocky Mountain National Forest, with its magnificent snow-capped peaks and alpine vistas. "I asked Temple if she did not feel a sense of their sublimity. She said she was puzzled by such words and had spent some time with a dictionary trying to understand them. She had looked up 'sublime,' 'mysterious,' 'numinous,' and 'awe,' but they all seemed to be defined in terms of one another." She was also puzzled by Sacks's reaction to an especially glorious sunset. " 'You get such joy out of a sunset,' she said. 'I wish I did too. I know it is beautiful, but I don't get it. . . . When I look up at the stars at night I know I should get a numinous feeling, but I don't. I would like to get it.' "[7] Although Temple is intellectually aware that people often use words such as *sublime* in relation to mountains, she does not experience them as sublime. Incidentally, Sacks discovered that Grandin is a *Star Trek: The Next Generation* fan, whose favorite character is Data, Spock's android successor!

To understand better what Temple's impairment prevents her from grasping, let us consider another case cited by Sacks, concerning a judge whose cognitive functioning was damaged by a shell fragment in the frontal lobe of the brain. As a result of the injury, the judge was left incapable of experiencing emotion—a condition one might suppose ideal for someone whose job is to render impartial determinations of guilt and innocence. But though he was able to understand the information presented by the lawyers and to draw correct inferences from it, he resigned from the bench because, as Sacks puts it, "he was no longer able to enter sympathetically into the motives of anyone concerned, and . . . since justice involved feeling, and not merely thinking, he felt that his injury totally disqualified him."[8] One part of determining guilt is ascertaining whether accused persons had sufficient motive to commit the acts with which they are charged. But to make such determinations requires that one be able to enter sympathetically into the motivational structure of other human beings, to "get inside their hearts," as it were. This often requires a sort of sympathetic understanding, a capacity to reason analogically from one's own case. This facet of judicial reasoning was exactly what the brain-damaged judge lacked.

Students of the emotions, from Aristotle to contemporary psychologists, note the crucial influence of early childhood training in fixing our initial emotional orientations as well as the subsequent pattern of emotional interactions with the world. Perhaps your parents commented to you from time to time about the plight of the disabled or the hungry and encouraged you to consider their welfare and your own good fortune. Perhaps after having flagrantly snatched your preschool buddy's truck to enlarge your own fleet of toy trucks, you found yourself dispossessed not just of the purloined vehicle but of your entire stockpile, and reprimanded with "Now you know how it feels to have someone take something from you. You don't like it, do you?" Such occasions constitute what Ronald de Sousa calls "paradigm scenarios," which establish for us the concerns by which we construe our experiences.[9] In addition to providing us with concerns, such scenarios equip us with the very terms of our emotional construals: *just, fair, guilty* and so on. The imprint of such scenarios in turn permits us to recognize other occasions calling for compassion, or other instances of injustice: I will simply construe as unjust, in a direct, quasi-perceptual way, future situations in which persons are unfairly dispossessed of their belongings. Or, in an indirect fashion, my anger at injustice will cause certain factors of a situation to be salient in my moral deliberations.

Temple's autism appears to have prevented her from acquiring in childhood a suitably rich repertoire of initial emotional orientations. Because most of us are schooled formally and informally to recognize and display emotions of solemnity, hilarity, guilt, remorse, indignation and hundreds more, we can also recognize departures from our initial framework; we can detect incongruities between the ways we have been schooled to construe our world emotionally and the expectations that such training instills, and what may be communicated to us in other ways. Because of my emotional training, I expect sincere apologies to be accompanied by certain gestures, tones and facial expressions; if you apologize in a sardonic tone of voice while rolling your eyeballs, this conflicts with my vocabulary of emotion, suggesting that you are not in earnest.[10]

Though right affections are indispensable for right reasoning in matters of interpersonal relations, public and private morality, religion and other matters possessing valuational dimensions, they do not direct us infallibly and can be badly trained. We can err both by misconstruing our surroundings and by investing them with too much or too little value. In Charles Dickens's *A Tale of Two Cities*, an aristocrat deliberately directs his coachman to drive pell-mell through the crowded city streets. When his team of horses tramples a young child, he flicks a coin to the grieving father, thinking himself to have offered just compensation. Obviously the aristocrat's thinking about the requirements of justice suffers from his investing the lives of peasants with too little value. And we are all too familiar with the anger and frustration that comes from investing our own selves, our plans, our ways of doing business with too much importance.

Because our affections can be badly trained, Aristotle was surely right to insist that the passions as well as the calculative intellect be properly trained. How I behave toward children, parents, neighbors and strangers will depend on my powers of estimating their value as persons and according them the treatment their status deserves. For parents to behave toward their children as they ought requires that they see them in their true light—as dependents who need care and nurturing.

Aristotle knew that properly trained affections are crucial ingredients in our becoming fully actualized moral agents and, for that matter, fully human *simpliciter*. While the following passage from Aristotle's *Nichomachean Ethics* may overstate the case, it nevertheless underscores an important theme: "So the difference between one and another training in habits in our childhood is not a light matter, but important, or rather, all-important" (2.1). Moral virtues fit us to perceive, to feel and to act properly. If I am a compassionate person, I am able to perceive the plight of the suffering, I am able to feel in a manner commensurate with their suffering, and I will be motivated to act appropriately to alleviate their suffering. The emotion of compassion is therefore not incidental to moral virtue but expressive of a disposition that is *constitutive* of it! Being emotional in the right way is simply part of what it means to be a moral person.

C. S. Lewis echoes Aristotle in claiming that we discern truths about our world only by investing it with the significance that it is due:

> It is the doctrine of objective value, the belief that certain kinds of attitudes are really true, and others really false, to the kind of thing the universe is and the kinds of things we are. . . . To call children delightful or old men venerable is not simply to record a psychological fact about our own parental and filial emotions at the moment, but to recognize a quality which demands a certain response from us whether we make it or not.[11]

The notion of a virtue allows us to see how closely our emotional, intellectual and behavioral lives are intertwined. Compassionate persons, for instance, combine reliable powers of moral perception, a sympathetic concern for the other and a disposition to act appropriately to alleviate the other's suffering. Note how our emotional nature not only makes up part of what it means to be virtuous but fosters our capacity to discern moral truths or make reliable moral judgments. Outrage, horror and anger may on occasion simply be the vehicles by which I see some feature of my world as unjust. In short, moral knowledge depends on properly tutored affections.

Thinking tempered by morality (and hence by proper affections) is what Aristotle called prudence, or practical wisdom, arguably the most important trait necessary for achieving human happiness. To the extent that we lack prudence, we lack the power to reason well about how to pursue our own happiness and the good life in the company of others. Whom should I marry, if anyone? What steps should I take to remedy my moral weaknesses? What career ought I to pursue? How should I raise my children? How can I motivate my employees and foster in them loyalty to the company? How can I diplomatically negotiate a dispute separating labor and management? These are not the sorts of questions for which the algorithmic thinking characteristic of "pure reason" offers complete and instant answers. They call for habits of character and mind such as insight, empathy, interpretive skill, creativity and the other traits making up practical wisdom.

The cases of the judge and Temple Grandin show how neurological damage causing emotional dysfunction can affect our ability to take in and understand certain features of the physical and social world, especially the richly textured sort of knowledge we have of other persons. We must now ask, however, whether a stunted emotional life and the diminished capacities for thinking that result from it are always owing to mental illness or a blow to the head. Might not a dwarfed capacity for interpersonal knowledge be owing to factors of a social and ethical sort over which we have some control and for which we bear some responsibility? (Of course we don't have control over many social factors—parents, place of birth and so on.) I think experience teaches that the intellectual limitations stemming from underdeveloped or improperly developed affections are due more often to nurture rather than the misfortunes of nature. The Gradgrind family from Dickens's novel *Hard Times* offers a classic example.

Thomas Gradgrind has undertaken an educational experiment on his children: to rear them as purely calculative, utilitarian reasoners. His is the home school from hell! Tables, charts, graphs, statistics and "plain facts" are the children's sole academic diet. "Bad books" containing fantasy, romance or anything that engages the emotions are strictly forbidden. While Thomas's motives are creditable (he wants his children to be fully rational, capable social agents), his methods yield the opposite effect. Because his children are not schooled to feel as they ought, they grow to be self-centered, unable to enter sympathetically into the suffering of others and unable to discern the demands of social justice for which their education was supposed to train them. The poor and suffering are seen merely as so many units destined for a place on a table of statistics about industrial accidents and urban mortality.

The Gradgrinds' adopted daughter Sissy Jupe receives her early education within a tightly knit circus community and, in contrast to Louisa and the other Gradgrind children, is acutely sensitive and empathetic. The children's tutor, M'Choakumchild, determines after a cursory questioning that Sissy is unfit for the Gradgrind educational regimen. A detached M'Choakumchild asks Sissy for her reaction to the fact that of 100,000 people recently undertaking sea voyages, only 500 were killed. Taking no solace from these "impressive" statistics, Sissy remarks that such a low number "is nothing to the relations and friends of the people who were killed" and that the people running such voyages should work harder to make them safe. Sissy's sensitive emotional nature allows her to perceive a person's immense worth and the gravity attached to a person's death, whereas these values remain opaque to those schooled in the Gradgrind educational regime. Martha Nussbaum contrasts M'Choakumchild's detachment with Sissy's empathic response:

> Intellect without emotion is, we might say, value-blind: it lacks the sense of the meaning and worth of a person's death that the judgments internal to emotions would have supplied. . . . The emotions do not tell us how to solve these problems; they do keep our attention focused on them as problems we ought to solve. Judge which approach would lead to a better public response to famine at a distance, to the situation of the homeless, to product testing and safety standards.[12]

Dickens's *Great Expectations* provides another example. Jilted at the altar as a young woman, Miss Havisham, now a vain and spiteful old woman, pursues her revenge on all men through her adopted daughter, Estella. She deliberately tutors the beautiful Estella in the art of mental cruelty, teaching her how to cause men to fall in love with her so that she can in turn break their hearts. Estella thus grows up emotionally and intellectually crippled. Miss Havisham also carefully oversees the life of the novel's main character, Pip, so that he will fall in love with Estella. And when, as a young man, he predictably declares his love to her, he meets with the following response:

> "It seems," said Estella very calmly, "that there are sentiments, fancies—I don't know how you call them—which I am not able to comprehend. When you say you love me, I know what you mean as a form of words, but nothing more. You address nothing in my breast, you touch nothing there. I don't care for what you say at all. I have tried to warn you of this, now, have I not?"[13]

Estella's tragic deficiencies are at once emotional, moral and intellectual; she fails to feel as well as to comprehend what is most precious about our relationships with others. And the central point thus far is that these two failures are related. Her failure to comprehend and feel as she ought is due not to a neurological disorder but to an impoverished home.

It is precisely because an impoverished upbringing can stunt us as effectively as a neurological disorder that Aristotle laid so much emphasis on the moral education of children. When we are properly trained in our affections as children, steeped in the right sorts of concerns, we are not only made fit to act justly in the public arena but inoculated against some of the more disastrous kinds of emotional traumas we might suffer as adults.

Aesthetic insight and interpretive understanding, no less than matters of personal relations, require the contribution of tutored emotions. Imagine asking a person of limited or stunted emotional development to provide a nuanced analysis of the characterization in a psychologically complex novel. To grasp sufficiently the motivational structure of its key personalities would require empathic skills sufficient to see things from the point of view of its characters. Someone emotionally shallow or perverse would likely be blind to these subtleties. Anyone with a dictionary can discover what the words of a poem mean, but not necessarily the sentiments such words are meant to convey. One part of understanding music and art requires that we grasp the devices artists employ to touch the emotional lives of their audience. Nelson Goodman writes:

> The work of art is apprehended through the feelings as well as through the senses. Emotional numbness disables here as definitely if not as completely as blindness or deafness. Nor are the feelings used exclusively for exploring the emotional content of a work. To some extent, we may feel how a painting looks as we may see how it feels. . . . Emotion in aesthetic experience is a means of discerning what properties a work of art has or expresses.[14]

Hence the art of novelists, musicians, poets and painters will be lost on persons whose affective lives, whose concerns, along with the emotions in which they are ingredient, are insufficiently developed.

While I have stressed the centrality of properly ordered affections for humanistic knowledge—knowledge of matters moral, religious, interpersonal and so forth—I have not shown that they are central to our thinking about chemistry, biology, physics and other sciences. Do emotional and moral qualities contribute to the work of scientists, or would Mr. Spock be better able to engage in scientific reasoning? Perhaps my claims about the importance of emotions to proper reasoning are correct only within the limited range of humanistic studies.

On the contrary, emotions enter in at virtually every phase of scientific inquiry, at the level of motivation, in the use one makes of scientific information and in ongoing scientific practice, including the way we perceive, interpret and communicate scientific information. Scientists are undeniably passionate *about* their work; they are intrigued by unresolved puzzles, exultant in discovery and confirmation, despondent in times of scientific crisis, and stirred even to awe by the beauty and elegance of the universe that their work reveals. Without a suitably rich set of life-characterizing concerns, the intricacies of nature would evoke none of these responses. Thomas Kuhn reports the swing of emotions reported by the physicist Wolfgang Pauli in a period of crisis over scientific theories:

> Wolfgang Pauli, in the months before Heisenberg's paper on matrix mechanics pointed the way to a new quantum theory, wrote to a friend, "At the moment physics is again terribly confused. In any case, it is too difficult for me, and I wish I had been a movie comedian or something of that sort and had never heard of physics." That testimony is particularly impressive if contrasted with Pauli's words less than five months later: "Heisenberg's type of mechanics had again given me hope and joy in life."[15]

Mathematicians too occasionally rhapsodize about the elegant, if severe, beauty of numbers, sets, proofs and other mathematical abstractions. Bertrand Russell writes:

> Mathematics, rightly viewed, possesses not only truth, but supreme beauty—a beauty cold and austere, like that of sculpture, without appeal to any part of our weaker nature, without the gorgeous trappings of painting or music, yet sublimely pure, and

capable of a stern perfection such as only the greatest art can show. The true spirit of delight, the exaltation, the sense of being more than man, which is the touchstone of the highest excellence, is to be found in mathematics as surely as in poetry.[16]

Mathematicians and scientists share an abiding concern for the truth, which in turn disposes them to a whole range of emotions—joy, excitement, depression, awe, aesthetic delight and so forth—as the circumstances of their scientific pursuits bear favorably or unfavorably on this goal.

But even if scientists are often moved to wide ranges of emotion *about* their work, the question remains whether proper emotions assist them *in* their work. The thinking of good scientists, claims Israel Scheffler, is marked by emotional dispositions that support characteristic patterns of thought, evaluation and actions constituting what he calls our "rational character."[17] Good scientists have a concern to make "cognitive contact with reality," to use Linda Zagzebski's phrase. This concern, in turn, motivates not just emotions but also actions symptomatic of the moral and intellectual virtues: a love for the truth; a contempt for lying, evasion and inaccurate or distorted reporting of data; a respect for the considered judgments of peers; joy at discovery; appropriate tenacity in one's research program in the face of anomalies; and humility concerning the significance and permanence of one's own work. Such emotions motivate our adherence to cognitive ideals that affect not just our motives for initially doing science but also our day-to-day scientific practice.

Scheffler comments in particular about what he calls "a capacity for surprise"; I believe *epistemic humility* would be a more apt phrase. Suitably humble scientists are alive to the possibility that their expectations about how nature should behave may be wrong, so that they will be required to revise their theories. "Receptive to surprise [being suitably humble], we are capable of learning from experience—capable, that is, of acknowledging the inadequacies of our initial beliefs, and recognizing their need for improvement. It is thus that the testing of theories, no less than their generation, calls upon appropriate emotional dispositions."[18] This sentiment is echoed by Nobel laureate physicist Subramaⱡyan Chandrasekhar, who was once asked why he was able to do innovative work in physics well past the age most persons retire, given that most of his fellow physicists peaked in their twenties. His response underscores the way a lack of humility may impede the scientist's efforts:

> For a lack of a better word, there seems to be a certain arrogance toward nature which people develop. These people have had great insights and made profound discoveries. They imagine afterwards that the fact that they succeeded so triumphantly in one area means they have a special way of looking at science which must therefore be right. But science doesn't permit that. Nature has shown over and over again that the kinds of truth which underlie nature transcend the most powerful minds.[19]

Testimonies from many scientists confirm that their capacity to love, respect and be fascinated or surprised by their subject influences not just their powers of perception but the way they select and appraise data, as well as their resolve to see a particular research program through. (Recall the discussion of "saliency" of evidence from chapter five.) Consider, for instance, Jane Goodall's groundbreaking research on the behavior of chimpanzees. Her devotion to the animals prompted her to spend extraordinary amounts of time earning their trust, with the result that she revolutionized the way scientists think about chimpanzees. Cannibalism, warfare, adoptions and the transfer of technology between chimp communities are just of few of the behaviors first documented by Goodall. "Had my colleagues and I stopped after ten years," says Goodall, "we would have been left with the impression that chimpanzees are far more peaceable than humans."[20] Surely we may reasonably suppose that Goodall's extraordinary concern for the apes positioned her favorably to see them in ways someone less devoted or more indifferent toward the animals would most likely have missed. The example of Barbara McClintock, mentioned earlier, attests to the fact that even scientists whose areas of research are quite far removed from anything having to do with humans nevertheless are emotionally involved in their work in ways that heighten their powers of perception and their persistence in problem solving.

8.2 Emotions, Intellectual Virtues and Religious Belief

Now we must ask what bearing a virtuous intellect has on religious belief. How do properly ordered affections shape our ability to secure justified religious belief? Christian thinkers such as Augustine, Aquinas, Pascal, Jonathan Edwards, John Henry Newman and others have insisted, contrary to the preachers of "pure reason," that we come to knowledge of God and other religious truths only if our affections are rightly ordered. Just as our ability to grasp scientific truths requires that we be equipped with the requisite training and abilities, so our capacity to grasp religious truths requires that we be the right sorts of persons.

These thinkers differ, however, in their accounts of the relationship between the intellectual and moral virtues and justified religious belief. Calvin, for instance, claims that with properly ordered affections we acquire what St. Paul calls "the eyes of the heart," whereby we have perceptual or quasi-perceptual experiences that allow us to see certain religious truths directly. The evidentialist Edwards, on the other hand, argues that a virtuous mind allows us to grasp certain religious truths indirectly, by enabling us to see and appreciate and reason correctly from the full range of evidence supporting various religious claims. (Here too nascent internalist and externalist intuitions are present.) Let us look at both of these positions more closely.

On Edwards's view, while evidence abounds to support God's existence, we may not have minds suited to grasp it and appreciate its force.[21] A problem drinker, for instance, may have evidence enough to be convinced that he is an alcoholic, but he discounts the evidence through self-serving rationalizations—"Oh, I could quit anytime. People with genuine drinking problems drink lots more than I do," and so on. The unbeliever, like the problem drinker, lacks not evidence but a mind, or perhaps a will, suited to acknowledge its force. Insufficiency of evidence doesn't bar him or her from believing in God, says Edwards; what the unbeliever lacks is mental and moral virtues and properly ordered affections.

Since intellectual vices such as self-deception and excessive self-interest impede our seeing evidence aright, they must be supplanted by virtuous traits that will put the evidence in proper perspective. Right affections don't manufacture evidence, on Edwards's view, nor do they motivate belief where evidence is lacking; instead they bolster our powers of reason, allowing us to see and correctly evaluate already existing evidence. Does it not stand to reason that an intellectually honest, morally sensitive person will be privy to the evidence behind moral arguments in a way a morally base person will not? Will not someone grateful for life and all its gifts be more inclined to see the world's beauty and design and reason to the existence of a Creator? But according to Edwards, the mental and moral traits required to reason correctly about religious matters cannot be cultivated on our own; they must be infused in us by God as an act of special grace.

Perhaps what moral and intellectual virtues make possible is not simply a capacity to detect and appraise evidence for God but a capacity to experience God more directly. When the psalmist stares into the heavens, he sees directly the handiwork of God. To see the world as God's creation, to see all of contingent reality as having its very existence in the sustaining power of God, is at the same time to experience our own dependence on God. And what is the normal way to grasp these truths about God's relation to the world if not through feelings of dependency and gratitude? And if the world really is as the psalmist perceives it to be, then we can say that his gratitude is genuinely a fitting response to the kind of place the world is and the kinds of creatures we are.

I have depicted the psalmist's belief that God created the world as emerging immediately from his having experienced the world with his affections ordered as they are. According to Calvin, God has engineered our noetic faculties so as to make this way of gaining divine truth normal:

> Since Perfection and blessedness consists in the knowledge of God, he has been pleased, in order that none may be excluded from the means of obtaining felicity, not only to deposit in our minds that seed of religion of which we have spoken, but to manifest his perfections in the whole structure of the universe, and daily to place

himself in view, that we cannot open our eyes without being compelled to behold him. (*Institutes of the Christian Religion* 1.5.1) The seeing Calvin has in mind is not purely cerebral and dispassionate but a sort of seeing with the eyes of the heart. If, however, we were left to infer God's existence from natural evidence, it is clear that some would be excluded from the "means of felicity," as Aquinas said. Instead we come to believe in God as Creator in an epistemically basic manner, as Plantinga argues. Now we can supplement Plantinga's idea that whether or not the experience of the world prompts us to take belief in God in the basic manner will depend on whether our noetic equipment is functioning properly. We now see that our affective nature, our emotions and moral nature, are not independent of our functioning properly but part and parcel of it. To function cognitively in a proper way is to function in a virtuous way.

It is also clear, however, that not everyone who beholds the starry heavens above gratefully acknowledges God's sustaining activity. Recall the example of Mary, Martha and Miriam: some look into the starry heavens and see no more than the Void, or a frighteningly cold, meaningless stretch of relatively empty space.

While moral reason, or seeing with the eyes of the heart, may be a common mode of human cognizing, it is by no means automatic, since not everyone possesses the requisite virtues to a suitably high degree. The Christian thinkers mentioned above also teach that it lies within our power to thwart reason by stifling the development of a virtuous nature. Sometimes an immature or perverse affective nature is traceable to an unfortunate upbringing or the powerful example of immoral company, as we have already seen. At other times, however, the responsibility we bear for our cognitive failings is more direct. Occasionally we willfully act to "suppress the truth in unrighteousness," as St. Paul says. More often than not, the vices impairing our cognitive apparatus arise the same way as most bad habits—bit by bit, by a series of very small, almost imperceptible steps.

The variableness of our cognitive makeups may explain why many beheld the miracles of Jesus, yet not all had "the ears to hear" or "the eyes to see," and consequently some walked away unmoved. What they needed was not more miracles but intellectual natures properly constituted to see the miracles in all their true significance. In sum, whether we function properly as intellectual agents depends on the contributions made by a properly cultivated moral, affective and volitional nature.

I have argued thus far that our ability to acquire many kinds of knowledge hinges on our cognitive power's functioning appropriately in conjunction with a suitably trained affective character. Emotions may be pivotal not just when we acquire beliefs but also when we modify or abandon them. After all, people do undergo changes of heart, by which the "eyes of the heart" are opened and new perspectives on old information are gained. How does this happen? Typically our initial emotional orientations are shaped over an extended period of time by our upbringing and the influence of the communities of which we are a part. I want to propose, however, that such changes often come about more suddenly by what I will call "transformative religious experiences."[22] Such experiences sometimes figure prominently in the process by which our beliefs are defeated.

8.3 Transformative Emotional Experiences
The plot of many a novel revolves around the transformation of a main character, so that we witness the events that contribute to the character's coming to see the world through new eyes. More often than not, suffering of some sort is a principal factor in such conversions. Recall the transformation of Mark Studdock, described in the first chapter. King Lear, Thomas Gradgrind and the characters of countless other stories come into their right mind only after a period of suffering.

Real life all too often imitates art. Happily, not all transformational experiences involve suffering; an encounter with great goodness can also touch our emotions in ways that result in our coming to see and think in a new way. Raskolnikov, the nihilist of Fyodor Dostoyevsky's *Crime and Punishment,* abandons his philosophical perspective not as the result of argument but in response to the powerful love of Sonya. After Raskolnikov confesses to having murdered a pawnbroker and her sister, Sonya perceives what a wretchedly tormented soul he is and moves to embrace and kiss him. He responds as follows:

> "You're so strange, Sonya—you embrace and kiss me, when I've
> just told you about that. You're forgetting yourself." . . . A feeling
> long unfamiliar to him flooded his soul and softened it all at once.
> He did not resist: two tears rolled from his eyes and hung on his
> lashes.[23]

Could not Raskolnikov have abandoned nihilism without undergoing this experience? Perhaps. We do sometimes change our minds on the strength of purely philosophical exchanges; we read or hear a rebuttal to our favorite ways of thinking about some intellectual matter and straightaway revise our thinking, with seemingly little emotional involvement. Not so with Raskolnikov. He does not merely observe Sonya's expression of love; he experiences himself as loved by her. And in virtue of his emotional experience, he suddenly construes himself as an object of value in someone else's eyes. His world is suddenly suffused with values and significance that his nihilism can't allow. His experience of himself as an object of value thus constitutes a defeater to his nihilism. It cannot simultaneously be true that the world is without value (the nihilist view) and that he is himself valuable. Raskolnikov allows his experience to override his philosophical theory; Dostoyevsky's phrase "he did not resist" suggests that Raskolnikov might have resolved the tension the other way, by allowing his prior philosophical commitments to undermine his experience as unveridical.[24]

Whittaker Chambers, the key witness in the famous perjury trial of Alger Hiss, writes of the pivotal event in his rejection of Marxist materialism.

> But I date my break [with the Communist Party] from a very casual
> happening. I was sitting in our apartment in St. Paul street in
> Baltimore. It was shortly before we moved to Alger Hiss's apart-
> ment in Washington. My daughter was in her highchair. I was
> watching her eat. She was the most miraculous thing that had ever
> happened in my life. I liked to watch her even when she smeared
> porridge in her face or dropped it meditatively on the floor. My eye
> came to rest on the delicate convolutions of her ears—those intricate,

perfect ears. The thought crossed my mind: "No, those ears were not created by any chance coming together of atoms in nature (the Communist view). They could have been created only by immense design." The thought was involuntary and unwanted. I crowded it out of my mind, But I never wholly forgot it or the occasion. I had to crowd it out my mind. If I completed it, I should have had to say: Design presupposes God. I did not know then, but at that moment, the finger of God was first laid upon my forehead.[25]

Chambers's abandonment of Marxist materialism likewise wasn't accomplished in the dialectical arena but in his heart, by his emotional inability to see his baby daughter as a mere piece of animated meat. There is no novelty in thinking that humans bear the mark of a Designer; this notion is a staple of most introductory classes in philosophy. To experience the world as purposive, however, is a different matter. Altered affections thus often bring an end to one way of seeing and thinking and the beginning of a new one.

The argument thus far appears to be open to an obvious objection. I have argued that proper cognitive functioning requires properly ordered affections. But how are we to identify which emotions are indispensable to right thinking and in what form and degree they must be present? To judge rightly here—obviously a cognitive task—usually requires that we already have properly ordered affections. So it looks as though we're caught in a vicious circle: to think right I have to feel right, but to know what feeling right amounts to, I must make correct judgments. Does the circularity here undermine the argument?

The circularity we have uncovered is not vicious but typical of the many hermeneutical circles we encounter in epistemology. Such circles require that we make use of information en route to gaining a better understanding of it. Recall our discussion of basic beliefs, where an analogous circle arises. We noted that what we initially take as epistemically basic stems largely from the belief communities that contribute to our early intellectual formation. Whether we think these beliefs are as suitable as others we might have received from different traditions depends on judgments we make while using these initial basic beliefs along with the other beliefs they support. Occasionally, however, experience and opposing perspectives lead to our revising or abandoning our initial basic beliefs. It was for this reason that I said such beliefs have prima facie justification—justification capable of being overridden.

Just as our reasoning about the adequacy of our beliefs stems from the initial deposit we receive from our various traditions, so our thinking about subjects we have mentioned above reflects the ways our traditions and experience have tutored our emotions. We have no alternative but to make our way in the world equipped with such emotions as early training and experience bequeath to us, and to do our thinking with them. But as the cases of Raskolnikov and Whittaker Chambers show us, our emotions and the thinking integrally bound up with them are subject to change, sometimes for the better. They also show a buried susceptibility to healthy emotional responses on which further healthy responses can be built.

Let us now review the argument of this last section. My central claim is that to flourish as intellectual beings, to grasp truths essential for our living full and happy lives, we must also flourish as emotional and moral beings. For as we have seen, if our lives are marked by deep, ongoing concerns, we will be moved by various circumstances to emotions and virtuous behaviors that in turn equip us to think in ways we could not otherwise think and to grasp truths we could not grasp were we lacking in these traits. But whether these traits become a deeply embedded part of our character is, in part, up to us. How we respond to adversity, and the affect it has on our character and our thinking, is a matter over which we have some control.

The Christian tradition, following Scripture, has also taught, however, that we are not alone in our efforts to cultivate life-characterizing concerns and the virtuous emotions and behavior that stem from them; God is ready to assist us. We can hardly do better than to recall the words of James: "If any of you is lacking in wisdom, ask God, who gives to all generously and ungrudgingly, and it will be given you" (Jas 1:5).

Suggestions for Further Reading

Reference Works
Dancy, Jonathan, and Ernest Sosa. *A Companion to Epistemology.* Oxford: Blackwell, 1993.

General Introduction to Epistemology
Audi, Robert. *Epistemology: A Contemporary Introduction to the Theory of Knowledge.* New York: Routledge, 1998.
Moser, Paul K., Dwayne H. Mulder and J. D. Trout. *The Theory of Knowledge: A Thematic Introduction.* New York: Oxford University Press, 1998.
Steup, Matthias. *An Introduction to Contemporary Epistemology.* Upper Saddle River, N.J.: Prentice-Hall, 1996.

More Advanced Reading
Alston, William P. *Epistemic Justification: Essays in the Theory of Knowledge.* Ithaca, N.Y.: Cornell University Press, 1989.
Audi, Robert. *The Structure of Justification.* Cambridge: Cambridge University Press, 1993.
Bonjour, Laurence. *The Structure of Empirical Knowledge.* Cambridge, Mass.: Harvard University Press, 1985.
Chisholm, Roderick. *Theory of Knowledge.* 3rd ed. Englewood Cliffs, N.J.: Prentice-Hall, 1989.
Foley, Richard. *The Theory of Epistemic Rationality.* Cambridge, Mass.: Harvard University Press, 1987.
Goldman, Alvin. *Epistemology and Cognition.* Cambridge, Mass.: Harvard University Press, 1986.
Kvanvig, Jonathan. *Intellectual Virtues and the Life of the Mind.* Savage, Md.: Rowman & Littlefield, 1992.
Lehrer, Keith. *Theory of Knowledge.* Boulder, Colo.: Westview, 1990.
Moser, Paul. *Knowledge and Evidence.* Cambridge: Cambridge University Press, 1989.

Plantinga, Alvin. *Warrant: The Current Debate.* Oxford: Oxford University Press, 1993.

————. *Warrant and Proper Function.* Oxford: Oxford University Press, 1993.

Plantinga, Alvin, and Nicholas Wolterstorff, eds. *Faith and Rationality.* Notre Dame, Ind.: University of Notre Dame Press, 1983.

Pollock, John. *Contemporary Theories of Knowledge.* Savage, Md.: Rowman & Littlefield, 1986.

Rorty, Richard. *Philosophy and the Mirror of Nature.* Princeton, N.J.: Princeton University Press, 1979.

Wainwright, William. *Reason and the Heart.* Ithaca, N.Y.: Cornell University Press, 1995.

Wolterstorff, Nicholas. *John Locke and the Ethics of Belief.* Cambridge: Cambridge University Press, 1996.

Zagzebski, Linda. *Virtues of the Mind.* Cambridge: Cambridge University Press, 1996.

Notes

Chapter 1: The Nature of Epistemology

[1] Norman Malcolm, "The Groundlessness of Belief," in *Philosophy of Religion*, ed. Louis Pojman, 2nd ed. (Belmont, Calif.: Wadsworth, 1994), p. 464.

[2] One prominent philosopher of the twentieth century, W. V. O. Quine, writes: "For the theory of knowledge has its origin in doubt, in skepticism. Doubt is what prompts us to try to develop a theory of knowledge." Quoted from "The Nature of Natural Knowledge," in *Mind and Language*, ed. Samuel Guttenplan (Oxford: Clarendon, 1975), p. 67.

[3] Fyodor Dostoyevsky, *The Brothers Karamazov*, trans. Richard Pevear and Larissa Volokhonsky (New York: Vintage, 1990), p. 296.

[4] See, for example, William Brown's *Character in Crisis: A Fresh Approach to the Wisdom Literature of the Old Testament* (Grand Rapids, Mich.: Eerdmans, 1996). "In short," writes Brown, "a crucial aim of the proverb is to help develop practical wisdom, to cultivate what Aristotle would identify as the chief virtue, prudence" (p. 14).

[5] See, e.g., Frederick Schmitt, ed., *Socializing Epistemology: The Social Dimensions of Knowledge* (Lanham, Md.: Rowman and Littlefield, 1994).

[6] St. Thomas Aquinas *Summa Theologiae* 1-2 Q53.1-3. See also 1-2 Q94.4-6.

[7] C. S. Lewis, *That Hideous Strength* (New York: Macmillan, 1968).

[8] As Samuel Johnson writes, "Adversity has ever been considered as the state in which a man most easily becomes acquainted with himself, and this effect it must produce by withdrawing flatterers, whose business it is to hide our weaknesses from us, or by giving loose to malice, and license to reproach; or at least by cutting of those pleasures which called us away from meditation on our conduct, and repressing that pride which too easily persuades us, that we merit whatever we enjoy." Quoted in "Self-Deception," in *Vice and Virtue in Everyday Life*, ed. Christina Hoff-Sommers (New York: Harcourt Brace, 1997), p. 418.

[9] Lewis, *That Hideous Strength*, pp. 245-46.

[10] Philosophers of science teach us that a scientific theory has a career, which at one moment of its history may be underdetermined by the evidence or plagued by unsolved anomalies. The success of the theory, however, is best measured by its fertility over the length of its career. Analogously, assessing the epistemological merits of belief at just one point in time not only may not prove especially accurate but actually may very well deprive you of a perfectly good belief.

[11] Jonathan Kvanvig, *The Problem of Hell* (Oxford: Oxford University Press, 1993), p. 80, distinguishes between the role the will plays in complex theoretical commitments and in simple day-to-day beliefs. He writes:

> Perhaps willfulness is beyond the pale of possibility in simple, ordinary cases of belief formation and sustenance (for example, I do not choose now to believe that there is a computer screen in front of me; it is not somehow directly "up to me" whether I believe this claim); yet, when we come to more global issues, such as the refusal to allow experience to count against a view of the world or certain parts of it, there surely is a possibility that such a response pattern is something I choose and for which I am responsible.

As I will claim in later chapters, our overall theological orientations are the sorts of global issues which are more readily subject to the influences of the will, passions and moral character.

[12]René Descartes, *Discourse on Method*, in *The Philosophical Works of Descartes*, trans. Elizabeth Haldane and G. R. T. Ross (New York: Dover, 1955), p. 101. One finds similar remarks in Plato; see *Phaedo* 65d-66.

[13]Robert Wright, *The Moral Animal—Why We Are the Way We Are: The New Science of Evolutionary Psychology* (New York: Pantheon, 1994), pp. 324-25. Of course Wright may face a potential problem of self-reference here. Are we to suppose that his claims here do not subserve evolutionary ends?

[14]Recent epistemology going by the name "naturalized epistemology" has placed great emphasis on ways our intellectual life is captive to our bodies. In fact, these philosophers have developed accounts of justification that turn on whether our bodies (especially the senses and the brain) were in proper working condition in producing our beliefs. See Hilary Kornblith, ed., *Naturalizing Epistemology* (Cambridge, Mass.: MIT Press, 1985).

[15]Aquinas *Summa Theologiae* 1-2 Q.57.3.

[16]Simple, uncontroversial beliefs of this sort are a kind of philosophical "lab rat." They are easy to handle and good subjects on which to test new theories.

[17]Søren Kierkegaard, *Concluding Unscientific Postscript to Philosophical Fragments*, trans. Howard V. Hong and Edna H. Hong (Princeton, N.J.: Princeton University Press, 1992), 1:197-98.

Chapter 2: Exploring the Intellectual Virtues

[1]Of course a good number of our beliefs do not fit this pattern. I cannot recall when I first came to believe that there is an external world. Still less can I recall having to defend this belief, teach it to someone else or apply it in any obvious way.

[2]I am assuming that Mary holds correct moral beliefs about the moral propriety of her journalistic practices. If not, Mary could find that being intellectually virtuous eventuates in her changing her beliefs.

[3]Timothy Ferris, *Coming of Age in the Milky Way* (New York: Anchor/Doubleday, 1988), p. 302.

[4]Edith Eisler, "Setting the Stage: How Dorothy Delay Turns Pupils into Performers," *Strings*, May-June 1995, pp. 45-49.

[5]Ibid., p. 49.

[6]Emotions last varying lengths of time. We might be angry for an instant or all afternoon, or so given to anger that we are considered to be angry persons. But this last sense of anger depicts a ready disposition to feel anger, and not necessarily the occurrent feeling of anger. So it might be more accurate to say that compassionate persons are marked by a ready disposition to feel sadness at another's suffering, gladness when such suffering is eased, anger at those who cause unnecessary suffering and so on.

[7]I don't wish to suggest that the order of causation always goes from flawed judgment to inappropriate feelings. Sometimes it goes the other way, as I will argue later on: improperly tutored affections lead to poor judgment.

[8]"For I do not do the good I want, but the evil I do not want is what I do. Now if I do what I do not want, it is no longer I that do it, but sin that dwells within me. So I find it to be a law that when I want to do what is good, evil lies close at hand. For I delight in the law of God in my inmost self, but I see in my members another law at war with the law of

my mind, making me captive to the law of sin that dwells in my members" (Rom 7:19-23). See Bonnie Kent's *Virtues of the Will: The Transformation of Ethics in the Late Thirteenth Century* (Washington, D.C.: Catholic University Press, 1995).

[9]From Zenkei Shibayama, *Zen Comments on the Mumonkan*, in John Koller and Patricia Koller's *Sourcebook In Asian Philosophy* (New York: Macmillan, 1991) p. 361.

[10]The notion of flourishing or failing to flourish is evident in the words of a personified Wisdom in Proverbs: "For whoever finds me finds life and obtains favor from the LORD; but those who miss me injure themselves; all who hate me love death" (Prov 8:35-36).

[11]Some recent epistemologists have equated "intellectual virtue" simply with one's having reliable cognitive faculties. "Virtue reliabilists," as they are sometimes called, depict intellectual virtues as a function of one's having natural powers of sight, hearing, memory, introspection and so forth that regularly lead one to arrive at truth and avoid error in a given field of inquiry. "Virtue responsibilists" find this account of intellectual virtue too thin, for it fails to embody the idea that being intellectually virtuous is something over which one has a measure of control, something one can be more or less conscientious in cultivating. Whether or not, or to what extent, we are creative and introspective is, in measure, up to us. By exerting effort we can either stifle or develop these traits within us. These two senses of intellectual virtue are contrasted in Guy Axtell's "Recent Work on Virtue Epistemology," *American Philosophical Quarterly* 34 (January 1997).

[12]While moral virtues paradigmatically come accompanied by some sort of feeling, they do not always do so. Virtues such as patience, forbearance and justice do not always come accompanied by emotion, still less by some exact emotional correlate.

[13]C. S. Peirce, "The Fixation of Belief," in *Philosophical Writings of Peirce*, ed. Justus Buchler (New York: Dover, 1955), pp. 5-22.

[14]Quoted in the chapter devoted to Barbara McClintock in Sharon Bertsch McGrayne's *Nobel Prize Women in Science* (New York: Birch Lane Book Press, 1993), p. 167.

[15]Ibid., p. 172.

[16]Ibid., p. 157.

[17]Aristotle *Nichomachean Ethics* 2.1.

[18]Again, I am using the term *intellectual virtue* in what Guy Axtell calls the "virtue responsibilist" sense. Having 20/20 vision is a relatively enduring trait that allows me to acquire truths about the world I would miss if I had uncorrected 20/200 vision. In this way, good eyesight improves my condition epistemically. But having good eyesight falls short of what is ordinarily meant by intellectual virtue in its fullest sense. I play no role in having this trait, I don't superintend the faculty, it is not integrated with my moral and emotional life, nor am I a fit subject of praise for having it. See note 11 in this chapter.

[19]See Linda Zagzebski's discussion of the distinction between virtues and skills in her *Virtues of the Mind* (Cambridge: Cambridge University Press, 1995), especially section 2.4.

Chapter 3: An Extended Look at Some Intellectual Virtues

[1]William James, *The Will to Believe and Other Essays in Popular Philosophy* (New York: David McKay, 1911), p. 17.

[2]Robert Coles, *The Call of Stories* (Boston: Houghton Mifflin, 1989), p. 195.

[3]Augustine *Confessions* 10.35.

[4]Charles Dickens, *Bleak House* (New York: Penguin, 1985), p. 360.

[5]"Knowledge itself is power," wrote Francis Bacon nearly four hundred years ago. The idea that knowledge is a tool we employ to dominate and oppress others has been voiced anew in writers like Michel Foucault. See the discussion below on intellectual honesty.

[6]See Stan Godlovitch's discussion of the moral propriety of making use of such information in his article "Forbidding Nasty Knowledge: On the Use of Ill-Gotten Information," *Journal of Applied Philosophy* 14, no. 1 (1997).

[7]Samuel Johnson, *Rasselas*, chap. 41.

[8]Medical research proves a veritable Pandora's box for the curious. *Biomedical Ethics*, an anthology edited by Thomas Mappes and Jane Zembaty (New York: McGraw-Hill, 1981), contains several interesting articles pertaining to limiting scientific inquiry. See, for example, "Inquiry into Inquiry" by Robert Sinsheimer and "When May Research Be Stopped?" by Carl Cohen.

[9]Augustine's concern does not undermine the legitimate place for recreation in our lives. For most of us, studiousness is best cultivated when study is punctuated by periods of leisure and rest that renew our minds, making them more productive when they are applied to more serious concerns.

[10]Evelyn Waugh, *Brideshead Revisited* (Boston: Back Bay Books/Little, Brown, 1944), p. 192.

[11]Ibid., pp. 192-93.

[12]John Locke *An Essay Concerning Human Understanding* 4.20.17, 12.

[13]John Bailar, "The Real Threats to the Integrity of Science," *The Chronicle of Higher Education*, April 21, 1995, p. B2.

[14]Francis Bacon *Novum Organum* 1.49.

[15]Locke and Bacon were not, of course, the first to observe the way certain emotions interfere with sound thinking. Centuries earlier Aquinas wrote: "In an emotional state objects appear to be greater or less that they are in reality. What is loved seems better than it is to the lover and what is feared seems more terrible to a frightened man. Thus by interfering with sound judgment emotions act essentially as a hindrance to the capacity for wise deliberation" (*Summa Theologiae* 1a-2ae Q44.2).
In fairness it should be mentioned that not every emotional state impedes good thinking. Chiefly Aquinas has in mind inordinate emotions such as excessive anger, unbridled lust or uncontrolled fear. Actually, some emotions like love, compassion and pity might *aid* our ability to perceive the world rightly and to make sound judgments about it. Those interested in a full account of Aquinas's theory of the emotions should read Robert C. Roberts, "Thomas Aquinas on Emotions," *History of Philosophy Quarterly* 9, no. 3 (July 1992). See also *Summa Theologiae* 2a-2ae Q110-13, where Aquinas deals with various vices opposed to the truth, among them lies of many different sorts, boasting, hypocrisy, dissimulation and irony.

[16]Charles Dickens, *Bleak House* (New York: Penguin, 1971), p. 648.

[17]Locke *Essay Concerning Human Understanding* 4.20.11.

[18]Michel Foucault, in *The Foucault Reader*, ed. Paul Rabinow (New York: Pantheon Books, 1984), pp. 72-73.

[19]See Merold Westphal, *Suspicion and Faith: The Religious Uses of Modern Atheism* (Grand Rapids, Mich.: Eerdmans, 1993). See also Westphal's article "Taking St. Paul Seriously: Sin as an Epistemological Category," in *Christian Philosophy*, ed. Thomas P. Flint (Notre Dame, Ind.: University of Notre Dame Press, 1990).

[20]Westphal, "Taking St. Paul Seriously," p. 218.

[21]I am grateful to the work of Robert C. Roberts on honesty for informing and clarifying

my own thinking on the subject of honesty. See his article "Honesty," in *New Dictionary of Christian Ethics and Pastoral Theology*, ed. David J. Atkinson et al. (Downers Grove, Ill.: InterVarsity Press, 1994), pp. 454-55.

[22]St. Thomas Aquinas *Summa Contra Gentiles* 1.4.4 (available in a 1975 edition from the University of Notre Dame Press).

[23]Ibid. *Summa Theologiae* 2-2, Q45.

[24]See Joseph Pieper's *The Four Cardinal Virtues* (Notre Dame, Ind.: University of Notre Dame Press, 1966). An extensive treatment of the virtue of prudence (well repaying the effort spent working through it) can be found in Aquinas *Summa Theologiae* 2-2 Q47-56.

[25]Notice the similarity between Homer and the writer of Proverbs. The personified Wisdom in Proverbs says: "For whoever finds me finds life and obtains favor from the LORD, but those who miss me injure themselves; all who hate me love death" (Prov 8:35-36). The idea that folly results in harm to ourselves is a common theme in most wisdom traditions.

Chapter 4: Foundationalism
[1]Foundationalism's chief competitor historically is coherentism. It too provides an account of how our beliefs ought ideally to be ordered. And it too sees justification as depending in part on the way our beliefs are ordered or related to each other. I will be discussing the coherence view in the next chapter.

[2]René Descartes, *Meditations on First Philosophy*, in *Philosophical Works of Descartes*, 2 vols., trans. Elizabeth Haldane and G. R. T. Ross (New York: Dover, 1955) 1:144.

[3]René Descartes, *Discourse on Method*, in *Philosophical Works of Descartes*, trans. Elizabeth Haldane and G. R. T. Ross (New York: Dover, 1955), 1:90.

[4]Nicholas Wolterstorff holds the controversial view that Descartes was not concerned with knowledge in our contemporary sense but with *scientia*, an intuitively apprehended knowledge of nature. Wolterstorff discusses the differences between Descartes's and Locke's projects in *John Locke and the Ethics of Belief* (Cambridge: Cambridge University Press, 1996); see especially chapter 3.

[5]See Susan Haack's "Recent Obituaries of Epistemology," *American Philosophical Quarterly* 27, no. 3 (1990). Nicholas Wolterstorff writes: "On all fronts foundationalism is in bad shape. It seems to me there is nothing to do but give it up for mortally ill and learn to live in its absence" (*Reason Within the Bounds of Religion* [Grand Rapids, Mich.: Eerdmans, 1976], p. 52).

[6]Perhaps I should mention now (I will discuss more fully later) that philosophers have used the concept of justification ambiguously. As will be discussed in chapter five, some have used the term as a way of indicating that one has satisfied all that can reasonably be expected in acquiring a belief, that no blame attaches to the person for believing as he or she does. Others have used the term to identify what must be added to true belief in order to have knowledge.

[7]See Timm Triplett's "Recent Work on Foundationalism," *American Philosophical Quarterly* 27, no. 2 (April 1990). Triplett's article also contains an outstanding bibliography for those wishing to explore the dozens of different brands of foundationalism.

[8]One frequently hears in these postmodern days that foundationalism is dead. Unfortunately, these obituaries seldom identify the exact identity of the deceased. Some authors seem to think that all versions of foundationalism are essentially of the form proposed by Descartes, Locke or logical positivists. Not only were there different versions of foundationalism available during the Enlightenment (Thomas Reid's

being a notable example), but there are now different versions as well.
[9]It is possible that people's ability to grasp self-evident truths varies. A mathematical truth that is self-evidently obvious to one person, a normal adult, might not be so to another, a three-year-old. Medieval philosophers would have explained this by saying that different people display in varying degrees the virtue of understanding.
[10]I will ignore for the moment the fact that this second condition can be met by any necessary truth that one believes. If I believe that the square root of 625 is 25, then it is impossible that I believe it and it be false, regardless of the reason I have for believing it. Suppose I decide to believe that the square of 625 is 25 because I like the sounds I make when I assert this proposition aloud. Strictly, it is impossible that I believe the claim and am mistaken, since the claim is necessarily true. One should add what Keith Lehrer calls an "irresistibility condition"—that if it is logically necessarily that a claim is true, then you believe it (and not for reasons independent of that claim's truth).
[11]Foundationalism can thus be seen to cut across the rationalist-empiricist divide. It is possible to find basic beliefs satisfying the criteria of proper basicality both from among the a priori deliverances of the domain of consciousness, as rationalists maintained, and from the immediate deliverances of sense experience, as held by empiricist foundationalists.
[12]This view, which was held by the early Bertrand Russell, Moritz Schlick and A. J. Ayer, is succinctly stated by another adherent, C. I. Lewis: "When I perceive a door, I may be deceived by a cleverly painted pattern on the wall, but the presentation which greets my eye is an indubitable fact of my experience. My perceptual belief in a real door, having another side, is not an explicit inference but a belief suggested by association; nevertheless, the validity of this interpretation is that and that only which could attach to it as an inductive inference from the given visual presentation. The given element is this incorrigible presentational element; the criticizable and dubitable element is the element of interpretation" (C. I. Lewis, "The Given Element in Empirical Knowledge," in Empirical Knowledge, ed. Roderick Chisholm and Robert Swartz [Englewood Cliffs, N.J.: Prentice-Hall, 1973], pp. 370-71).
[13]Being self-reflectively aware that one possesses knowledge, justifiably believing this to be the case, knowing this to be the case and showing that this is the case are all distinctive requirements, many or all of which do not appear in some versions of foundationalism. Failure to keep these separated leads to what William Alston calls "levels confusions in epistemology." See his article by the same title in Midwest Studies in Philosophy, vol. 5, 1980 Studies in Epistemology, ed. Peter French, Theodore Uehling and Howard Wettstein (Minneapolis: University of Minnesota Press, 1980), pp. 135-50.
[14]This line of argumentation can be explored in greater detail in Alvin Plantinga's "Reason and Belief in God," in Faith and Rationality, ed. Alvin Plantinga and Nicholas Wolterstorff (Grand Rapids, Mich.: Eerdmans, 1982), pp. 59-63. Also interesting is the series of exchanges on this and related points between Plantinga and Phillip Quinn, beginning with Quinn's "In Search of the Foundations of Theism," Faith and Philosophy, October 1985.
[15]Wilfred Sellars, "Empiricism and the Philosophy of Mind," in Challenges to Empiricism, ed. Harold Morick (Indianapolis: Hackett, 1980), p. 100. While it may be the case that even my most primitive beliefs depend on prior concepts, it won't follow that my primitive beliefs are based on those concepts. Sellars's argument is thus best construed as an attack against the incorrigibility of basic beliefs. A similar argument is made by Frederick Will in his Induction and Justification (Ithaca, N.Y.: Cornell University Press,

1974), p. 203. He writes: "If knowing any truth about a sensation, if indeed *having* a sensation of the kind that is specified in that truth, involves the employment and sound working of a vast array of equipment and resource extending far beyond any individual and what can be conceived private to him, then the possibility that this equipment and resource is not in place and working soundly cannot be discounted in the philosophical understanding of the knowledge of such truth. If the sound discrimination of the sensation of X, in its character *as* X, can be made only by correctly utilizing something further, say Y, and if, in a case like this, discrimination of a sensation as X can be made while yet, for some reason, Y is not being used correctly, then a discrimination of X need not be a sound discrimination." Roderick Chisholm defends the possibility of a noncomparative use of "This is red" in *Theory of Knowledge*, 3rd ed. (Englewood Cliffs, N.J.: Prentice-Hall, 1989), pp. 22-25.

[16]See Keith Lehrer, "Skepticism and Conceptual Change," in *Empirical Knowledge* (Englewood Cliffs, N.J.: Prentice-Hall, 1973), pp. 47-58.

[17]Sellars, "Empiricism and the Philosophy of Mind," pp. 99-100.

[18]Arguments similar to this are given in Laurence Bonjour's "Can Empirical Knowledge Have a Foundation?" *American Philosophical Quarterly* 15, no. 1 (1978): 1-13; and in Keith Lehrer's *Theory of Knowledge* (Boulder, Colo.: Westview, 1990), pp. 73-75.

[19]C. S. Peirce called the sort of inferential support I am describing "abduction." For an explanation of the differences between induction and abduction see Thomas Goudge, *The Thought of C. S. Peirce* (New York: Dover, 1969), pp. 195-99. The following two articles will also be helpful for anyone wishing to explore this point further: Ernan McMullin, "Structural Explanation," *American Philosophical Quarterly* no. 2 (April 1978): 145-46; Paul Thagard, "The Best Explanation Criteria for Theory Choice," *Journal of Philosophy* vol. 75 (1978): 76-92.

[20]See Chisholm's *Theory of Knowledge*, pp. 69-71.

[21]Hans Georg Gadamer, *Truth and Method*, 2nd ed. (New York: Continuum, 1993), p. 279.

[22]In "Two Types of Foundationalism," *Journal of Philosophy* 73 (1976): 165-85, William Alston argues forcefully against foundationalism's having to satisfy higher-level requirements. There he distinguishes between what he calls "iterative foundationalism," championed by people like Descartes, and "simple foundationalism," which dispenses with such requirements. This paper is included in his book *Epistemic Justification* (Ithaca, N.Y.: Cornell University Press, 1989), pp. 19-38.

[23]The notion that the body is an impediment to reason is at least as old as Plato and is a recurring theme in Western philosophy. Consider the following quotation from *Phaedo* (66), in which Socrates questions Simmias about the ideal conditions of knowing: "Don't you think that the person who is likely to succeed in this attempt most perfectly is the one who approaches each object, as far as possible, with the unaided intellect, without taking account of any sense of sight in his thinking, or dragging any other sense into his reckoning—the man who pursues the truth by applying his pure and unadulterated thought to the pure and unadulterated object, cutting himself off as much as possible from his eyes and ears and virtually all the rest of his body, as an impediment which by its presence prevents the soul from attaining to truth and clear thinking?"

[24]Merold Westphal, "Taking St. Paul Seriously: Sin as an Epistemological Category," in *Christian Philosophy*, ed. Thomas P. Flint (Notre Dame, Ind.: University of Notre Dame Press, 1990), pp. 209, 218.

[25]Quoted in Steve Pyke, *Philosophers* (London: Cornerhouse, 1993).

[26]Some modest foundationalists deny that one's foundations take the form of a belief.

In other words, they resist the doxastic assumption that only *beliefs* confer justification on other beliefs. Instead they say that one's foundations consist of certain cognitive states one is in (say, certain perceptual or memory states), without these states necessarily taking the form of a belief or proposition one has consciously formulated. This has been argued for by Ernest Sosa in "The Raft and the Pyramid: Coherence Versus Foundations in the Theory of Knowledge," in *Midwest Studies in Philosophy*, vol. 5, *1980 Studies in Epistemology*, ed. Peter French, Theodore Uehling and Howard Wettstein (Minneapolis: University of Minnesota Press, 1980), pp. 3-25; and by John Pollock, *Contemporary Theories of Knowledge* (Totowa, N.J.: Rowman and Littlefield, 1986), especially chap. 2.

[27]Nicholas Wolterstorff pointed out to me that Reid here failed to distinguish between beliefs that we take for granted—such as the general reliability of memory—which may never be brought to consciousness, and immediate beliefs produced by our cognitive faculties on which we base other nonbasic beliefs.

[28]Lehrer, *Theory of Knowledge*, p. 65.

[29]Richard Taylor, *Metaphysics* (Englewood Cliffs, N.J.: Prentice-Hall, 1963), pp. 86-87.

[30]*Thomas Reid's Inquiry and Essays*, ed. Keith Lehrer and Ronald Beanblossom (Indianapolis: Bobbs-Merrill, 1975), p. 153.

[31]Thomas Reid, *Essays on the Intellectual Powers of Man*, ed. Baruch Brody (Cambridge, Mass.: MIT Press, 1969), p. 745.

Chapter 5: Epistemic Justification

[1]What else one needs besides justification to convert true belief into knowledge depends on how one handles the infamous Gettier problem, an issue I intend to bypass. A comprehensive review of recent answers to the problem can be found in Robert K. Shope, *The Analysis of Knowing: A Decade of Research* (Princeton, N.J.: Princeton University Press, 1983). As the next chapter on reliabilism will show, some epistemologists think that a true belief produced in the right way can be an instance of knowledge without the justification component.

[2]W. K. Clifford, "The Ethics of Belief," in *Philosophy of Religion*, ed. Louis Pojman, 2nd ed. (Belmont, Calif.: Wadsworth, 1994), p. 426.

[3]Ibid. p. 425.

[4]For an excellent discussion of the difference between truth-dependent evidence and pragmatic reasons, see Gary Gutting's *Religious Belief and Religious Skepticism* (Notre Dame, Ind.: University of Notre Dame Press, 1982), pp. 79-108.

[5]John Pollock, *Contemporary Theories of Knowledge* (Totowa, N.J.: Rowman and Littlefield, 1986), p. 19.

[6]Some epistemologists think that when an experience functions in the automatic way I have indicated, it doesn't serve as the basis for any inference and thus ought to be called not "evidence" but "grounds." This constitutes more than a mere terminological dispute, but I shall set this issue to one side.

[7]J. L. Mackie, *The Miracle of Theism* (Oxford: Oxford University Press, 1982), p. 10.

[8]See Stephen J. Wykstra's "Toward a Sensible Evidentialism: On the Notion of Needing Evidence," in *Philosophy of Religion: Selected Readings*, ed. William Rowe and William J. Wainwright (Orlando, Fla.: Harcourt Brace Jovanovich, 1989). Perhaps the requirement as stated is still too strong. One might require of an agent that they could meet a subjunctive condition by making themselves aware of the evidence possessed by a community were they challenged to do so. Other more sophisticated versions of evidentialism are offered in Norman Kretzmann, "Evidence Against Anti-evidential-

ism," and Richard Feldman and Earl Conee, "Evidentialism," in *Philosophical Studies* 48, no. 1 (1985).

[9]Using the formula

(probability x payoff) - cost = rational expectation

we can determine what sorts of bets it makes best sense to place. Suppose horse *A* has won two-thirds of its races and is paying at a rate of 5 to 1. If you wager 9 dollars on the horse, you would expect to win 45 dollars. Figuring in the odds of winning minus the cost of betting, you get a rational exception of 23. Horse *B* pays out at 30 to 1 but has won only one-third of all its races. Which horse should you bet on? The same nine-dollar bet will yield 270 dollars if horse *B* wins. Figuring in the likelihood of winning minus the cost of betting, you get a rational expectation of 81. Obviously, the smart money will be on horse *B*.

[10]Aristotle *Nichomachean Ethics* 1094.24-25.

[11]Further discussion of our standards of evidence, especially the salience that evidence has for us, will be discussed in chapter 7.

[12]I haven't here delved into the issue of how we assess the probative force of evidence. Why do two philosophers equally aware of all the evidence for God's existence disagree as to its force? I will take up this issue in chapter eight.

[13]Ernest Sosa, "The Raft and the Pyramid: Coherence Versus Foundations in the Theory of Knowledge," in *Midwest Studies in Philosophy*, vol. 5, *1980 Studies in Epistemology*, ed. Peter French, Theodore Uehling and Howard Wettstein (Minneapolis: University of Minnesota Press, 1980), pp. 3-25.

[14]Alan R. White, "Coherence Theory of Truth," in *Encyclopedia of Philosophy*, ed. Paul Edwards (New York: Macmillan, 1967), 1:130. White's remarks could be interpreted as addressed to a coherence theory of truth rather than a coherence theory of justification. The former specifies what conditions must be satisfied for a belief to be considered true, whereas my concern in this chapter is with justification. But I think his suggestion can be applied to coherence theories of justification as well.

[15]W. V. O. Quine, "Two Dogmas of Empiricism," in *From a Logical Point of View* (Cambridge, Mass.: Harvard University Press, 1961), p. 43. Unfortunately, Americans have witnessed this very ability to achieve coherence "come what may" in the writings of white militia groups following the bombing of the federal building in Oklahoma City. They accuse the FBI of having blown up the building itself in order to generate favorable public opinion for its crackdown on militia groups.

[16]Similar "coherent" webs of belief include the claim that aliens crashed at Roswell Air Force Base and that this fact is being covered up by the government. Oliver Sacks, *An Anthropologist from Mars* (New York: Alfred A. Knopf, 1995), p. 46.

[17]Keith Lehrer, *Theory of Knowledge* (Boulder, Colo.: Westview, 1990), chap. 6. By saying Lehrer's is an account of personal justification, I mean that he is attempting to specify what conditions I must satisfy if I am to be justified. His is thus a first-person, subjective account of justification.

[18]Lehrer's formal definition of competition is as follows: "c competes with P for S on the basis of the acceptance system of S at t only if it is less reasonable of S to accept that p on the assumption that c is true that on the assumption that c is false on the basis of the acceptance system of S at t" (*Theory of Knowledge*, p. 118).

[19]Ibid., p. 121.

[20]In Keith Lehrer's "The Coherence Theory of Knowledge," in *Empirical Knowledge*, ed. Paul Moser (Lanham, Md.: Rowman and Littlefield, 1996), he writes: "It is important to notice, however, that beating all competitors, though sufficient for justification, is

not necessary" (p. 126). Sometimes justification requires only that we be able to "neutralize" skeptics, not defeat them. Lehrer shows by example what neutralizing amounts to: "If the skeptic attempts to undermine my claim that I see a [computer] monitor by pointing out that people sometimes hallucinate, thus suggesting that I may be hallucinating, the way to neutralize the suggestion is to point out that I am not hallucinating. The conjunction of statements that people sometimes hallucinate and that I am not now hallucinating is as reasonable for me to accept as the single statement that people sometimes hallucinate. The conjunction does not compete with the statement that I now see a monitor. Consequently, the statement that I am not now hallucinating neutralizes the competitor that people sometime hallucinate. The competitor of my claim that I see a monitor is thus neutralized" (p. 127).

[21] Arguments similar to the one posed here can be found in Richard Fumerton, "A Critique of Coherentism," in *Theory of Knowledge*, ed. Louis Pojman (Belmont, Calif.: Wadsworth, 1993), p. 242; see also J. M. Fritzman, "Against Coherence," *American Philosophical Quarterly* 29, no. 2 (April 1992): 187.

Chapter 6: Reliabilism

[1] This is true on the assumption that each has "justification" rather than some other form of epistemic merit uppermost in mind.

[2] W. K. Clifford, "The Ethics of Belief," in *Philosophy of Religion*, ed. Louis Pojman, 2nd ed. (Belmont, Calif.: Wadsworth, 1994), p. 425.

[3] Here it is useful to recall a point made in the first chapter about different epistemic desiderata or merits. The intellectual life offers many merits we are better off having than lacking. Justification is one such state, which has been depicted thus far as the condition of being fully entitled to hold the beliefs one does or, put a bit differently, of not being an appropriate subject of blame for believing as one does. One might be justified in this sense and still believe falsely, as was noted. Another epistemic merit accrues to us when we believe in a reliable fashion, that is, in a manner that makes it highly probable that our beliefs are latching onto the truth. Unfortunately, philosophers have also used the term *justification* to refer to this merit, thereby causing confusion in discussions about justification. Still another epistemic merit is having knowledge, which, for now, we can describe as justified true belief. But which sense of justification, the first or second, is crucial for knowledge? Reliabilists are best read as championing the second sense of justification as the most important and the one that when added to true belief yields knowledge. I will endeavor to make these two senses of justification unambiguous in the ensuing discussion.

[4] D. M. Armstrong and Robert Nozick pose their conditions as necessary for knowledge, but they are easily adapted to justification.

[5] Robert Nozick, *Philosophical Explanations* (Cambridge, Mass.: Harvard University Press, 1981), p. 172.

[6] Alvin Goldman, "What Is Justified Belief?" in *Justification and Knowledge*, ed. George S. Pappas (Dordrecht, Holland: D. Reidel, 1979), p. 20.

[7] Ibid., p. 17. This has the unsettling consequence that no one can be justified in believing the content of revealed religion, since it is only by God's intervention that we acquire these beliefs.

Thus no one can justifiably accept what St. Thomas calls "the mysteries of faith."

[8] We may still have to expend effort to open our eyes, turn our heads and fix our attention on a visual display long enough for a visual belief to be reliably generated. Even so, my being justified doesn't include as an ingredient my having striven

conscientiously to believe in accordance with the evidence, or some such requirement.
[9]Skepticism can be formulated to cast doubts on both claims to have knowledge and claims to have the sort of justified belief required for knowledge.

[10]Some philosophers are happy to accord science pride of place in epistemological matters. W. V. O. Quine has written: "Epistemology is best looked upon, then, as an enterprise within natural science. . . . Science tells us that our only source of information about the external world is through the impact of light rays and molecules upon our sensory surfaces. Stimulated in these ways, we somehow evolve an elaborate and useful science. How do we do this, and why does the resulting science work so well? . . . They are scientific questions about a species of primates, and they are open to investigation in natural science, the very science whose acquisition is being investigated" ("The Nature of Natural Knowledge," in *Mind and Language*, ed. Samuel Guttenplan [Oxford: Oxford University Press, 1975], p. 68).

Elsewhere Quine says, "Epistemology, or something like it, simply falls into place as a chapter of psychology and hence of natural science. It studies a natural phenomenon, viz., a physical human subject. This subject is accorded a certain experimentally controlled input—certain patters of irradiation in assorted frequencies, for instance—and in the fullness of time the subject delivers as output a description of the three-dimensional external world and its history. . . . The old epistemology aspired to contain, in a sense, natural science; it would construct it somehow from sense data. Epistemology in its new setting, conversely, is contained in natural science, as a chapter of psychology" ("Epistemology Naturalized," in *Naturalizing Epistemology*, ed. Hilary Kornblith [Cambridge, Mass.: MIT Press, 1985], p. 24).

[11]Richard Feldman, "Reliability and Justification," *The Monist* 68, no. 2 (April 1985): 159-74.

[12]As John Pollock notes, anytime one describes the relevant process so narrowly as to include its having a true output or a false output, the processes will again have a reliability of either 1 or 0 with nothing in between. See his *Contemporary Theories of Knowledge* (Totowa, N.J.: Rowman and Littlefield, 1986), p. 118.

[13]Oliver Sacks, *An Anthropologist on Mars* (New York: Alfred A. Knopf, 1995), pp. 166-67.

[14]See Laurence Bonjour, "Externalist Theories of Empirical Knowledge," in *Midwest Studies in Philosophy*, vol. 5, *1980 Studies in Epistemology*, ed. Peter French, Theodore Uehling and Howard Wettstein (Minneapolis: University of Minnesota Press, 1980), p. 62.

[15]Ibid., pp. 54-55. Also see Laurence Bonjour, "Externalism/Internalism," in *A Companion to Epistemology*, ed. Jonathan Dancy and Ernest Sosa (Oxford: Blackwell, 1992), pp. 132-36. He writes: "The main objection to externalism [reliabilism] rests on the intuition that the basic requirement for epistemic justification is that the acceptance of the belief in question be rational or responsible in relation to the cognitive goal of truth, which seems to require that the believer actually be aware of a reason for thinking that the belief is true (or at the very least that such a reason be available to him)" (p. 134).

[16]Keith Lehrer, *Theory of Knowledge* (Boulder, Colo.: Westview Press, 1990), p. 168. Lehrer's entire chapter "Externalism and Epistemology Naturalized" is an especially lucid argument for the insufficiency of reliability for knowledge.

[17]William Alston, *Epistemic Justification* (Ithaca, N.J.: Cornell University Press, 1989), p. 5.

[18]Bonjour, "Externalist Theories," p. 65.

[19]John Greco, "Internalism and Epistemically Responsible Belief," *Synthese* 85 (1990): 245.

[20]I say "appropriately" to indicate that our being personally invested in our intellectual lives does not require attentiveness to the point of neurotic anxiety; it need not bar our trusting the testimony of others or prevent us from accepting our creaturely limitations as knowers. One aspect of a being a virtuous knower might just be the capacity to judge which beliefs require investigation and to what degree they require it. Recall Aristotle's comments about the marks of a wise man in book 1 of the *Nichomachean Ethics*.

[21]Alvin Plantinga contrasts "warrant" and "justification." The latter, he thinks, is virtually indissolubly connected to notions of duty fulfillment, to doing one's level best. Justification and deontological normative notions go hand in hand.

[22]Alvin Plantinga, "Justification in the Twentieth Century," *Philosophy and Phenomenological Research* 1 (Fall 1990): 70.

[23]Alvin Plantinga, "Précis of *Warrant: The Current Debate* and *Warrant and Proper Function*," in *APA Book Symposium* 27 (March 1993): 447.

[24]Mark Twain, *The Adventures of Huckleberry Finn*, ed. Shelley Fisher Fiskin (Oxford: Oxford University Press, 1996), pp. 123-24; see also Jonathan Bennett, "The Conscience of Huckleberry Finn," *Philosophy* 49 (1974): 123-34. My thanks to Linda Zagzebski for bringing this example to my attention.

[25]Linda Zagzebski includes a "success component" as a part of her analysis of intellectual virtue. "A kind, compassionate, generous, courageous, or just person aims at making the world a certain way, and reliable success in making it that way is a condition for having the virtue in question" (*Virtues of the Mind* [Cambridge: Cambridge University Press, 1995], p. 136).

[26]Thomas Reid, *An Inquiry into the Human Mind on the Principles of Common Sense*, in *Thomas Reid, Inquiry and Essays*, ed. Keith Lehrer and Ronald Beanblossom (Indianapolis: Hackett, 1983), p. 4.

Chapter 7: Epistemology & Religious Belief

[1]Thomas Aquinas *Summa Contra Gentiles* 1.4.4 (Notre Dame, Ind.: University of Notre Dame Press, 1975), p. 67.

[2]Nicholas Wolterstorff, "Can Belief in God Be Rational If It Has No Foundations?" in *Faith and Rationality*, ed. Nicholas Wolterstorff and Alvin Plantinga (Notre Dame, Ind.: University of Notre Dame Press, 1983), p. 149. Wolterstorff gives an excellent introduction to the central ideas of Thomas Reid as well as a compelling presentation of the bearing of these ideas on religious belief.

[3]Thomas Reid, *Inquiry and Essays*, ed. Keith Lehrer and Ronald Beanblossom (Indianapolis: Hackett, 1983), p. xxi.

[4]Ibid., p. 84. Again, let me draw your attention to the distinction between what Reid "takes for granted" and what he "believes as basic." See note 27 in chapter four of this book.

[5]Thomas Reid, *Essays on the Intellectual Powers of Man* (Cambridge, Mass.: MIT Press, 1969), p. 295.

[6]My earlier discussion of modest foundationalism explained the hopeless circularity that ensnares anyone who endeavors to vindicate the practice of taking as reliable the deliverances of our perceptual faculties. For any such argument will perforce make use of some faculty or other whose reliability is also open to question. For a more detailed presentation of this argument see William Alston's "Plantinga's Epistemology of Religious Belief," in *Alvin Plantinga*, ed. James Tomberlin (Dordrecht, Netherlands: D. Reidel, 1985), p. 303.

[7] Again, see Nicholas Wolterstorff and Alvin Plantinga, eds., *Faith and Rationality* (Notre Dame, Ind.: University of Notre Dame Press, 1983).

[8] Scholars within the Reformed tradition debate among themselves whether Plantinga's claims about Reformed thinking are true to the actual claims of the Reformers themselves, but I shall not pursue these in-house controversies. Anyone so interested might start with John Beversluis, "Reforming the 'Reformed' Objection to Natural Theology," *Faith and Philosophy* 12 (April 1995): 2.

[9] Immanuel Kant, *The Critique of Pure Reason*, trans. Norman Kemp Smith (New York: St. Martin's, 1961), p. 520; emphasis mine.

[10] Alvin Plantinga, "Reason and Belief in God," in *Faith and Rationality*, ed. Nicholas Wolterstorff and Alvin Plantinga (Notre Dame, Ind.: University of Notre Dame Press, 1983), pp. 83-84.

[11] See Sigmund Freud, *The Future of an Illusion*, trans. W. D. Robson-Scott (New York: Anchor, 1964), especially chap. 4.

[12] Phillip Quinn, "In Search of the Foundations of Theism," *Faith and Philosophy* 2, no. 4 (October 1985): 484. Alvin Plantinga's reply is in "The Foundations of Theism: A Reply," *Faith and Philosophy*, July 1986.

[13] Plantinga, "Foundations of Theism," *Faith and Philosophy*, July 1986, pp. 310-11.

[14] Reid, *Intellectual Powers of Man*, p. 291.

[15] The idea that a theory of knowledge must accommodate itself to an antecedent set of concrete instances of knowledge is clearly and forcefully defended in Roderick Chisholm's "The Problem of the Criterion," in *The Foundations of Knowing* (Minneapolis: University of Minnesota Press, 1982), pp. 61-75.

[16] Plantinga, "Reason and Belief in God," p. 76.

[17] Plantinga, "Foundations of Theism: A Reply," p. 302.

[18] Ibid., p. 303.

[19] Readers are urged to explore the full account of warrant in Alvin Plantinga, *Warrant and Proper Function* (Oxford: Oxford University Press, 1993).

Chapter 8: The Role of Emotions & Virtue in Proper Cognitive Functioning

[1] Erasmus of Rotterdam, *In Praise of Folly*, cited in Daniel Goleman, *Emotional Intelligence* (New York: Bantam, 1995), p. 9.

[2] Most of what I say here stems from the work of Robert C. Roberts, whose work on the nature of emotions is, in my judgment, unsurpassed. See his "What an Emotion Is: A Sketch," *Philosophical Review* 97, no. 2 (April 1988), and "Emotions as Access to Religious Truth," *Faith and Philosophy* 9 (January 1992), among others. Martha Nussbaum advances a view similar to Roberts's in the chapter "Rational Emotions" in *Poetic Justice* (Boston: Beacon, 1995).

[3] This is not to deny that feelings and other bodily states often accompany the construals or beliefs that make up our emotions, but they are not what is central to them. Anger, for instance, is commonly accompanied by elevated blood pressure, a flushed face and a rapid pulse, but these are not what is essential to anger, for there are brooding and "cool" ways of being angry that do not come accompanied by such feelings.

[4] Gilbert Harman, *The Nature of Morality* (New York: Oxford University Press, 1977), p. 4.

[5] Temple Grandin's story is told in Oliver Sacks's chapter titled "An Anthropologist on Mars," in *An Anthropologist on Mars* (New York: Alfred A. Knopf, 1995).

[6] Ibid., p. 288.

[7] Ibid, pp. 293-94.

[8]Ibid., p. 288. The case of the judge resembles that of Phineas Gage, discussed at length in Antonio D'Amasio, *Descartes' Error: Emotion, Reason and the Human Brain* (New York: Avon Books, 1994). Due to an injury to the frontal lobes, Gage is rendered incapable of reasoning in accordance with social conventions and ethical rules. "The unintentional message in Gage's case," writes D'Amasio, "was that observing social convention, behaving ethically, and making decisions advantageous to one's survival and progress require knowledge of rules and strategies and the integrity of specific brain systems" (p. 17).

[9]Ronald de Sousa, *The Rationality of Emotion* (Cambridge, Mass.: MIT Press, 1987), p. 180.

[10]Actually, Temple has developed compensatory means of detecting people's inward states. She has built up an immense catalog of situations from which she is able to reason inductively: "Oh, this is one of those situations where it is appropriate to offer someone condolences." She does not detect sadness in others experientially but *infers* that people might be feeling that way. So while it is possible that I come to know that you are sad by a process of reasoning, this is not the normal way. Typically I simply construe you as sad based on my own powers of sympathetic imagination.

[11]C. S. Lewis, *The Abolition of Man* (New York: Macmillan, 1947), p. 29.

[12]Nussbaum, "Rational Emotions," p. 69.

[13]Charles Dickens, *Great Expectations* (New York: Signet Classics, 1963), p. 389.

[14]Nelson Goodman, *Languages of Art*, 2nd ed. (Indianapolis: Hackett, 1976), p. 248.

[15]Thomas Kuhn, *The Structure of Scientific Revolutions*, 2nd ed. (Chicago: University of Chicago Press), pp. 83-84.

[16]Bertrand Russell, *Mysticism and Logic* (New York: Doubleday/Anchor, 1957), p. 57.

[17]Israel Scheffler, *Science and Subjectivity*, 2nd ed. (Indianapolis: Hackett, 1982), p. 141. See especially his chapter "In Praise of the Cognitive Emotions." See also Michael Polanyi's discussion of the relation of proper passions to science in the chapter "Intellectual Passions" in his work *Personal Knowledge* (Chicago: University of Chicago Press, 1958).

[18]Scheffler, *Science and Subjectivity*, p. 152.

[19]Subramanyan Chandresekhar, quoted in *A Passion to Know: Twenty Profiles in Science*, ed. Allan L. Hammond (New York: Charles Scribner's Sons, 1984), p. 5.

[20]Jane Goodall, in *National Geographic Magazine*, December 1995, p. 108.

[21]For a more thorough discussion of Edwards's views of intellectual virtue, see William Wainwright's *Reason and the Heart: A Prolegomenon to a Critique of Passional Reason* (Ithaca, N.Y.: Cornell University Press, 1995), from which my brief remarks are taken.

[22]See C. Stephen Evans, "Transformative Religious Experiences," *Faith and Philosophy* 8, no. 2 (April 1991): 180-92.

[23]Fyodor Dostoyevsky, *Crime and Punishment*, trans. Richard Pevear and Larissa Volokhonsky (New York: Vintage, 1993), p. 412.

[24]Dostoyevsky's passage suggests that whether Raskolnikov's experience of love defeated his nihilism was in some measure up to him. This raises the prospect that the will plays an important indirect role in the way we accept and reject beliefs.

[25]Quoted in Martin Gardner, *The Whys of a Philosophical Scrivener* (New York: Quill, 1983), pp. 196-97.

Name Index

Subject Index